Two Against
The Sahara

Two Against The Sahara

On Camelback from Nouakchott to the Nile

MICHAEL ASHER

Photographs by

MARIANTONIETTA PERU

William Morrow and Company, Inc.
New York

Library of Congress Cataloging-in-Publication Data

Asher, Michael, 1953–
Two against the Sahara: on camelback from Nouakchott to the Nile
Michael Asher: photographs by Mariantonietta Peru.
p.   cm.
ISBN 0-688-08926-7
1. Sahara—Description and travel. 2. Asher, Michael, 1953–   —
Journeys—Sahara. 3. Peru, Mariantonietta—Journeys—Sahara.
I. Peru, Mariantonietta. II. Title.
DT333.A753   1989
916.6'04328—dc19   89-30800
                                                                  CIP

Printed in the United States of America

First U.S. Edition

1 2 3 4 5 6 7 8 9 10

TO MARIANTONIETTA

Neither I nor anyone else knows the Sahara.

The last words of
General Henri Laperrine, 1920

Two can do together what is impossible for one.

Arab proverb

Contents

List of Illustrations

Color photographs

1. In Moorish dress at the door of our house in Chinguetti.
2. On the edge of the emptiness: Chinguetti oasis. The building on the left is a grain store.
3. High noon under the palms of Ganeb.
4. Mafoudh leading the caravan across the plains of Aoukar valley.
5. The real spirit of Ténéré: the face of the Tuareg herdswoman in Wadi Borghat.
6. Making bread the nomad way.
7. Yet another stoppage: fixing a nose-ring in the Grand Erg of Bilma: Mu'min is supervising.
8. Kababish girls carrying a *girba* at Greywit wells.
9. Searching for a well: Abu Tabara lies somewhere among these rocks.
10. Guide Adam climbs a great dune to look for Abu Tabara.
11. The edge of darkness: hitching up the caravan near Tegaru plateau.
12. A long-dreamed-of sight: the river Nile after 256 days.
13. The going gets tougher: Marinetta grabs a rest near Tegaru.
14. The wild man collects fodder for the camels on the banks of the Nile.

Black-and-white photographs

1. The first day out: a crowd watches as we saddle the camels for the first time. Sid'Ahmed's house in the background.
2. Threading a nose-ring: Li'shal, the small camel from the Mauritanian Adrar.
3. Handing out aspirins to the crowd at Talmoust.
4. The butterfly saddle: Mafoudh adds the finishing touches.
5. A Berabish boy, Mali.
6. A Kababish tribesman: his rosary beads hang around his neck.

Author's Note

As dialects vary considerably throughout the Sahara, I make no apology for standardizing common names. The flowing shirt worn by most Saharan tribes in one form or other is referred to here as *gandourah*. The Moors call it *dara'a*, a word which few Westerners can pronounce correctly: this is probably why the French named it *boubou*, a word the natives never use and one which I detest. In the eastern Sahara this garment is called a *jallabiyya*. I use the spelling *girba* for a waterskin, in preference to the more common *guerba*, which bears no relation to its pronunciation in any dialect. I have no intention of getting bogged down in Saharan tribal names. It is sufficient to say that most names have plural, masculine singular and feminine singular forms: for example, Haratin (plur.), Hartani (masc. sing.), Hartaniyya (fem. sing.). The principal nomadic groups of the Sahara are (from west to east) the Moors (who call themselves *bidan* or 'whites'), the Tuareg, the Toubou (more correctly called Teda or Gor'an) and the Arabs. Nomadic tribes of the eastern Sahara have been labelled 'Afro-Arabs' by those who make a business out of labelling races. Their name for themselves is, simply, 'Arabs'.

For place names I have mostly followed the map, except where a degree of anglicization has made for simplicity. Thus 'Ouadane' appears as 'Wadan' and 'Oualata' as 'Walata'. Nigérien refers always to the Niger Republic and never to the state of Nigeria, whose adjective is Nigerian. Finally, I have referred to 'western', 'central' and 'eastern' Sahara as integral parts of the great expanse of desert that lies between the Atlantic and the Nile. It was the custom in colonial times, and still is in some quarters, to believe that the 'Sahara' ends at the borders of the Sudan and Egypt, beyond which it is mysteriously transformed into the 'Western Desert' or the 'Libyan

Desert'. If anyone is in doubt, I can assure him or her, having walked and ridden by camel every inch of the way, that the Great Desert is all in one piece.

Foreword

In April 1986 I travelled to Mauritania with my wife, Mariantonietta, to begin preparations for a journey across the Sahara desert, from west to east, by camel and on foot. Our route lay through Mali, Niger, Chad, the Sudan and Egypt, a distance of 4,500 miles. No Westerner had made such a journey before.

Mariantonietta and I were no newcomers to Africa: we had both lived there for some years and spoke Arabic fluently. To each other, though, we were little more than strangers. When we arrived in Mauritania we had been married for exactly five days. She, an Italian born on the island of Sardinia, and I, an Englishman, were from cultures as alien to each other, almost, as Saharan ways were to both of us.

This book is the story of our journey across the world's greatest desert by camel and on foot. It is also the story of a man and a woman from very different backgrounds who had come to terms with each other in a harsh environment and of how they managed, just, to survive.

For six years I had dreamed of crossing the Sahara from west to east by camel. Meanwhile, I had been living and travelling with desert nomads in the Sudan. In March 1985 I was in Khartoum, on my way back from a desert journey, when I received an unexpected message from the representative of the United Nations Children's Fund (UNICEF), asking me for advice on the use of camels in their aid project in the Red Sea hills.

It was at UNICEF's headquarters in Khartoum that I first set eyes on the woman who was to become my wife.

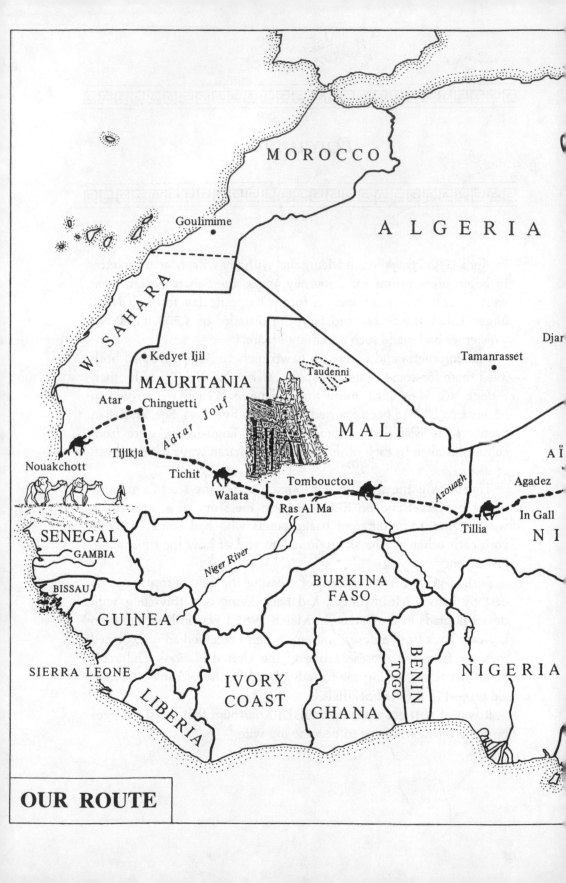

OUR ROUTE

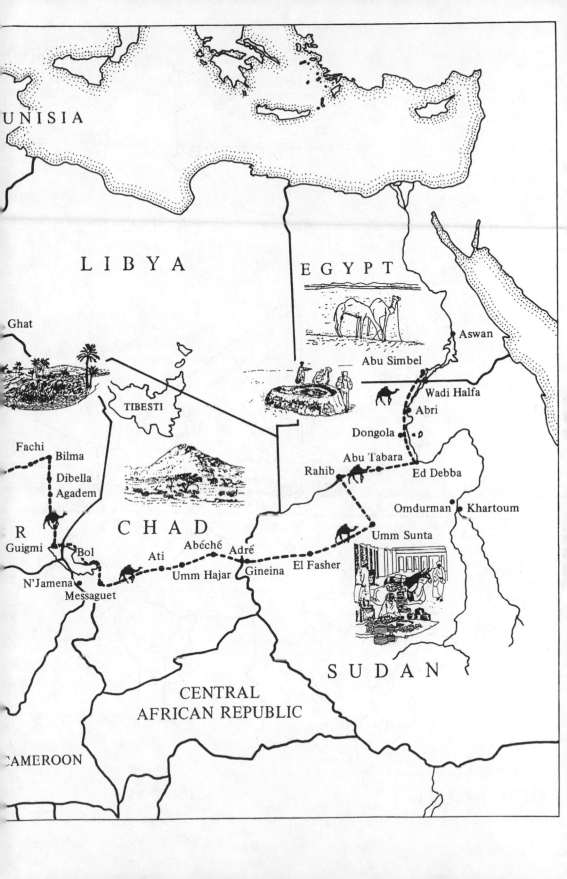

Mariantonietta

She was sitting behind a desk in the smallest office on the highest floor of the UNICEF building. Her appearance confirmed my worst fears: she was beautiful.

Her face was square, precise and Mediterranean, her perfect nose almost imperceptibly angled down. The lips, when closed, were the shape of a flattened-out heart. The page-boy-style hair swirled glossily when she moved her head. The best thing about her face was the eyes. They were enormous brown pools, partly hidden under enormous spectacles. The spectacles were strangely irritating. You felt like pulling them off to get a better look at the marvellous face.

'So you're the writer who's an expert on camels!' she said, looking me up and down through the giant spectacles. There was a hint of disapproval on her face as she took in my faded shirt, my jeans and my battered flip-flops. I hid my feet under the desk instinctively as I sat down on the proffered chair. 'Did it take you long to drive here?' she asked. 'The office is a bit far out, isn't it?'

'I didn't drive,' I told her. 'I haven't got a car. I walked.'

'Oh!' she said, pursing her lips. 'Don't you find it difficult to get around without a car?'

'Not really,' I said. 'I've never been one for cars. Camels are more in my line.'

'Yes,' she said snootily, 'but you can't take a camel to the Hilton, can you? I mean, what do you do when you want to go out to dinner?'

'I don't,' I told her. 'And I've never been to the Hilton.'

She looked down again at my jeans, probably thinking that I would never be allowed in the Hilton anyway. The nose was perfectly constructed for looking down, I decided.

The telephone rang and I jumped. She spoke into it coolly while I looked around the room. It was crammed with books and pamphlets about UNICEF. An air-conditioner blew an arctic gale in my face. On the wall was a poster showing a cherubic African child wearing a UNICEF hat, and there was a black-and-white photo of a burly Latin-American policeman immunizing a little boy. From the outside came the insistent jingle of other telephones and the clack of typewriters.

It was only when she put the phone down and stood up that I realized how small she was. From a distance, you might have mistaken her for a child. She excused herself and ran out of the room.

She came back eventually, walking gracefully, as if trying to erase the childish impression given by her hasty departure. I watched her squeeze past the desk with admiration, attracted by the sleek, suntanned body. Yet I was repelled by the thought of how the tan had been acquired. I could imagine the yachts, the beach parties and the cocktails. I could imagine tennis with the well-heeled boyfriend; I could see the Mercedes-Benz. The men in her life wore polished shoes and safari suits. They didn't ride camels, I thought.

'Oh, yes,' she said as she sat down, 'the representative told me to brief you about my work. Basically, I promote COBI.'

'The only Gobi I know is the desert,' I said, grinning weakly.

She frowned. 'GOBI means Growth-monitoring, Oral rehydration, Breast-feeding and Immunization,' she lectured me. 'It's UNICEF's master-plan for ridding the world's children of all major problems by the end of the century.'

'I see,' I lied grimly, looking around for a way of escape. I was dying to get out of the office. I felt that I didn't belong there, and I had been out of the company of women for so long that her proximity made me nervous. I asked a few desultory questions, and she replied dreamily. Soon she yawned and looked at her watch.

Taking the hint I said, 'I'd better be going,' and poised myself for the getaway. I stood up and offered my hand. Hers was very small, soft and delicate. 'Nice to meet you,' I said. 'I'll probably see you in Port Sudan.' I turned and marched towards the door. I didn't make it. On the second step one of my flip-flops broke. The little plastic knob that held the strap in place must finally have worn through. In a moment it was hanging from my foot, making me stagger clumsily.

'Excuse me,' a voice said, 'but isn't your shoe broken?'

I felt myself flushing. 'It's rather awkward,' I stammered. 'I've got nothing to fix it with.'

Marinetta giggled. It was a fresh, childish giggle that seemed suddenly to change the atmosphere from icy-cool to warm. 'I bet I can find something,' she said, rummaging in an elegant handbag. She produced a small, blue pin-badge, with a smiley face and the words 'UNICEF is for children' printed on one side. It did the trick. When I showed her the worn-out sole with 'UNICEF is for children' etched across it, she laughed delightedly. The laugh did for me: it was a lovely laugh. 'Don't forget to give it back when you get a new pair!' she giggled. It must have been precisely then that I fell in love with Mariantonietta Peru.

The next time we met was in Port Sudan on the shores of the Red Sea. I was there assisting UNICEF with their camel project, and she had been sent to compile a photographic report of our progress. Photography, I discovered, was only one of her many talents. She looked ravishing.

'So you bought a new pair of flip-flops!' She smiled. 'Now where's my badge?'

'I'm afraid it's gone the way of the old flip-flops,' I said. 'But I want to make it up by inviting you out to dinner.'

'I thought you didn't go out to dinner,' she said mischievously.

'There are always exceptions,' I told her. 'How about it?'

'All right,' she said.

We ate at a small, open-air restaurant on the dockside where they fried fish and grilled shish kebab. It was full of displaced Eritreans trying to find ships to America and foreign sailors with raucous voices. There were lights blinking out on the seaways and the honking of unseen ships coming in. The stars were out in their thousands, and the rich smell of the sea was everywhere.

Marinetta told me that she was Italian, born on the island of Sardinia but based in Rome. Her father was a retired army general who had been captured at Tobruk and had spent five years in a British prison camp in India. Her mother was a teacher of English. She was an experienced photographer but preferred to call herself a linguist.

She had studied Arabic, French and English at the University of Rome and had perfected her Arabic in Tunis and in Cairo, where she had spent a year with an Egyptian family. She had been UNICEF's information officer in Somalia for two years and had travelled for the organization in Ethiopia and Kenya. Travel was a passion that she had inherited from her parents. She had been all over Africa, Asia, the Caribbean and the United States. Despite my earlier misgivings, I was impressed.

In turn, I talked about my life as an English teacher in the Sudan and how I had given it up to live full-time with the nomads.

Now she seemed interested. 'What about the future?' she asked me later. 'You can't live in the desert for ever.'

'I'm planning something really big,' I said. 'I'm going to cross the entire Sahara desert from the Atlantic to the Nile, by camel.' I wondered if she would think I was mad. Instead she looked at me attentively. I explained that I had been fascinated by the Sahara since I had first seen it spreading out west from the banks of the Nile six years before. I said that I had dreamed of traversing the whole of that desert, all 3,000 miles of it, in one go and by camel. I explained that the trek would actually cover more than 4,000 miles, since a straight-line march would be impossible, and that it would mean crossing six of the world's most arid countries, some of them unstable, one of them at war.

Marinetta fell silent and I thought that my enthusiasm must have put her off. I sat back and lit my pipe. The restaurant was quiet now. Most of the sailors had gone. The Eritreans had gathered on the waterfront and were talking in soft, wistful voices and smoking cigarettes. Marinetta was looking at me with a dreamy, meditative air. Two flecks of light burned in the corners of her spectacles. Her face was smoothed by the lamplight and framed in the dark halo of her silky hair. 'God, you're so lucky, Maik!' she said. 'I wish I could do something big like that, something really *exciting*. Then they'd know that I'm tougher than I look.'

We had dinner in the same place the following night. And the night after. And the night after that. The restaurant became a special place for us. No one else existed. The two of us seemed enough. We talked and talked. We talked about nomads, about the Sahara, about Africa, about the aid agencies, about photography.

By day we met and walked along the waterfront under the parasols of the *nim* trees. We strolled through the streets, beneath the façades of the tall, Indian-style buildings with their verandahs and arched balconies. We laughed at the fat camels that wandered unperturbed among the hooting traffic. We watched the Beja tribesmen with their plumes of knotted hair. We scoured the market for big, red apples. We bought hooks and fishing lines and tried our luck in the harbour. Marinetta always caught fish, but I caught nothing.

Before long it seemed that she was waiting for me to do or say something, to make some move. Like a fool, I was terrified, still unable to believe my eyes. Why should a marvellous woman like Marinetta be interested in an eccentric like me? It was only the romantic setting, I thought, the sea and the stars. It was three weeks before I kissed her goodnight, clumsily, on the balcony of her borrowed flat. She seemed to like it. 'Maik,' she asked me, 'are we having a relationship?'

'Yes,' I said, 'I do believe we are.'

It was like all the romantic films I had ever seen, played simultaneously and all happening to me. I had spent six years in remote backwaters of the Sudan, where women were few and far between. Now a quiet kind of madness had beset me. Our restaurant had become a sacred place. Those evenings, entranced by the flow of her syllables, the reflection of the lamplight in her eyes, the soothing glow of the stars on the inky water, are held in my memory like a magic spell. It was a long time since I had felt so tranquil.

One afternoon, as we were walking, the air cooled suddenly and the sky misted over with slate-grey clouds. Marinetta grew excited. 'It's going to rain!' she shouted. A moment later the rain fell, the drops splashing across the sand. We laughed like children. 'It's the beginning of a new life!' she cried. 'I can feel it! The beginning of a new world!'

Caught up in her excitement, I took her hands. I was about to blurt out that I wanted to marry her and be with her always. But the words, blocked by years of caution, refused to emerge. Right on cue the rain stopped. The wind pushed the clouds away. The magic spell was broken.

In Khartoum Marinetta returned to her gloomy office and her GOBI. I settled down in my rented apartment to work on a book about the Great Drought and its effect on the Sudanese nomads. I still saw a great deal of her.

She was restless, disillusioned with her job. 'I can't stand much more of this GOBI,' she told me once. 'I dread the meetings we have. So many people using long words. They use big words, but when you listen to what they are really saying, it's crap. I don't want to spend my life telling nomads about breast-feeding. I want to know what they have to teach *me*. I want to know what their lives are really like.'

One evening she said, 'I was always so little. At school they treated me like a baby – the teachers and the pupils. It was because I was so small. You know, they called me Perina – it means "little pear". I've always wanted to do something really big so that they would know what the little pear can do.'

She must have been a lonely, shy little girl, I thought, always wanting to sit at the back of the class and always being made to sit at the front. Her small size and strict Sardinian upbringing had made her different from the rest. As she grew older, her estrangement had grown into aloofness. She had despised the smoking and the drinking, the casual sex and the experiments with drugs. She had been a serious girl, top of the class in languages, sensitive and artistic, with a streak of relentless steel. It must have been a chagrin for all those other girls when she turned into a ravishing beauty.

'They used to laugh at me because I didn't have a boyfriend,' she said, 'and because I went on holiday with my parents. Most of them were married by the age of twenty. They're not laughing now.'

The book on which I had been working, *A Desert Dies*, was nearing completion, and my Saharan project was looming. I hated the thought of leaving Marinetta, but the dream of the desert crossing had been a part of me for so long that I could not abandon it. I suppose that sooner or later I might have asked her to accompany me, without much hope of success. As it happened, I didn't need to.

One evening, having spent a particularly depressing day with GOBI, she said, 'Maik, I want to cross the Sahara with you.'

'You *what*?'

'I'm serious, Maik. I've thought about it for a long time. I think I could do it. I bet you wouldn't even consider me. You'll say I'm too soft, as everyone else does.'

'It would mean leaving UNICEF,' I said.

'I don't care!'

'It will be very dangerous.'

'I don't care about the danger.'

'Steady on,' I said. 'See how you feel about it in a few days.'

A week later she was still adamant. Nothing I said seemed to put her off. I felt that she had no idea what difficulties she would be taking on. 'Over four thousand miles!' I told her. 'Riding on a camel through blazing sun, scorching wind and freezing cold. Monotonous food and dirty water. Marching all day, every day, without even stopping to pee. No man has ever done it — at least no Westerner. It's a longer journey than any of the old explorers of the past made.'

'Who were all men!' she scoffed.

'They call the Sahara "The Land of Men".'

'Crap! I'll prove them wrong!'

I shrugged and hoped she was right. My conscience bothered me. The truth was that I agreed to take her on the expedition only because I was in love. Was it right to drag this petite mannequin into a devil's cauldron, into the least hospitable environment on earth, for my own sake? How could she possibly survive? She wasn't in the least the outdoor type. She had never climbed a mountain or carried a rucksack. She had never known thirst or hunger or physical exhaustion. She looked so small and vulnerable. What if our lives were threatened? What if she were raped or injured or mutilated?

I was aware of some advantages in taking her. She spoke Arabic and French. There was no denying that she was an excellent photographer. And, as a woman, she could penetrate the harem side of nomad communities, something I had always failed to do. It would be a fascinating experiment, a man and a woman in the Sahara. I half persuaded myself that it was a good idea.

I admired her obstinacy. That alone was an encouraging sign. And I didn't realize then that I was dealing with Sardinian stubbornness at its most gritty. The Sards are a tough, mountain people, an island race like my own. For centuries they endured drought and poverty, taking to their wild mountains and resisting all attempts at invasion by the Muslims. Sicily fell, Spain fell, but Sardinia never. What better pedigree, I thought later, for someone taking on the earth's greatest desert?

I showed her some of the letters that I had received from Saharan experts. They demonstrated how slim were our chances of succeeding. One veteran of many vehicle-borne expeditions actually wrote, 'If I had to bet money on it, I'd say it's impossible.' There was also a letter from Geoffrey Moorhouse. He was the English writer who had attempted to make the west–east crossing by camel in 1972. He had set out from the Mauritanian oasis of Chinguetti and, after a record-breaking trek of 2,000 miles, had given up in Tamanrasset, Algeria. Three of his camels had died, and he had been plagued by sickness on the way. I had read Moorhouse's excellent book about his journey three times, with increasing trepidation. I understood why he had chosen to call it *The Fearful Void*.

I had earmarked Chinguetti as our starting point. It stood near the borders of the Sahara and would be the ideal place to train with camels before undertaking the journey. From there we would head south-east to the legendary caravan town of Tombouctou in Mali. Our next major stopping place would be Agadez in Niger, almost due east of Tombouctou and the centre of the Tuareg people of the Aïr mountains. The salt oasis of Bilma would be the third major port of call, across the featureless sand-sea of the Ténéré Erg. After Bilma we should have to find a way to cross war-torn Chad, then the Sudan, and to enter Egypt. Our major problem would be crossing Chad. The north of the country was the site of a fierce civil war between Chadian factions, one of them supported by Libya. The Chadian Ambassador in Khartoum warned us not to enter the country north of the sixteenth parallel, which made a long deviation necessary.

The Saharan authority Théodore Monod advised me that five camels and three people would be the ideal caravan size for such a journey. Mostly we would hire local guides for navigation, which was where our fluent grasp of Arabic would be essential. We would take maps and compasses but nothing in the way of advanced technology, which would spoil the spirit of the adventure. At the last minute we added a set of pencil flares for emergencies.

Moorhouse had begun his journey in November, during the Sahara's cool period. Travel was more comfortable then, but I reckoned that it was a mistake: that way you ran the risk of getting stuck in the hyper-arid eastern Sahara during the following hot season, the heat coming on you just as you were at your weakest point. I thought we could average 25 miles a day with our camels. Allowing for a non-marching day of one in three for watering and bureaucratic delays, this meant that the journey would take about nine months in all. To finish before the summer in the east, we should have to start in August. It would still be seething-hot then, but the onset of the rains, if there were any, would bring occasional cool days. We agreed that it would be easier to face the intense heat at the beginning of the journey, when we were still fresh, than at the end, when we would be exhausted.

Every day we jogged and swam, preparing our bodies for the challenge to come. Marinetta excelled in the swimming-pool, but on the track she was less than proficient. One day, after she had fallen behind for the fifth time, she bawled, 'What's the point of this? We won't be running in the Sahara!'

'You're useless!' I shouted back. 'You'll never even damn' well make it to Tijikja – and that's the first stop!'

I took her to the least salubrious type of Sudanese restaurant, where they served raw liver and fly-blown sheep's heads. They didn't give you a knife and fork. 'You'll have to get used to eating with your hands,' I told her. 'It's the custom in the desert.'

'I'm not eating a mouthful until I get a fork,' she said. 'Why shouldn't I eat like a Christian?'

'What will you do in the desert?'

'We're not in the desert yet.'

Sometimes I doubted if we ever would be. We still lacked what we needed most: money. We had tried everywhere to get support. An Italian magazine had expressed interest, and its director had invited Marinetta to his base in Milan during her leave. Then the director was mysteriously removed. We never heard from the magazine again.

It was almost out of the blue that I received a telex from Penguin Books, offering me a reasonable sum for the rights to my book about the journey. We were in business. Wildly excited, I ran to Marinetta with the news. For the first time I saw her worried.

'What's the matter?' I asked. 'This means it's no longer a dream.'

'I know,' she answered. 'That's what I'm afraid of. Now we really have to make decisions.'

My worst suspicions seemed to have been realized. It had all been talk. She had no intention of giving up her secure and well-paid job with the UN for a wild adventure in the Sahara. For days she hovered, undecided, while I cursed the fickleness of women. Then, half way through November, she handed in her resignation. Four months later we were married in London, and the same night we flew to Paris *en route* to Nouakchott, Mauritania.

Our honeymoon in Paris was the most miserable five days of my life. Every day the rain dribbled down the rue Kepler outside our dismal hotel room, but it was not the life-giving rain of Africa. Every morning we woke on opposite sides of a giant bed, seeing each other as if for the first time, two strangers in a foreign land on the eve of a terrifying adventure. Perhaps it was fear that prevented us from making love. 'I feel flat,' was Marinetta's way of expressing it. 'The last thing I feel like is sex. I just don't feel sexy at all.'

By day we wandered, exhausted and depressed, through the wet streets. Paris seemed cold, the architecture austere, the people overdressed and unfriendly. We visited the Mauritanian embassy in St Germain and found a dingy, dilapidated building with grease-smeared walls, where a gaggle of black men crowded around a desk.

'What do you want?' one of them asked rudely.

'Visas for Mauritania.'

'Why?' came the aggressive response.

'Tourism.'

'Ah, tourism!' Was the inscrutable look on his face mockery or surprise? The Malian embassy next door was more stately, but inside there was no reception, only a maze of doors without labels. In desperation, Marinetta pushed one of them open and discovered a huge room with a man in an immaculate suit sitting behind a mahogany desk. 'Is this the room for visas?' she piped up.

'No, it's not!' the man snapped. 'Now get out and shut that door.'

'Do you think that was the Ambassador?' she whispered, giggling, as she closed it.

In the evenings we walked down the boulevard des Italiennes, through the pools of light cast by the crowded cafés. Everywhere there was the bustle of life and good spirits, a joy that we were unable to share. Already we felt like aliens on the way to a far-off planet. Yet the worst was that we felt alienated from each other. It was as if the magic had somehow been washed away like the glitter from a Christmas star. 'Jesus!' Marinetta said once. 'I thought it was bad when all the girls I knew got married because they were pregnant. *We* only got married for a bloody expedition!'

When we returned to the hotel at night the desolation covered us like a blanket. We had loved each other once, but now the fever had gone. I began to regret having wanted Marinetta with me on the expedition. I saw that weakness and my own selfishness had ruined me. I would have been far better off alone after all.

The only relief of those days was our meeting with Professor Théodore Monod, the octogenarian who was considered the world's leading expert on the Sahara. He was a small man, slightly bent but very active for eighty-five. He had penetrating blue eyes, a manner that was cool but not impolite, enthusiastic at moments but not effusive. I wondered how many hopeful Saharan explorers had come and gone in his small office in the rue Cuvier. He showed us maps and geological specimens, holding them up to the light. When I mentioned Moorhouse, he sighed. 'Ah, Moorhouse. He sent me a postcard from Tamanrasset saying, "I have seen enough of your beautiful desert!" But Moorhouse was a good man.'

An hour later I felt refreshed. After all the warnings and discouragement here was someone, and the leading expert at that, who believed that we could succeed. On our way out I thanked him for his confidence.

'Listen,' he told me paternally, 'nothing is impossible. Only, some things are difficult.'

I looked at my new wife. It was the best advice I could have been given.

Later, the night before we were due to fly to Nouakchott, we lay awake, afraid and excited, until the bleary light of dawn came crowding in. We were on the verge of not one but two adventures: the Sahara and marriage. In the chalky dawn of our last day in Europe I wondered which of them would prove the more dangerous.

The Atlantic lay beneath us, deep Prussian blue and frayed at the edges by a white spume of spindrift. At midday we passed the Atlas mountains, looking like giant upturned scallops of grey and ochre veined with pale streaks of snow and plumed in mist. Beyond them lay the desert, an umber plain criss-crossed with wadis like coiled brown snakes. Nothing and no one moved down there. I wish I could describe how the sprawl of Nouakchott looked from the air, how through the porthole we saw the Sahara coming closer and closer, stretching on for ever and ever until it reached the Nile. The truth is that after passing the Atlas range the aircraft was enveloped in fog, and we saw nothing more until it came to rest outside the terminal.

We stepped out into the oppressive April heat and queued up for the immigration procedures. The airport was crowded and claustrophobic. Beyond the bars that separated 'Arrivals' from the multitude a current of faces bobbed, peering through at us like those of prisoners. The faces covered the spectrum of African shades — khaki, coffee-cream, brown and black. Some of them were wrapped in brilliant-blue headcloths that displayed only the eyes. They gave the impression that their owners had stepped out of the desert that moment. (More likely they had come from the local shanty town on bicycles.)

The first character whom we met in Mauritania was a bored-looking official in an ill-fitting uniform. He stamped our passports and thrust a pair of green forms into my hand. They were currency-declaration forms on which, according to instructions, you had to declare all the foreign currency you were carrying. This gave me a problem. I had about £5,000 in French francs and dollar traveller's cheques, almost all of which were in a money belt under my shirt. I wasn't sure of the exact amount, but neither was I keen on opening my belt and counting the notes, displaying to that sea of inquisitive faces how much I had and where it was kept. Making a quick estimate, therefore, I wrote a sum down on the form. I made a small error – one that almost cost us the expedition.

Marinetta and I were last in the queue. Between us and freedom lay a dingy cabinet like a changing booth at a third-rate swimming-pool, into which, one by one, the passengers were disappearing with a slit-eyed soldier wearing a beret. It occurred to me only as my turn came that they were being searched for foreign currency. The man allowed Marinetta through without searching her. Then I was thrust up against him, in a few feet of space behind a filthy curtain, while he slowly and ham-fistedly counted the notes in my belt. He examined my declaration form, then counted the notes again. Finally he said in broken French, 'There are over 6,000 francs here not declared. That's bad. Very bad.' I opened my mouth to protest, but already I was being marched like a convict through the mob outside and into a small office, where a narrow-featured supervisor sat.

'You have failed to declare 6,100 francs,' the supervisor said, after listening to the story. 'We do not like currency smugglers in Mauritania. Now, not only are we entitled to confiscate the amount you have tried to smuggle, we can also charge you a fine of five times the amount. That will be 30,500 francs.'

Staring at him incredulously, I almost gagged. Three thousand pounds! My head spun dizzily. My mouth dried up and my heart thumped. For a moment I thought I would faint. I tried to explain that I couldn't possibly have made such a big mistake, but no articulate sentence came out. I had to cling to the desk to steady myself. 'What if I don't pay?' I finally managed to stammer.

'Then you'll go to prison,' he snapped. 'And I'll keep your passport here until you do.'

We stood outside the airport like refugees with our bits of luggage scattered around us. I still couldn't believe that I'd made such a mistake. All the years of dreaming and planning were wasted, ter-minated on our first day in Mauritania by a stupid error and intran-sigent officials. I have never, before or since, felt so useless.

Marinetta had a friend in Nouakchott. His name was Charles Habis, and he was consular officer at the US Embassy, responsible for health projects. A phone call brought Charles and his lovely Ecuadorian wife, Mariana, to our rescue. Later, in their house in the suburbs, I had a chance to explain the problem. At the same time I re-examined my copy of the currency form. I noticed that something was amiss. I had clearly written 25,000 francs on the form. They had found 26,100 francs on me. There was certainly a discrepancy but nothing like as large as the amount they had mentioned. The larger mistake had been theirs. The difference that this made was the difference between success and humiliating failure.

Charles and Mariana were sympathetic. Charles was a stocky, fit-looking man with a black beard and a serious, friendly face. He had led an interesting life. Born a Roman Catholic in Jerusalem, he had emigrated with his parents to Ecuador when his father had foreseen the emerging problems in Palestine. He had grown up speaking Spanish like a native and, after finishing school, had emigrated once again, this time to the United States. He had been a social studies teacher and had run a drugs-abuse programme. Then he had been enlisted by the State Department for their USAID projects in Somalia, where he and his wife had met Marinetta. It was our great good fortune that Charles and Mariana happened to be in Nouakchott when we arrived.

'This kind of thing happens all the time here,' Charles said. 'Never saw a country like it for bureaucracy. Everything can be worked out, though. It just needs diplomacy and patience.' Charles said that everything in Mauritania worked by personal acquaintance. One of his staff, a Moor called Abbas, was a fixer who generally handled delicate diplomatic problems for him. 'Abbas is a white Moor,' he explained, 'and from a noble tribe. They say all that stuff about nobility is in the past, but, believe me, it still works wonders. Abbas knows everyone who's anyone.'

We met Abbas the following day. He was a tall young man, nut-brown, with a dignified face and a graceful bearing. Like most Moors we saw in Nouakchott, he was dressed in a flowing gandourah of bright blue and extremely baggy Arab trousers, or *sirwal*. 'It's not difficult,' was his opinion when he'd heard the problem, 'but it will take some negotiation. You have to start at the bottom and work your way up.'

For the rest of the day we worked our way up, starting with the airport supervisor who had confiscated my passport and walking or driving from office to office, each one representing a grade higher in the pecking order of officialdom. At last, in the afternoon, we were granted an interview with the Director of Customs himself.

He was a gaunt, silent man with an inscrutable look, and with him were the airport supervisor and another official. The four of us took up places in a row before his desk like a trade delegation and accepted the tea he ordered. After preliminary polite greetings, Abbas began to talk smoothly about our case. He said that we were guests in the country and had made a mistake in the confusion of our arrival. A mistake was a bad thing, but we were good characters and there had been mistakes on both sides. The expression on the Director's face never changed. He made some challenging remarks. Abbas countered politely. The discussion went on and on until it seemed they must have forgotten about us.

Suddenly I sensed a relaxation of the tension. The Director was smiling. Even the supervisor was smiling. 'We welcome guests in this country,' the Director told us, 'so we'll let the matter drop. You will fill in the declaration form again. But do it right this time.'

That was my first taste of the Moors. Discussion was a way of life for them. Even in pre-Arab times the nobility had been composed of families of mediators. The mediators had been deposed by warrior tribes of Arab stock but had soon reasserted their status by converting to Islam and learning classical Arabic, while the warriors remained illiterate. The present nobility of Mauritania comprised just these elements, the Arab warriors and the Berber mediators or marabouts. Together with a third, vassal, class descended from the ordinary Berber herdsmen, these castes formed the *bidan* or white Moors. Their language was Hassaniyya, a dialect of Arabic.

Nouakchott was not part of the traditional Moorish state. It had been built in the 1960s to serve the newly independent government of Moukhtar Ould Dadda. The city was a blend of many half-remembered styles. Little chunks of Africa, the street stalls and the artisans, were tucked under the verandahs of modern office blocks and scattered along boulevards shaded with mesquite trees. The

Sahara drifted along the streets, blowing into the lobbies of the hotels with every swing of a plate-glass door, dragging down the highways, frosting the traffic lights and piling up in the gutters.

The city seemed a tranquil place, but its appearance was deceptive. It was ringed with hundreds of thousands of makeshift houses constructed of old timber and flattened-out tins. Thin goats and old women in ragged black robes could be seen wandering among these shanty streets. The Moors who lived here were nomads who had been forced out of the desert by the Great Drought of the previous five years. They had lost their animals – their camels, goats and sheep – and now they could no longer survive in the desert. They were in the city as refugees. More than half of Nouakchott's population were displaced nomads.

There was a mixed reaction to our proposed journey. Some expatriates laughed outright. A young volunteer from the Peace Corps told us confidently, 'It's not possible to do a trek like Moorhouse's any more. Too many of the wells have dried up in the drought.'

A UN worker assured us with equal confidence that there were few camels left now in Mauritania. 'Most of them died in the drought,' he said.

That, at least, was not true. There were camels in plenty within the city itself. We were walking one day, near sunset, by the football stadium when a battalion of dark shapes came marching into view. There were three separate camel herds, more than 200 animals, streaming two or three deep from the battlements of the city. They were being driven by two men on foot who were dressed in faded blue gandourahs and oily headcloths. They carried sticks across their shoulders in time-honoured herdsman style. As the procession stomped by we caught the pungent smell of camel and heard the *ssh-ssh* cries of the herdsmen. Most of the camels were females, their udders strapped to prevent their calves from suckling. Among them was a large red bull camel, which foamed at the mouth and blew out his floppy pink bladder. Here, under the eaves of the city, the old life of the desert went on. When they had gone Marinetta said, 'You look like a child who's been given his favourite food. You're only satisfied when you're in the desert. Sometimes I think there's no room for me in your life at all.'

We were anxious to leave for the oasis of Chinguetti, where we intended to spend the summer months acclimatizing and learning Hassaniyya. It lay in the Adrar mountains of northern Mauritania. The only way to get there was by Peugeot taxi, which you shared with six or seven others, and to spend a cramped five hours as far as Atar, the capital of the region. From there Chinguetti could be reached by Land-Rover through the tortuous Amogjar pass.

Before leaving, though, we wanted a last look at the ocean. We visited the fish market. The sky was grey over the Atlantic and an off-shore breeze riffled the waters and whipped up a thick surf. Rows of fishing smacks belonging to the Imraguen fishermen were drawn up out of the current, and the fisher-folk hurried back and forth in their yellow oilskins with trays of tunny and mullet, which they gutted, filleted and laid out on acres of trestles to dry in the sun. The smell of high fish was everywhere. Some men carried lobsters and other shellfish, which were sold live on brine-soaked slabs of wood, sculpted into totems by generations of fishermen's knives. 'We won't see anything like this again till we reach the Nile,' Marinetta said. And as we turned back and saw the desert stretching before us, I remembered just how far away that was.

Sid'Ahmed

From the door of our house in Chinguetti you could see an ocean of dunes, amber, cream and ivory, cascading down to the wadi, where palm trees grew and the sand was white and smooth as snow. The wadi cut the oasis neatly into halves, so that the inhabitants regarded themselves as two distinct divisions. Our landlord, Sid'Ahmed Ould Aidud, was sheikh of the western division. His house was almost the last on the west bank of the wadi, a manor built of stone and surrounded by the tents and sack-cloth shacks of retainers and poor relations. I suppose that we were also regarded as Sid'Ahmed's satellites. Chinguetti clung to its feudal traditions, and everyone was expected to have a protector. As the hereditary leader of the Awlad Ghaylan, the dominant Arab warrior tribe of the oasis, Sid'Ahmed fitted this role perfectly.

The official ruler of Chinguetti was the *préfet*. He was a Pular from the Senegal river, a polite, educated man who had studied in Paris. He was often to be seen walking in the market with a long face, so that white Moors like Sid'Ahmed would screw up their eyes and say, 'That man's not happy here.' The *préfet* thought Chinguetti about as far from civilization as you could get and yearned for the intellectual café society of Paris. Sid'Ahmed longed for the old days when the warriors ruled, but he knew those days had gone for ever.

Sid'Ahmed was a big man with a bull-like neck and an upright bearing. A paunch of good living showed under the folds of his gandourah, but he carried his weight as regally as an emperor. Still, he was not above showing you the scars on his legs made by a saddle. 'I'll carry those scars for life,' he would say. 'I was a *méhariste* with the French. I've been everywhere there is to go on a camel. And I can still ride, by God!'

When Marinetta and I arrived in Chinguetti, it was the *préfet* who directed us to Sid'Ahmed. 'I've got a house for you,' the big man told us. 'Just what you're looking for.' It was a single-roomed house of stone, standing not two hundred yards from Sid'Ahmed's manor. On one side was a staircase that led to the roof and, at the back, a cubicle for washing. There was no furniture except for an Arab carpet and three foam-rubber mattresses. On two sides stood the Sahara and, on the other two, a wall that for some reason had never been completed. He asked for 3,000 ougiyyas a month. We beat him down to 2,000 ougiyyas and accepted. It was, as he had said, just what we wanted.

Sid'Ahmed's house was an austere mansion of several rooms, set in a high-walled courtyard. There we met his buxom wife Mahjouba, two very buxom daughters and a spindly son called Boyhin. Boyhin was so thin, in fact, that it seemed he had sacrificed any spare flesh he might have been born with for the sake of his sisters. Both they and their stepmother were plump enough for two, but this was normal among Moorish women. For them fat was beautiful, and no self-respecting lady would be seen in public without a goodly layer of flesh on her bones. They even fed their daughters a special diet of milk and peanuts so that they would grow up desirably colossal. Naturally they looked askance at Marinetta's sylph-like figure. You could hear the pity in their voices when they told her, 'You don't eat enough, by God!'

'She'll never make it,' was Sid'Ahmed's opinion when he heard our plans. 'She's too weak. Why don't you leave her here and go on your own?'

'I'm not weak,' Marinetta cut in indignantly. 'The reason why I'm not fat is because I work hard!' This probably lowered our standing even more in the eyes of the *bidan* women. They did nothing and were proud of it. One of them even boasted to us, 'I've never in my life made a glass of tea.'

It was the Haratin who did all the work. The Haratin washed, cleaned, cooked the meals, fetched the water, tended the domestic animals, cultivated the palm gardens and, more often than not, looked after the children. Haratin men and women were as lean and sinewy as the palm trees they tended. They were black but not negroid, and

they had been in the Sahara far longer than the Arabs or even the
Berbers. 'A long, long time,' Sid'Ahmed told us. 'Since before the
Arabs came. Since before the time of the Prophet, may peace and
blessing be upon Him.' But the term 'Haratin' had become confusing.
Once it had meant a distinct caste of settled people, superior to
slaves. They were the free sharecroppers who worked the palmeries
for their white overlords. Slaves, on the other hand, were bound to
their masters and worked for them as servants. As recently as 1980
the government had abolished slavery and decreed that all former
slaves would be known henceforth as 'Haratin'. Naturally the real
Haratin had been livid. 'My father had slaves,' Sid'Ahmed said, 'and
my grandfather. All my ancestors had slaves. I am the first of my line
who doesn't have slaves. I have Haratin.'

The Hartani we got to know best in Chinguetti was a lad called
Dada. Every day he brought us a goatskin of water from the well,
carried on his donkey. He was about fifteen, a tall, slim youth with
a face already grained with the effects of outdoor work. We looked
forward to the raucous singing that announced his arrival each
morning. Together, he and I would unload the heavy *girba* and hang
it from our wobbly frame. Then Dada would point to his donkey
and say, 'The old so-and-so is worn out. Look at him!' Almost
daily he would repeat, 'A new donkey will cost more than 10,000
ougiyyas. Now where will I get *that* kind of money?' Then he would
vault into the wooden pack-saddle with a flourish and drive the
animal into a terrific gallop towards the well. He never got very far.
After a moment the animal would grind to a halt and Dada would
be flung off. Then he would pick himself up, curse, dust off his
ragged clothes and drive the donkey back, singing the same jaunty
song.

Our *girba* frame stood at the door of our house, and if the waterskin
was not tied very tightly, we would be plagued all day by the
maddening drip-drip of water on the sand. After hours of this I would
explode. 'Marinetta! Haven't you learned to tie a *girba* yet?'

To which she would politely reply, 'But it was you who last drew
water.'

The frame was something like a clothes-horse and was made of
bits of wood lashed together with string. It never inspired our

confidence and got more wobbly with each new hanging. Finally it collapsed in a heap, almost depositing the swollen *girba* at Marinetta's feet. After that I looked for somewhere else to hang it and eventually found a metal ring fixed in the rear wall of the house. 'It's too far away!' was Marinetta's verdict after I had struggled for two hours to hang it. Exasperated, I went to cut it down. No sooner had I severed the first strand than the wall crumbled and the whole Heath Robinson arrangement collapsed. The knife was knocked out of my hand and stuck in my foot just behind the big toe. I looked down in surprise at the blood welling out of the wound and thought longingly of tap water.

When we started cooking with charcoal I understood why the Moors used Haratin cooks. Even cooking for two was a full-time job. First you had to hunt for straw or paper, which meant some serious scavenging in the streets. Once the charcoal was alight, you had to fan it frantically with a tray until the orange stain of fire crept through the carbon. If there was no wind, you had to keep fanning at intervals until your arms ached and your brow ran with sweat. It sometimes took twenty minutes to boil water. I suggested moving the iron stove up to the roof where there was more wind. There fanning was unnecessary. Instead the charcoal exploded with sparks, which blew into our clothes, leaving scorch-marks like cigarette burns. The charcoal became so hot that everything we put on it was instantly charred to a frazzle. It drove Marinetta mad. 'How the hell do they do it?' she grumbled, presenting me with a plate of blackened rice. From thereon, at sunset, the smell of burning food became familiar and a little later she would appear, smiling bravely, with yet another platter of burned-out pellets, saying, 'I think it's a bit better today.' Once she announced that she would make bread to end the monotony of rice. She had never made it before in her life. After an hour of silence I went to investigate. Guiltily she held up one of our precious cooking pans with a half-inch hole neatly burned through the bottom.

The Moor women who visited our house had plenty of advice for her but rarely lifted a finger to help. They would come waddling up to inspect the *nsara* (as they called Christians), their plump behinds undulating beneath thick wraps of indigo cotton. The cotton looked mercilessly hot, but they claimed it was the coolest material of all.

They preferred it even though it left a tell-tale stain of blue on their skin, which gave them a ghostly appearance. Sitting well-padded on our rug, they would tell Marinetta, 'You should hire a Hartani to do the work. A respectable woman shouldn't be washing and cooking.' They pressed her constantly to eat more. 'Your husband won't desire you unless you put on more weight,' they whispered to her more than once.

Sex seemed to be their main preoccupation. They joked about it when I was there and talked about it *ad nauseam* when I was absent. Marinetta told me that they always asked, 'Is this your first man?' They seemed surprised when she answered, 'Yes.' Many of them had been married and divorced several times and were 'between marriages', waiting for someone to pick them up. Marinetta thought that this was why so many of them came to our house and sat there without speaking, fluttering their eyelids and looking pretty. 'They're after you!' she said. 'They remind me of loose women in Europe.' I was flattered, knowing that she was joking but remembering that Muslim custom allowed up to four wives.

They spent an extraordinary amount of time prettifying themselves, trying out perfumes, dressing their hair and applying henna in geometric designs on their hands and feet. I returned one day to discover Marinetta sitting on the rug with her hands and feet tied up in plastic bags. 'They insisted on my trying the henna,' she said. 'They said, "You should look nice for your husband, then he will desire you more."' The plastic bags were supposed to help the henna dry, but when she had scraped off the soggy clots of manure the effect was less than erotic. The women did persuade her, however, to try out local dress. She scorned the indigo robe, with its prestigious blue stain, and chose a light-orange one. It looked elegant when she was sitting, but as soon as she moved there were problems. It trailed around her feet, tripped her up, caught in the door, fluttered into the cooking pans and got scorched by the charcoal. 'I'm never going to wear *that* on a camel!' she said.

I felt the same about the gandourah I tried out. It was as stately as a Roman toga on the Moors, but on me it looked like a sack tied in the middle. It was really no more than a square of cotton with a hole cut for the head and a pocket stitched on the outside. In the wind it bellied out and wrenched at me like a kite, and on calmer days it tripped me up constantly. It was the worst possible dress for camel-riding. I soon noticed that, when working, the herdsmen and Haratin wore trim Arab shirts, layered headcloths and floppy *sirwel*. We decided that this would be the ideal dress for both of us.

Our occasional adoption of Moorish dress did nothing to disguise our strangeness from the hordes of children who dogged our foot-steps in the street, shouting, '*Nsara! Nsara!*' If it hadn't been for them, we would certainly have delighted in the beauty of this little town squatting on the sides of the wadi. There was a huddle of mud-brick shops clustered around a grain store, each shop skirted by the tiny stalls of Haratin women selling eggs, dried gazelle meat, tomatoes and fresh-baked bread. Beyond the shops was a sandy square where camels hustled around a rusting water-tank, bordered on the other side by the battlements of the old French fortress, with its Saharan 'meat-ball' walls and moresco arches. The fortress now housed the *préfet* and the town police. Behind the fort were streamers of narrow, crooked streets fanning out as far as the sand dunes and the ring of palmeries that stood below them.

But the children made our visits to the market a misery. They would pour into the shops behind us, pointing and staring, repeating what we said and asking for gifts. Perhaps they thought that if their presence was obnoxious enough, we would pay them to go away. But I have never believed in blackmail. Their grubby hands remained empty, causing them to follow us home again, still chanting, '*Nsara! Nsara!*' And even at home there was no escape. They would camp outside in little squads, and the bolder ones would make forays to peek through our windows and the cracks in the door. When I had had enough I would sally forth waving a camel stick and trying to look ferocious, sending them scattering into the distance and giggling at the fun.

Often people would stop us and bring out little bundles of cloth, neatly tied, displaying an array of flint axe heads, arrow tips and ornaments for which they asked exorbitant prices. They seemed disappointed when we turned them down, saying, 'The other *nsara* always bought them!'

'Which other *nsara*?'

'The *nsara* of the film *Fort Saganne!*'

It turned out that the previous year a French film company had virtually taken over the oasis for the making of a desert epic called *Fort Saganne*. They had employed hundreds of the locals as extras, hired cars and planes and helicopters, imported horses and camels and put on the payroll the entire operational strength of the Corps Méhariste. The oasis had enjoyed a ten-month festival. It had become transformed into the battleground of a fierce colonial war for possession of a fortress, the 'Fort Saganne' of the title, which had been built especially for the film and stood at the top of the waterless Amogjar pass, where no fortress could ever have stood. The real fort of Chinguetti had been used as a hotel by the film crews and supplied with a generator, electric lights and a waterpump that now stood idle.

The French had showered everyone with money, not least Sid'Ahmed, who had been given a walk-on part. 'I'm not going to tell you how much they paid me,' he said. 'You'd never believe it anyway.' His part had lasted fifteen minutes and he had played the 'Chief'. I never discovered what he had been the 'Chief' of, but no doubt they had cast him well. To the children it must have seemed suddenly very quiet when the film company pulled out. Chinguetti was one of the oldest settlements in the Sahara, one of the seven holy towns of Islam and the former capital of Mauritania. I once met two Belgian tourists there who said they had come only to see 'Fort Saganne'. The irony was that the real Fort Saganne was in Algeria.

Even the children would disappear in the searing heat of midday, when the shops closed and the streets cleared as if by magic. The heat lay like treacle on the sweltering afternoon, pressing in through the windows and bulging through the cracks in the door. You could feel the hot stones throbbing like oven bricks, and the heat seeped into every ligament and muscle, clogging up the motion of your body and dizzying your head. To walk just half a mile in that heat was a challenge. To travel 4,500 miles by camel over the world's most arid terrain, to plan the longest trek ever undertaken by Westerners in the Sahara, that seemed like an impossibly arrogant dream.

Despite the women's interest in sex, the Moors did not follow the Mediterranean habit of sleeping with their wives in the afternoon siesta. It was too hot for that. Our sex life, already moribund after a few dismal failures, died the death in Chinguetti, what with the flies and the heat and the lack of privacy. Instead we fought like caged dogs. 'You only married me for this expedition!' was Marinetta's favourite line. She missed the carefree life of the single girl. She felt nostalgic for home. 'I should never have got married,' she said. 'I've let my parents down. I should never have left them when they needed me most.' She confessed that she'd always been shy of sex. Even in her late teens she had blushed when people talked about pregnancy and having children. The bawdy jokes of the classroom had passed over her head like smoke. She had longed to be out of the lust-choked place by the end of the day. The others said she was living on pink clouds.

She had always been determined not to marry an Italian. There had been boyfriends, of course, many of them. There had been the American anthropologist in Pago-Pago and the Austrian gynae-cologist in India. In Somalia there had been a Swede and an Iranian and a Frenchman and another American, but they were always short-lived romances. 'When they got too serious, I dropped them,' she said. 'I loved dressing up and going out with a handsome man to a nice restaurant. I loved the idea of romance. But when it went any further I ran a mile.'

Often she cried. Sometimes she screamed. 'It's a nightmare!' she said. 'I wish it was all a dream. I wish I could wake up and find myself at home in my own room in my parents' house.' It was security she longed for, I thought, an escape from the knowledge that she now had responsibilities that might last longer than our expedition. 'My mother warned me,' she told me. 'She said that I knew nothing about the problems of life. She said all that was to come.' There was no reprise of the romantic episode in Port Sudan. She seemed almost a different person now. 'I realize that I did the wrong thing in getting married,' she said. 'It was a big mistake. We've made the biggest mistake of our lives. God, I don't even think I love you!'

'You mean you only agreed to get married to go on this ex-pedition?'

'Yes,' she sobbed. 'Only for a bloody expedition. How stupid I was to give up my freedom for this!'

Sometimes, when I became fed up with the tirade, I would escape and talk to Sid'Ahmed. His perspective was refreshingly different.

'Mahjouba's my eleventh wife,' he told me. 'A man's got to have a change. When a woman's no good, just get rid of her and get another. There's plenty of hares in the desert, by God!' He said that although Islam allowed you four wives at once, he'd sooner have one at a time and change her often. 'Two can make your life hell,' he said, 'especially if you don't treat them the same.'

'Even one can make your life hell,' I said.

'We have a saying,' he went on. 'Nothing hurts like a toothache and a bad wife. If you have a bad tooth, you pull it out, don't you?'

According to Sid'Ahmed, it was a woman's duty to conceive as soon as possible. Marinetta's dereliction in this respect must have worried him because he asked me, 'Isn't she pregnant yet?'

I thought wryly of the number of times we had actually made love and said, 'No.'

'What if she gets pregnant in the Sahara?' he asked. 'What will you do?' I sighed, not wanting to start on the juggernaut question of the Pill. 'The desert is hard for a woman,' Sid'Ahmed said. 'Look at Mahjouba. She was born a nomad and even she finds it hard to get on a camel.'

I felt like commenting that this was hardly surprising considering her size. Instead I told him, 'I thought you were townspeople, not nomads.'

'There are no townspeople in Mauritania,' he scoffed. 'Not unless you count the Haratin. Every white Moor comes from a tent. Ours is still rolled up there in the store with Mahjouba's camel litter. I've got camels too. They're grazing in the south near Tichit. If we get any rain this year, they'll be brought up here and we'll go and camp with them.'

'On camels?'

He looked shamefaced. 'We usually hire a Land-Rover now,' he admitted. He explained that you needed at least five camels to move a household like his, what with the tent, two massive poles, waterskins, cooking stuff, bedding, rugs and carpets and a sort of table that supported everything once the tent was erected. In Chinguetti he had only two female camels with their calves, which he kept for milk. They wouldn't even have carried the tent poles. 'Ah, but it's not the same in a car,' he sighed. 'You can keep your cars and your planes. Give me a camel and a cool, moonlit night, a skin of milk, a pouch of tobacco and nothing before me but the emptiness. That's freedom! The Arabs are camel men. They always have been.'

Things had changed since Sid'Ahmed's youth, when Chinguetti had been full of camels, and raiders had come hunting for them from as far away as the Spanish Sahara. 'You had to be a *man* in the time of raids!' Sid'Ahmed said. He would whip back his gandourah and display a grey bullet scar on the arm. 'Nineteen forty-three that was,' he would say. 'Some Rigaybat came up from the south driving 500 camels and some slaves they'd taken from the tribes. We went after them and caught them at Aghuedir. What a battle there was, by God! We killed thirty Rigaybat and got all the camels back!' Those were the days Sid'Ahmed longed for. Now the Rigaybat had been recruited into the popular resistance movement, the Polisario, and the Spanish Sahara had become the Western Sahara. The Polisario were armed with rocket-launchers and machine-guns. Now they played for different stakes. The Polisario had attacked Chinguetti a few years before, and the oasis walls still bore the scars. The power station had never worked since they had punched three neat shell holes in its side. 'The Libyans built it, and the Polisario finished it,' Sid'Ahmed said. 'No God but God, what a world we live in!'

I had already asked Sid'Ahmed to find us some camels in Chinguetti. After a few weeks of searching he told me, 'It won't be easy now, Omar. So many camels died in the drought. There are only about forty left in the oasis now, and most of those are females kept for milk.' He advised me to go to Atar. 'There's a daily market there,' he said.

But even Atar was suffering from a camel shortage. Camels were brought there from the south, and prices were high. We visited the market twice and found nothing but calves and females and untrained bulls. They were of no use to us. The Moors trained only geldings to be ridden. They were easier to handle than bulls because they weren't bothered by the mating instinct, which could transform a docile male into a frothing, demonic man-killer within days. We found what we were looking for at last in a butcher's yard. They were two big geldings, one red, the other white. They were lithe and tall and supple, with well-padded humps and well-muscled legs. They were the camels that would take us to Tombouctou and perhaps even Agadez. We paid over £500 each for them, which made them easily the most expensive camels I had ever bought. The red one we named Shigar, which denoted his colour, and the white Gurfaf, or 'hyena', because he was bad-tempered and greedy. 'He wasn't gelded until after he had matured and mated,' the butcher told us. 'No wonder he's bad-tempered. Wouldn't you be?'

We spent the rest of our time in Atar buying saddles and equipment. An entire section of the market was given over to the stalls and workshops of the smiths. They made everything from saddles to jewellery and were another distinct caste in Moorish society. The other castes, the white Moors and the Haratin, regarded them with a mixture of fear and distrust. No self-respecting Moor would have let his daughter marry one. 'You can't trust a smith,' Sid'Ahmed told us. 'Don't pay him anything until you get what you ordered. Otherwise you'll never get it!'

In Chinguetti Sid'Ahmed advised us to hand the camels over to the keeping of a man called Mohammed. He was a Hartani built like a wrestler, with the biggest calf muscles I had ever seen. He was the town herdsman who took charge of the forty or so camels left, picking them up from each house before sunrise and driving them far out into the plateau to feed during the day. At sunset he would drive them back into the oasis for the night. Sid'Ahmed said that Mohammed had acquired his muscles in the salt quarries at Kedyet Ijil, where he had worked with the *azalais*, the great caravans that had transported salt to the West African states for centuries. There were few *azalais* left now. Most of the salt trade had been taken over by lorries. They used the new main road of asphalt that went via Nouakchott, by which they could make Nema, on the Mali border, in three days instead of thirty. Mohammed had grown tired of the work and had come to Chinguetti looking for a job and a wife. He had married Dada's sister and they lived in one of the makeshift tents that surrounded Sid'Ahmed's house.

Mohammed told me that there had been very little grazing on the plateau since the Great Drought and advised me to supplement it with camel cake. This was someone's bright idea for making use of peanut shells. They were ground up, mixed with oil and churned out as hard slugs an inch long. The cake was cheap and nutritious, and you had to soak it in water and serve it as a mash. The camels loved it. They fought to get at it in the evenings, when Sid'Ahmed and I fed our camels together. It was a messy business, which Sid'Ahmed could easily have got his Haratin to do. But Sid'Ahmed was a simple man beneath the bluster and, like me, he enjoyed it.

We became accustomed to the slow rhythm of life in the oasis. Our visitors no longer seemed like intruders. The children seemed just children. The only things that got worse were the heat and our arguments. The afternoon was a prison in the suffocating darkness of our room. The heat seemed to eat away at us. We lay prostrate on our mattresses and argued about the past.

'I can't understand why you agreed to marry me,' I told Marinetta.

'It seemed so romantic at the time.' She sighed. 'It was the idea of adventure with a writer, an explorer. What girl wouldn't have been excited by it?' She had never wanted a real relationship, she said. Real relationships gave you problems. The idea of love and marriage was romantic, but in reality it was just a trap. Now all she wanted was to be free.

Sometimes the blackness of despair covered me, and I longed to escape. All the love I had felt drained out of me. I almost shivered with apprehension when I thought of the vast distance that we had set out to cover together. 'When you get to the Nile you can do what the hell you like,' I said. 'But until we get there, let's at least pretend we're friends.'

'Friends!' she scoffed. 'We're not even friends. Friends *like* each other.'

In the evenings, though, these battles were forgotten like a passing dream. We moved our beds up to the roof and basked in the cool of sunset as peace settled among the houses. The oblongs of shade moved around the buildings, swelling then dissolving into the sand. The grey sky was threaded with the last ribbons of rose-pink, and the settling half-light gave new purpose to the moving figures. First the goats would troop out of the desert, marching in grim order, each squadron with its leader and the weaker stragglers bringing up the rear. Finally the camels would come into view, appearing like a rash of black spots against the white sand of the wadi, getting closer until the individual animals were recognizable, followed by the dark, lonely form of the herdsman Mohammed. As they passed each house two or three camels would peel off and make for the place where their evening mash would be served. Sid'Ahmed's blunt figure would be seen performing the sunset prayers on the dunes, and from somewhere the sonorous voice of a muezzin would sound.

We were on a platform among the stars with only the desert beyond. The Sahara was everywhere around us and everywhere across the horizon of the closing darkness. Sitting on the roof was like sitting on the quayside of a vast ocean of nothing stretching half way across the world. Its far shore was the bank of a river 4,000 miles away.

A week after our camels arrived in Chinguetti we decided to make our first training run. We chose as a goal the mysterious crater of Guelb Richat. It stood on the very edge of El Jouf, the great eastern emptiness that stretched 1,000 miles until it merged with the gloomy gravel plains of the Tanezrouft. It was now high summer, the worst time of year for such a journey.

Sid'Ahmed seemed horrified. He did his best to put us off. 'It's forbidden to travel in the Sahara at this time of year!' he exclaimed. 'No Moor who knows the desert would do it. You should wait till the Pleiades rise.'

I knew that the Arabs gauged the changing seasons by the rise and fall of the constellations and that the rise of the Pleiades announced the onset of the rains in late July. We intended to be on our way to Tombouctou by then.

The day we set off for Richat I did something else no Moor would have done, at least not in Chinguetti. I went down to the well and, standing shoulder to shoulder with the Haratin, I stripped off my shirt and began to water my own camels. The Moor women gathered in the shade, pointing and gesticulating as if scandalized. It was deeply satisfying to hoist up the cool, clear water from the bowels of the planet and to watch my own camels slurping it up with relish. It was good to mix with these lean Haratin at the well and hear their cheerful banter, to feel the blood flowing fresh through my muscles and to be in tune once again with the heartbeat of the earth after days of hiding from the heat. I knew that the well was a Haratin place, and I was flouting convention. But the children of Chinguetti had never let us forget that we were *nsara*, and everyone knew the *nsara* were half crazy.

When he realized that we couldn't be dissuaded, Sid'Ahmed laughed and said, 'It will be a real test for you, and especially for Mariam. If she survives this, no one will say she is weak!' Then he showed us how to strap on the peculiar Moorish saddles that we had bought in Atar. They were like miniature armchairs, painted in garish colours, yellow and scarlet, with upthrust wings like those of a giant wooden butterfly. He demonstrated how the brilliantly coloured saddle bags fitted on behind and how the furry *girbas* dangled down on either side. These waterskins were our most precious pieces of equipment. 'You'd last about a day without water in this heat,' he said. 'Remember, always hang the *girbas* up. Never leave them on the ground, or your water will run out very quickly.'

When his demonstration was finished he walked with our small *azalai* as far as the dune barrier on the edge of the town and showed us the direction of Wadan. It was the last oasis in the region, and the Richat crater lay a little beyond. 'Go in the safe-keeping of God,' he told us and shook each of us solemnly by the hand. Then we were alone with the desert.

The journey to Guelb Richat lasted nine days. Never have I seen the desert so violent, so numbingly hot. We travelled over a landscape desolate and deserted. At midday the torrid sun flamed across the dunes, setting the sand ablaze with blinding light. The rocks glittered like steel over the broken plains, and the far horizons vaporized into a mist of scorching dust. Along the wadis the trees stood lifeless. Not a foot of shade remained in the thornscrub. The dread wind

called the *rifi* began its oppressive progress south, searing the desert
with its furnace blast, withering the plant life left on the open scree
sides and eddying into the valleys, tearing at the nomad tents and
the shelters of the Haratin. Most of the nomads had fled from the
high pastures, driving their flocks down below, rolling up their
heavy tents and stashing them in the thorn-tree branches. They had
abandoned their shelters in the wadis, leaving a scattering of twisted
tins and broken *girbas*, seeking refuge among the palmeries and in
the clefts in the valley floor.

Each day we were up before sunrise, struggling with the heavy
equipment and the waterbags. I was used to the easier Sudanese
system, by which you just slung everything over the saddle horns.
Moorish saddles had only one horn, and the gear had to be tied on
with a series of intricate knots. If you got one of them wrong, the
whole rig came crashing down as soon as the camel rose to its feet.
This happened to us several times in the first few days.

When the loading was complete we would string the camels
together and start walking. We walked for two or three hours into
the swelter of the morning. The *rifi* gusted behind us, tearing across
the dunes and sharpening their knife-blade edges with a spindrift rasp
of sand. The dust sandpapered our faces raw as we plodded on,
tramping up the sides of great crescent dunes and skidding down
with our camels in tow. The bulbous, orange sun of first light shrank
into a glowering ball of white-hot fire. When we could walk no more,
we stopped and mounted.

At first Marinetta was nervous of getting into the saddle. Her
height was a disadvantage, for her legs couldn't reach the camel's
shoulder to ensure a steady foothold. She would scramble up the
equipment, using it as a stepladder, while I held the bridle tensely,
afraid that her camel, Gurfaf, would leap up despite my solid grip.
The first day was a comedy. The great Gurfaf snorted as she settled
herself into the saddle. Then he rose like a leviathan, holding his head
high and bubbling with irritation. I handed her the bridle. 'It seems
OK,' she said.

Just then Gurfaf started to wander off, as if he realized she was a
novice.

'Tug the headrope!' I yelled at her.

She tugged as sharply as she dared, making little 'Hey! Hey!' sounds, which were scarcely audible. 'You've got to shout at the sod!' I told her. 'Let him know you're the boss! Dig your heels in!'

She tried to bounce her tiny feet on the camel's shoulder. Her legs were an inch too short, and she managed only to kick against the saddle. This produced as much reaction from Gurfaf as did the flies buzzing around his muzzle. He veered haughtily in a circle and started mooching back towards Chinguetti. 'Maik!' she shouted. 'Stop him!'

'Pull his head round!' I called. She strained vainly on the rope, and a moment later she committed the worst of all camel-riding sins: she dropped the headrope. The camel was out of her control. She sat there, terrified, both hands frozen to the saddle while Gurfaf continued his meandering voyage home. I ran desperately to catch him, working around in a semi-circle and praying he would not bolt.

'Thank God!' she said, when I grasped the headrope.

'Never, never, drop the headrope,' I said.

After that I towed Gurfaf behind me. We would continue until noon, when we couched the camels and dumped the equipment. Then we would hobble them by the forelegs. This was always a dangerous job, since once you had knelt down to twist the rope around his legs, the camel could give you a smashing kick with his back feet. Marinetta showed great aptitude for this job. She had no fear. She would crouch like a doll in the shadow of the huge animal, fitting a thong of rope about his ankles without a thought for the twitching legs and stamping hooves. When this was done we built a shelter of blankets and sticks, which gave us a tiny pool of shade. It was generally too windy to cook, and instead we made the Moorish drink zrig. It was a mixture of milk, made up from the powder we carried, sugar and water. It was ideal food for these conditions, and we swallowed it in massive draughts from an enamel bowl, trying to finish it before it filled with grit.

Each of these midday halts was a three-hour mini-hell. We could do nothing but curl up foetally in our few feet of shade, waiting for the time to pass. The rifi beat over our prone bodies, sucking out the moisture we had just poured into them. It dehydrated the waterbags too, and often we found no trees to hang them from, so that more water escaped by osmosis. To cap it all, one of them developed a leak. We watched our water dripping into the sand with dismay.

When the sun began to wane we fetched the camels. They were usually reluctant to be loaded. They would squirm as we tried to fit the headropes into their nose-rings, roaring and spluttering and snapping their canine teeth threateningly. Roping difficult camels like these was a job for two. One person had to grab their nostrils, about the only thing that made them docile, while the other threaded the headrope carefully through the ring. Marinetta's job was to thread the rope through. She would stand there, steeling herself, while I wrestled with the beast's nostrils, shouting, 'Come on! Come on!' I would watch with admiration as she determinedly threaded the rope and knotted it.

Afternoon was another passage through the barbecue grill of sun and wind. After sunset we would halt and unload the camels again. By that time both of us were exhausted, stiff from the riding and sore from the rubbing of the saddles. But there was no time for rest. The camels had to be fed their meal of grain. We measured it out and set it before them on a canvas sheet. They had poor manners. Always they fought and lunged at each other, each trying to drive the other away from the food. Quite often they would give each other nasty bites, and there would be a roar like thunder and an eruption of sand as the serpent-like necks twisted around themselves. Up would come the canvas sheet and the grain would be spilled in the sand.

After they had eaten it was time to look for firewood. Although this region was called Rag as Sder or 'Plain of Trees', most of the forest that had given it that name had long since disappeared, leaving only the occasional stump like a scarecrow in the dunes. If often took us half an hour to find wood. Then we had to struggle with the fire and the cooking. Mostly we ate rice, though its standard was rarely higher than that of the rice we had eaten in Chinguetti.

Only then would we lie down on our blankets and try to sleep. 'I could have led such an easy life,' Marinetta told me. 'When I'm exhausted during the day I think all this is a stupid waste of time. But when I arrive at the camp in the evening it seems a small victory. Then I'm glad I did it.'

We rarely got a good night's sleep. We would be woken by a

fresh outbreak of hostilities between the camels or by mice scuttling about after the tidbits of grain that had been spilled. It was the black beetles that Marinetta feared the most. Their scratching woke her from sleep, quivering. 'They're like monsters,' she told me. 'The noise makes me think they're coming to get me!'

It took us three days to reach Wadan, a fortress of stone buildings set on a cliff overlooking a wadi rich in palms. This oasis was one of the first places in the Sahara to have been reached by Europeans. The Portuguese had set up a trade mission here in the fifteenth century to tap the rich caravan trade between Morocco and Tombouctou. Now the oasis had a derelict look. More than half the stone houses were in ruins, and a hotel built to attract tourists had been shelled by the Polisario. Many local inhabitants had left for other parts. There was no caravan trade through Wadan now. Ours was probably the first *azalai* to visit the place in years.

We spent a night in the wadi beneath the town, plagued by ragged children with their packets of arrow heads for sale. The next day we pressed on towards Guelb Richat. We climbed out of the wadi and rode across a flat plain for hours until we saw a sheer wall of silver-grey stone rising out of the desert. This was the Guelb. It looked like the shell of an extinct volcano, though there was no evidence of volcanic activity in the area. Monod believed that it was the crater of an enormous meteorite that had crashed here in prehistoric times.

We remained at the crater for only a few hours and were back in the wadi by sunset the following day. As we climbed out of the depression the next morning, the *rifi* hit us head-on. We wrapped our headcloths around us and plunged into the tide of dust. At mid-morning we mounted as usual and rode on in silence for two hours. The motion of the camels was almost hypnotic. We had no inclination to talk, which meant shouting over the wind. Occasionally I heard Marinetta humming snatches of a tune. Suddenly there was an ear-piercing roar, followed by a shriek of 'Maik! Maik!' I whipped around just in time to see Gurfaf bucking like a mustang and Marinetta sailing out of the saddle as if in slow motion. A second later she hit the sand, face down, with a resounding crump. A look of utter amazement was frozen on her face for a long instant. Then a water-bag hit the ground and split open, showering her with water. After it came a saddle bag, which burst and scattered utensils across the desert. I grabbed the headrope tightly, but by then the camel had lost all signs of fight. He regarded me coolly through big, black eyes.

I dismounted and picked her up. 'Are you all right?' I asked.

She looked as if she was unable to decide whether to cry or laugh. 'I think so,' she said.

'What happened?'

'The saddle bag collapsed on one side. It must have given him a prick or something.'

There was a pause while we both remembered who had fixed the saddle bag that morning. Me.

'Thank God it was sand, not rock!' I said.

As the days passed we began to master the small problems of loading. Marinetta gained confidence with the camels despite her fall. Soon she was hobbling and bridling as well as me and had even begun to grasp the intricacies of fire-making. The severe summer conditions, the blazing, merciless desert, began to weld us firmly into a tiny team.

One evening we were couching the camels in the half-light when I noticed that my map case was missing. The *rifi* was still howling across the landscape and quickly obliterating our tracks. 'You unload the camels and feed them,' I told Marinetta. 'I'm going to look for those maps.'

'Don't go!' she said, suddenly afraid. 'You'll never find your way back in this.'

'We need those maps,' I said and left her standing there in the near-darkness. I followed the faint traces of our path with torch and compass. The camp was soon out of sight behind me in the night. The trail went on and on. I cast around constantly with the torch beam, only half expecting to find the maps. The wind began to subside, as it usually did around sunset, and the going became easier. After almost half an hour I saw the transparent case lying like a fallen leaf in the sand. I vowed that I would never let this happen again.

I began to follow my own footprints back towards our camp. It was difficult going. Often I lost the direction and had to backtrack.

A few minutes later I saw a flicker of flame as fragile as a candle in the night. 'God!' I thought. 'She's made a fire!' It was the first time Marinetta had made a wood fire in conditions like these. It was like a beacon in the dead landscape, and I ran straight towards it. I found her standing by it, staring into the night. The camels had been unloaded, hobbled and even fed.

The first thing she did was hug me. 'You were so long!' she gasped. 'I thought you were lost!'

'What made you light a fire? I didn't tell you to.'

'I suddenly thought I might lose you,' she said.

As we neared Chinguetti we were consumed by a creeping exhaustion, which increased daily with the constant battle against deep sand, the heat and the relentless wind. On the afternoon of the ninth day we saw the shadows of palm trees on the horizon. We dismounted, both sore from the saddles, and continued on foot. We struggled though the sand for what seemed like hours, but the palm trees were no nearer.

Marinetta had to stop to relieve herself and told me there was blood in her urine. I hoped to God she hadn't been injured internally by her fall. I saw that she was in pain and wondered how long she had been hiding it. Now we were desperate to reach those palms. The terrible heat and the wind had worn us down. My legs felt like jelly and we carried on at a snail's pace. Every few minutes Marinetta had to squat down. I could see agony written on her face. I started to believe that the palm groves were an illusion. The sun dropped lower. We had been in sight of the palms for four hours.

Suddenly the palm fronds were above us like feather plumes, and there were houses and people. There were children clapping their hands and shouting, 'Nsara! Nsara with camels!' It sounded like a welcome. Moments later we were unloading outside our house. Neighbours poured out to meet us as if we were royalty. Sid'Ahmed was there, smiling and saying, 'They said you'd never do it without a guide! But I told them Omar is a man! This is the work of men!' And by the way he looked at Marinetta you could tell he was paying her the ultimate compliment. He was including her in that most elite of groups.

*

It was a week before Marinetta recovered completely. The bleeding was replaced by full-blown dysentery, which sent her dashing miserably into the desert many times a day. Yet somehow her resolution to complete the journey was stronger than ever. 'It's all changed somehow,' she said. 'Before it all seemed unreal, the idea of crossing the Sahara from west to east. The Sahara was just something out *there*. But now I've lived through those conditions anything seems possible.'

We felt more alert, our senses sharpened, our milk-fat, city bodies honed down and ready for the challenge to come. There was a change in the way people treated us too. They would stop us in the street and say, 'Did you really go to Richat without a guide?' The women looked at Marinetta with a new respect, if not with admiration. It was hard for us to settle down and wait the summer out, but we employed ourselves by learning Hassaniyya and prying into the workings of the township.

One of Sid'Ahmed's jobs, we discovered, was doling out sacks of wheat, marked 'Gift of the People of the United States of America', which piled up periodically in the town's warehouses. The grain explained the numerous tents of nomads that circled around the perimeter of the oasis. The nomads had become dependent on the free supplies, since half of the livestock on which they had once depended had been wiped out in the drought. It seemed a cruel irony that such people, notorious for their independence, were now unable to survive without help from a Christian country that most of them had never heard of.

This was true of the nomads we visited outside the oasis. They lived in four pyramid-shaped tents of thick goat's wool, pitched in the sand among some thornscrub. There were some young men with their wives and children. The men were small and trim, with the confident step of desert people. Their faces were smudged with beard, and their hair grew in wild masses. There were also two friendly old women with features of wizened leather, clad only in wraps of blue cotton. They invited us into the shade, and a young woman with a baby made *zrig* in a wooden bowl. Then one of the men made tea. This was a solemn business. The Moors drank green China tea in tiny glasses. It was brewed in a miniature pot into which they dropped a chunk of sugar hacked from a two-kilo conical loaf. The tea was very strong and very sweet. You received only a mouthful at a time and you had to swig it down in a gulp so that someone else could use the glass. There were rarely enough glasses to go round. When you had finished you were supposed to throw the glass back to the server with a twisting flick of the hand so that it landed by his knees. I was too unsure of my aim ever to attempt it. Your host served you three glasses of the stuff. Any less was an insult and any more excess.

While we drank I looked around at the tent. Streamers of brilliant light pierced the gloom from the seams in the roof, which was kept in place by massive V-shaped poles. The floor was covered by straw mats. On one side of the floor stood a frame with carved legs, which supported two nylon sacks of American grain. Around the opening were scattered some pack saddles and wooden funnels for milking, encrusted with milk stains. An old rifle leaned against a corner, rusty-looking and held together in places by surgical tape. Outside in the thornbush was a scrimmage of goats.

'We don't move far now,' one of the men told us. 'We used to go as far north as Bir Moghrein at one time. That was when we had camels. But most of them died in the drought, and we sold the rest off. You have to keep moving when you have camels. Now we have these goats and some date palms. It will be date harvest in a few weeks, then we'll leave the tents here and move into our shelters in the palmeries.'

'There's nothing like the life of the desert, by God!' one of the old crones cut in. 'There was once milk and meat, enough for you and your guests. The camels ate good grasses. We rode all over the desert, all the women of the family in litters. But that's gone now. The old life is finished. Now we get this *nsara* grain in Chinguetti, two sacks a family.'

The young men had been extras in *Fort Saganne*. They had earned more in a day than they normally earned in six months. They had formed part of the background of a million-dollar fantasy, while at the same time the roots that tied them to their environment were being severed. One day, I thought, they might become 'museum nomads', putting on shows for tourists, sad souvenirs of a way of life that was no more.

A few days later a Land-Rover pulled up outside our house. Out climbed a lanky, fair-haired Westerner in shorts. He produced a camera, took two quick shots of the house, then jumped back in the Land-Rover. As it pulled away I saw the words 'Oasis Tours' painted on the outside. 'It's the tourists,' Sid'Ahmed told me later. 'They come here every winter. They stay in the town for a few days, then they go for a ride round the hills on camels. This year I'm going to rent the house to them. They pay plenty of money.' I thought of the rusty rifle leaning against the corner of the tent. You had to be a *man* in the time of raids.

Sid'Ahmed was even more crestfallen next time I saw him. He told me that one of his female milch-camels was sick. 'It's that camel cake,' he said. 'It's swollen her belly. Now she won't eat.' He asked me to help Mohammed hold her while he fed her some evil-smelling medicine in a kettle. It was a traditional mixture of oil and baobab seeds, used as an emetic. The idea was to purge the camel's stomach of cake so that she could eat. She coughed and spat while he poured the disgusting stuff down her throat, but afterwards there was no improvement. The following day he called me to help again. This time the baobab sauce had been replaced by ten bottles of Pepsi, which he proceeded to administer to the sick beast. A few minutes later she groaned, and there was an eruption of dark-brown mess from her rear end. 'You see!' Sid'Ahmed said. 'The new ways are sometimes the best!'

The summer dragged on. Our Hassaniyya improved with constant practice. In mid-July we returned to Atar and bought another camel. Sid'Ahmed had advised us that three camels would be enough to take the two of us and a guide as far as Tombouctou. The new camel was of the small breed native to the Adrar region. It was named Li'shal because of its blond-coloured skin. We made a few more training trips up the wadis and across the plateau, but these short treks were no longer enough. We looked forward to getting out of the oasis and into the wilder world of the Sahara. Towards the end of July Sid'Ahmed brought us a guide. He was called Mafoudh, and he belonged to a marabout tribe, the Laghlal.

Marinetta and I had often discussed the ideal qualities of a guide.

Finding the right man was crucial because, once in the desert, we would be dependent on him, as he on us. We had prepared for any potential guide a list of questions about his opinions and preferences. But when we were introduced to Mafoudh we dropped it abruptly. Mafoudh was a good man. You could tell he was a good man by his face.

He had the deep, black, watchful eyes of the desert. Standing beside Sid'Ahmed, you could see at once that he belonged to a different class. There was none of our landlord's spare tyre about Mafoudh. He had the rope-muscled leanness of a nomad and carried not an ounce of unneeded fat. His face was broad and hard, pickled brown by the outdoors, but it split easily into a smile. 'I used to work on the caravans,' he said, 'but I haven't been that way these ten years. Still, you never forget it once you've been. The only problem will be the heat.'

'Does the heat bother you?' I asked.

'No,' he answered. 'It gets you down at midday, but by sunset the worst of it is past. Everything passes. That's the way of God.'

Mafoudh said that he would be prepared to take us as far as Walata, on the Mali border. He reckoned we could make it in under thirty days. Then he asked for 60,000 ougiyyas. To me the price seemed excessive, but after Mafoudh had gone Sid'Ahmed said, 'You can't blame him for asking so much. It's torture to travel in this heat, don't forget. He's got eleven palm trees to water, and that means hiring a Hartani while he's away. Then he's got his wife and children to provide for and his fare back to pay. You'll be lucky to get such an honest man for less than that. And he is completely honest, I can guarantee.' I said that we would consider it and spent the next few days searching for another guide. Either they asked for more than Mafoudh, or their faces didn't convince us. In the end we made a contract with Mafoudh.

The next day I almost regretted it. I asked him to help me brand our camels with the symbol that Marinetta had designed. It was a configuration of the letters 'we', which stood for 'West to East'. Mafoudh turned up to help me but seemed very reluctant to do the branding. 'You do it,' he told me, 'and I'll hold the camels' heads.'

I had never branded a camel before, but Sid'Ahmed showed me

how to heat the branding-iron on some charcoal. I applied it shakily to the camels one by one, while Mafoudh fought their wriggling heads. There was no smell of burning flesh, as I had expected. The iron was too cool and didn't penetrate far. The result was some spidery squiggles of lines at the base of the animals' necks.

'Those brands won't last a week,' said Sid'Ahmed after Mafoudh had gone away.

'I wanted Mafoudh to do it, but he refused,' I said testily. 'I'm not sure he's as good as you told me.'

'It's not surprising he refused,' Sid'Ahmed chuckled. 'He's a marabout. Branding camels is a smith's job. He'd have been laughed at all day if he'd done it himself.'

Mafoudh

We left Chinguetti on 6 August. Mafoudh turned up at first light, bringing with him nothing but a blanket, a camel stick and a much patched knapsack containing a teapot, a glass and a spare gandourah.

I envied him his simple gear. Ours seemed to cover every bit of ground outside the house: saddles, sacks, cushions, saddle bags, tent, poles and waterskins. We had even exchanged one of our butterfly saddles for the more comfortable woman's litter. Loading it was a marathon. A crowd of women and children gathered around to watch the spectacle. Sid'Ahmed made an appearance and started shouting instructions. Not to be outdone, Mafoudh shouted back, while every child who could walk tramped joyfully through our belongings, picking them up, putting them down and arguing with any adult who tried to stop them.

Slowly the piles of equipment grew smaller as each item found a place on one of the camels. Miraculously there was a place for everything. We got the animals to their feet, groaning and grumbling. 'Isn't it a bit heavy?' I asked.

'Nonsense!' Mafoudh replied. 'This is nothing. You should see what a *real* caravan carries, by God!' Then he grabbed the headrope of the leading camel. 'In the name of God,' he said, 'the way is long. Let's go!'

As he led the caravan off, there were cries of 'Go in peace!', which struck me as comically inappropriate amid the clamour. Sid'Ahmed walked us down to the bank of the wadi, saying. 'Omar is the boss, Mafoudh. When he says go, you go, and when he says stop, you stop.' Then he shook hands with us and said, 'Send me a letter when you reach the Nile. God go with you!' We left him standing there, a solid, proud old warrior on the edge of his domain.

Moments later we had crossed the wadi and plunged over the ridge of dunes, which for three months we had seen on waking. Now we were among them, and Chinguetti was blotted out, gone for ever. 'I feel like Jonah in the belly of the whale,' Marinetta said. 'We've just entered the whale's belly.'

All morning we trudged through the dunes. They were the visible expression of the unseen force of the wind, delicately moulded, rippled and coloured with watery pastels. There were places where the sand had been scooped out of the desert floor and layered over the rocks so that the sharp edges showed through the smooth carpet like ground-down teeth. We crossed bridges of sand where the surface cracked like ice and fell away; the camels stumbled down at incredible angles, drifting into narrow corridors where the dunes towered above us, dwarfing our tiny *azalai* with its arrogant mission of conquering the great Sahara.

Once I stopped to pick up a barbed arrow head. It was just like the ones that the people of Chinguetti had tried to sell us so often. I wondered how many thousands of years it had lain there, waiting for me to pick it up. It had belonged to a hunter, some time long ago, when this desert was a forest. The forest had gone, and the hunters had gone with it, but men had survived in this desolate land by changing their ways and adapting to the new order. Change was certain, but man survives by adapting. If we adapted to the ways of the Sahara, we too could survive.

At midday we reached the palm groves at Aghayla, where Mafoudh owned some young trees. The dates were red and squashy, ripe for the cutting. A host of people helped us to unload and set our gear down in the shade. Marinetta took the cooking things and went off to make lunch. Four old men came to talk, sitting cross-legged on our blankets, and I invited them to eat with us. They looked pleased, but I wondered if they would remain so when they saw the standard of the cooking.

Half an hour passed. The men shifted restlessly. Then the unmistakable smell of burnt rice drifted through the palm trees. A few moments later Marinetta appeared and slapped in front of us a tray of the familiar scorched pellets. Lost within the desert of rice were a few oases of dried meat, now reduced to lumps of charcoal. The men looked at the dish, and I saw their faces drop. Mafoudh grinned at me cheerfully. 'It's the wind,' he said. 'It makes the fire too hot. Come on, everyone, eat!' The old men each took a small amount with their fingertips and began to chew. They chewed and chewed, and the tension mounted as I wondered if anyone would take another handful. None of them did. One by one they whispered thanks and got up to leave. Before we departed, though, they brought us a gift of ripe dates. Was there a touch of pity in their eyes as they handed them over?

The afternoon was steaming-hot. Every half hour my mouth became so clogged with mucus that I had to take a sip of water from one of our canteens. Marinetta had the same problem. 'This water tastes like honey,' she gasped. 'I never knew water could taste so good.' For hours we stumbled on through one band of dunes after another, but before sunset we had emerged on to a plateau of black stone that allowed us to ride for the first time. We couched the camels, and I helped Marinetta into her new litter. I had chosen to ride the red camel, Shigar, even though he now carried an uncomfortable pack saddle with almost all the provisions. Mafoudh climbed aboard the smaller Li'shal, carrying a butterfly saddle, and led the way. We rode on silently until the last sparklers of the sun burned out and left the plain in thick darkness.

It was all confusion in the camp that night. It seemed strange to have a third person with us, and neither of us knew quite what to do. Mafoudh took everything in his stride, however. He collected firewood, lit a fire and made tea while we were still sorting out our equipment. 'I have to drink tea first,' he explained apologetically, 'or I get a tight feeling in my head. It makes me feel angry.' We all felt better after we had drunk tea and eaten a plate of macaroni and sardines. We sat back in the warm sand to watch the last flux of the fire. The dark screen of the night was awash with the familiar pattern of the stars. The camels, unseen in the darkness, made shuffling sounds as they hunted for shoots of grass. 'There may be some rain tomorrow,' Mafoudh predicted, sniffing the air. 'It's been hot today. The rain follows the heat at this time of year.'

'You think it's a mistake to travel at this time?' I asked him.

'In some ways the rainy season is better than winter for travellers,' he said, 'because although it's hot, the rain leaves pools of water in the desert. When you've got water you don't need to be afraid of the heat. Water is God's blessing.'

It was soon time for sleep, and I worried about the sleeping arrangements. It seemed ridiculous to concern myself with this in the middle of the world's greatest desert. There was no lack of space, but I felt protective about Marinetta. I was wary even of leaving the camp to relieve myself, afraid that Mafoudh might take advantage of her in my absence. Mafoudh solved the problem by taking his blanket and going off to sleep in the sand a good distance away. Marinetta and I spread out our blankets among the saddles and gear. We cuddled up close in the darkness, more contented with each other than we had been for weeks. 'Well, that was day one,' I commented. 'Do you think we'll make it to the Nile?'

'Yes,' she answered. A few minutes later she was asleep.

We saw the first signs of the storm the next afternoon as we crossed the Agfeytit valley. Before us was a vast line of grey cliffs stretching as far as the horizon. The base of the valley was a serpent of black powder on which lay a school of small, humpy dunes that reminded me of jellyfish washed up on a beach. The sky suddenly filled with a scud of cloud, and the wind carried a touch of dampness. Sloughs of silvery dust began to squirm across the ground, and we heard the distant boom of thunder. The sky was a ragged quilt of grey and blue, and there were places around us where the clouds seemed to be reaching down into the desert. The wind began to buffet us in waves that rose and fell successively. Suddenly there was a shocking crack of lightning directly in our path. For a split second I saw the distant flash pattern, like a many-branched, electric-blue tree as it forked down into the earth. It was followed by a shell blast of thunder, which made us jump. 'Jesus Christ!' Marinetta said. 'We'll all be fulminated!' We waited for the rain to come.

'We'd better make camp,' Mafoudh advised.

'No,' I said. 'Let's risk it and go on till sunset.'

That evening we erected our Arab tent in case the rain started. It didn't begin until the next morning at about 5 a.m., but when it came it hit us like an explosion. The wind railed through the camp, knocking down the tent with a single blow. The violence of the storm was frightening. Every few moments the darkness was slashed by brilliant streaks of lightning, and the thunder growled overhead like a barrage. Then the rain came gushing out of the night, roiling into the sand, soaking everything, dripping cold down our necks and running three inches above the ground so that we sat like ducks in the current. Every time the thunder boomed Marinetta let out a gasp and tried to crawl closer to me. We were already completely entwined in each other's arms, and it was somehow very comforting to feel her small, damp, warm body close to mine. How many times had we watched storms like this from the cosy safety of my flat in Khartoum? How different it was to be out in it.

'My God, the cameras!' Marinetta said suddenly. I pulled the cotton sheet of the tent aside and rushed out, barefoot, from its spurious protection. Mafoudh's body was a wet sausage under his blanket. He was lying on a hillock of sand, above the running water, and he had moved the most vulnerable of our equipment up there with him and had covered it with a plastic sheet. His narrow, drenched features peered at me through the night. We laughed at each other. 'God is generous!' he said. But it didn't sound as though he meant it.

The dawn came, bleak and freezing. The rain stopped and was replaced by the cutting edge of the wind. We shivered uncontrollably in our wet clothes as Mafoudh tried to make a fire for the morning tea. The rain had washed off the light topsoil and liberated the colours beneath, which showed in a mandala of patterns across the plain. Our tea was soaked; our loaves of sugar had dissolved into a damp mass mixed with sand and grit. Marinetta's flip-flops had been carried off, and my leather sandals were so wet that they folded up as soon as I put them on. Mafoudh said that we should dry out everything well before we started, as the saddles would fall to pieces if we tried to use them while they were wet.

'I've never seen a night like *that*!' Marinetta said, and laughed.

'God is generous!' Mafoudh repeated, then he laughed too. 'But the rain is hell, isn't it?' he said.

For the next three days we crossed a landscape where water had taken over the job of sculptor from the wind. The black plain had become a blotch of blood-red, amber, orange and gold, overlaid in places by slicks of mud as smooth and creamy as milk chocolate. The rain had excavated narrow canals that fed into pools among the rocks. We never lost an opportunity to fill our *girbas* from them. Mafoudh reckoned that rain water was far better than well water, since it was never salty or sulphurous. That it tasted of camel urine and was full of camel droppings didn't seem to bother him.

'In fifteen days there will be grass everywhere,' he informed us. 'That rain was enough for all Adrar.' We heard later that the wadi in Chinguetti had been awash like a river, and in Atar the flood water had boiled through the market, demolishing buildings and drowning four people. 'You can't win in the desert,' Marinetta commented. 'Either you get too little water or too much. We were lucky the lightning didn't strike us.'

'That all depends on the will of God,' Mafoudh replied. 'I once knew a man who was just sitting inside his tent and the lightning killed him. Burnt a hole through the roof as clean as a bullet, by God! Another time I saw seventy sheep killed by lightning while they were sheltering under a tree. Killed the lot! You never know when your time has come.'

As we travelled, we gradually got used to each other's ways. Mafoudh had a great deal to put up with. He sometimes watched me tying on the luggage in the morning, shaking his head sorrowfully as I tried to tie knots as secure as his. 'You'll have to learn to tie knots better than that if you want to travel in the desert,' he told me once. 'When I was a boy working on the caravans, the custom was that anyone whose knot came undone had to buy a goat or a cone of sugar. That's what we should do.' I agreed and threw myself into the knot-tying with new vigour. By the end of that day I owed two goats. 'Don't worry, Omar,' Mafoudh said, smirking. 'Everyone has to learn.'

The following day a *girba* that he had tied came undone and showered water across the sand. Later we almost left one of the camels behind when the headrope came unfastened. Mafoudh had tied that one too. 'I think that's two goats each,' I said smugly.

He looked as though he regretted having mentioned it. 'Goats were a lot cheaper in those days,' he said.

We generally walked for the first three hours, then rode until noon. As midday approached we would start looking for a tree around which we could build our shelter of ropes and blankets. There were few trees that were more than brittle skeletons, yet still we argued about which was the best. 'That one's no good,' Mafoudh might comment. 'It's got no branches to hang the waterbags on.'

'We can't camp there,' I would respond. 'There's not enough shade.' When the intense heat finally drove us to accept one or the other, we couched the camels near it. Tired, thirsty and very hot, we had to spend long minutes picking at the knots that had slowly tightened during the morning. Even Mafoudh, his head already throbbing from the lack of tea, would get angry and swear like a trooper as he struggled with the rope. We drank *zrig*, and then Mafoudh would make tea. He always looked tense and harassed until he had downed his first glass. Then he relaxed, and a smile spread across his face. We drank the tea, nibbling dates or biscuits.

Marinetta made lunch, choosing from our menu of rice, pasta, couscous, tinned sardines and dried gazelle meat. It was usually too hot to eat much at midday, and often we ended up tipping the remains of the food into the desert. Mafoudh would shake his head and declare that this was 'forbidden'. It was worse when Marinetta threw away excess water from the cooking pot. 'Getting water is hard work in the desert,' he told her. 'It's a crime to throw it away.'

We ate from a communal steel plate with our right hands, in the Arab fashion. Although the Moors didn't generally eat with women other than their wives, Mafoudh never turned a hair at eating with Marinetta. He told me once that it would have been a disgrace to refuse. What did cause him to raise his eyebrows was her appalling manners. The rice was invisibly divided into 'territories', and it was as impolite to reach into someone else's 'territory' as it would have been for us to take food off someone else's plate. Marinetta constantly dived into Mafoudh's portion for tasty morsels of dried meat or sardine. 'Keep to your own bit!' I had to tell her several times before she understood.

Eating rice was a problem that she found hard to resolve. You were supposed to thrust your fist into the food, squeezing the rice into a ball between fingers and thumb. Then you transferred the ball to your mouth and popped it inside with the thumb. It was unseemly for the fingers to enter the mouth. When Marinetta tried to make a ball, it would inevitably crumble before it got anywhere near her mouth, leaving a scattering of rice across the sand. Furiously, she would crush the gluey stuff into her palm and chew it out of her closed fist, drawing disgusted glances from Mafoudh.

The reason why the Moors used only the right hand for eating was that the left was exclusively for cleaning themselves after defecating. They thought toilet paper disgusting and used water to clean themselves when it was available. In the desert they used sand or stones. Marinetta tried sand and found it painfully abrasive. Often she pined for 'Scottex Supersoft'. Answering nature's call was always a dilemma for her. In the daytime there was nowhere to hide, and she had to pull her long Arab shirt over her knees and hope no one was watching too closely.

After we had eaten Mafoudh would whip through his afternoon prayer. He prayed at sunrise, noon, afternoon, sunset and evening. The prayer consisted of bowing, kneeling and the repetition of certain verses from the Quran, like a meditation. Before each prayer he would make ritual ablutions, covering his hands and face with sand. He always seemed to be in a hurry with his prayers, though, as if they were something to be got out of the way before he drank his tea.

As the days passed any doubts that I may have entertained about Mafoudh dissolved. He seemed completely trustworthy. I felt foolish for having been over-protective about Marinetta. Still, we had to behave very formally with each other while he was around, never touching or showing any sign of affection, which might have upset his sense of propriety. In Chinguetti, with a measure of privacy, we had fought like cat and dog, rowed and argued and raged. Perversely, now that there was no privacy at all, our desire for each other increased in leaps and bounds, and I found Marinetta more attractive every day as her clothes became more stained and dishevelled and her appearance wilder. Often when Mafoudh's back was turned we found ourselves exchanging secret smiles and, occasionally, the forbidden delight of a kiss. Mostly, though, we maintained the distance of strangers, hardly able even to talk.

Marinetta always kept her hair covered in the Moorish fashion.

For a woman to show her hair in their culture was as much a green light to men as flashing a naked breast in ours. She had always detested hats of any kind, and keeping her thick headcloth on, even in the cool of evening, was the worst torture she had to bear. Throughout the journey she dressed like a man, and the bulky Arab shirt and *sirwel* neatly disguised any alluring feminine curves she might have shown. This brought us problems of its own. When we arrived at a well on 11 August two women who were watering goats there refused to greet her. They backed away, giggling, when she held her hand out. 'They think she's a man,' Mafoudh chortled. 'Moor women never shake hands with a man.' Both the women were dressed in faded indigo shifts and even more faded cotton skirts. One of them was quite an old lady with a face like parchment, but the other was young, slim and willowy with creamy, smooth shoulders and pert breasts. To me she looked decidedly sensuous as she dipped the rubber bucket in the well. But Mafoudh hardly gave her a second glance. Watching Marinetta beside her, I realized with a jolt what a weird, hermaphroditic figure she must have seemed to them, with her feminine smallness and her masculine dress.

When they learned that she was a woman their behaviour changed dramatically. They hustled up to her, examining her clothes and touching her skin. They fingered her wedding ring and earrings and peered into her camera bag, continually demanding presents. They seemed like wild things. Once she presented the young girl with a cheap bracelet from Chinguetti; the girl said, 'This is nothing!' and asked for more. When they became aggressive in their demands I went to her rescue and told them gruffly to leave her alone. They did so immediately. I found myself wondering about this culture in which women could touch any other woman, even a complete stranger, but a man couldn't touch his own wife.

The well was in the Khatt, the great fault in the desert crust that divides the regions of Adrar and Tagant. The water was salty, but the women said it was all they had, since no rain had fallen here or farther south. 'That means there'll be no tents for us to rest in,' Mafoudh said testily. 'We'd better fill a *girba*, even though the water's bad. A man who doesn't fill his waterbags when he gets the chance knows nothing about the desert.'

The heat was back with a vengeance, and a hot wind raked us, scorching the sand and drumming up a shroud of dust that raged in the sky like sea-froth, obscuring the sun. 'This is the worst type of day to travel on,' our guide declared. 'It's hot, and with this mist you can't tell the north from the south.' The heat got us all down. Mafoudh became prickly and argumentative, lapsing into sullen moods of silence, then waking up and yelling, 'Come on! Come on!' even though we were right behind him and going no more slowly than usual. Instead of laughing, he glared at me nastily when one of my knots came undone and, when he saw me tying a *girba*, commented crabbily, 'I thought you knew how to tie a *girba*. You should tie it on the left, not the right.'

'Rubbish!' I snapped back. 'It doesn't make any difference. You just want everything done your way!'

The heat did this: it made you argue. Yet I knew that beneath the arguments was the ancient, ugly question that has plagued all men at all times: 'Who's the boss?' No one travelling in the desert with desert people can avoid that issue for long. Sooner or later, in ways subtle or obvious, there will be a struggle for power.

Ours came that night, when Mafoudh told me, 'The way you march is wrong. We should get up two hours before dawn and travel in the coolest time. That way is better for camels and men. We should rest most of the day and travel at night. The day is our enemy in this heat. When you find grazing you should stop for a day or even two.'

I told him that I had developed my own system of marching in the Sudan. I knew that Arabs marched haphazardly, resting for two days when they found grazing, then rushing on madly for twenty hours to make up. That style was no good for our journey of 4,500 miles. It was a journey that most Arabs would not have undertaken. I was convinced that it required a more methodical approach, a blend of the Orient and the Western. Mafoudh would be with us only till Walata, then we should have another guide, then another, and another. We couldn't change our ways continually to accommodate the whims of each new guide. Our guides would have to adopt our way. And our way was to march by watch and compass, going by day and covering the same distance daily, come hell or high wind, from Changuetti to the Nile. I remembered the story of Harry St John Philby, the explorer of Arabia's Empty Quarter. His bedouin guides had threatened to kill him because he insisted on travelling by day. He had won only by refusing to eat with them. I doubted if such drastic measures would be needed with Mafoudh. I reminded him of what Sid'Ahmed had said before we left, and he stomped off to bed, muttering. By the following day it was forgotten.

The next morning we saw the palm groves of Talmoust sprouting from a depression in the middle of a dusty, black plain. The palm trees looked temptingly green, but when we got nearer we saw that they bore no dates. The Moors who were at the well inside the groves told us that there had been no rain there for five years and that dates no longer grew. 'The palms need water just like the grass,' one old man said. 'If we don't get rain next year, Talmoust will be finished.' There were no Haratin in Talmoust. The people here were *bidan* of the Kunta, an Arab tribe of noble origin found throughout the Sahara. They herded goats and camels around Tijikja and retired to these palm groves in the season of the date harvest. Their tents were rolled up and stored on wooden frames outside the huts of palm fibre that they used in summer. The village of huts was bleak. The buildings were grey and derelict, inhabited by naked, brown children and shy women in the usual faded blue. The men were very Arab-looking, stringy as thorn trees, with wisps of beard and ragged gandourahs. A few scraggy camels were being watered at the well, and around it lay butterfly saddles, stained and broken, and heaps of old ropes and saddle bags.

The men crowded round to greet us, and Mafoudh and I shook hands with each of them. The greeting always followed the same ritual. First you wished the whole crowd, 'Peace be on you!' and they would reply in chorus, 'And on you be peace!' Then you grasped each man firmly by the hand and, putting on your most earnest expression, repeated, 'How is your condition? Nothing evil, I trust!' 'How is the news? Only good, I trust!' You jabbered this as if in competition with an opponent, and your adversary would repeat, 'No evil, thank God!' 'The news is good, praise God!' The news was always good, even if your father had died or your entire camel herd had contracted the mange.

When all this had finally died down, someone would diffidently inquire which tribe you belonged to. It was really an inquiry after your social position because in Mauritania your status depended on how high up the social scale your tribe stood. Mafoudh belonged to a marabout tribe, which, while still nobility, didn't figure very highly in relation to these Kunta. They considered themselves descendants of the family of the Prophet Mohammed, a distinction that earned them the title of Shurfa. The Shurfa were top-drawer in Moorish society. Curiously enough, *nsara* were considered nobility because it was said that they were descended from a branch of the Prophet's tribe that had left Arabia before the time of Islam.

When status had been established, they would get down to the real news. The first question was always about grazing. Had there been rain? Where had it fallen, and how much? Had the grass bloomed yet? Where was it, and of which type? When that topic had been exhausted, they would move on to questions about people and places. Had you seen so-and-so in Chinguetti? He was a cousin. Had you seen a she-camel of such-and-such a description? Someone had lost one a few days before. They were always avid for the news, and their grapevine was very efficient, yet they much appreciated the luxury of a radio. Mafoudh constantly chided us for not having one. 'It tells you everything,' he said, 'even where the rain has fallen. It can be very useful.'

Next morning, in a stream of thick, silent heat, we saw Tijikja below us. It lay in a rocky groove in the middle of a valley from which the purple stain of date palms spread for several miles in both directions.

'Well, you've made it to Tijikja,' Mafoudh said.

'You said I'd never make it!' Marinetta laughed at me.

'Anyone can be wrong,' I said, 'and there's still another 4,350 miles to go.'

We made camp by a thorn tree above the town. It was like coming into a great harbour and dropping anchor without reaching the quayside. As soon as we had unloaded, Mafoudh said he wanted to look up an old friend and set off on foot. Marinetta and I put the tent up. It was our first moment of privacy since we had set out. She looked very attractive, and it was all I could do to stop myself dragging her into the tent that moment. 'How do you feel?' I asked her, massaging her shoulder.

'I certainly don't feel flat any more,' she admitted, smiling.

I was just about to move a little closer when there was a buzz of voices. We looked up to see a crowd of Haratin children who immediately surrounded us, shouting, 'Nsara! Nsara with camels!'

'There's the end of our privacy,' Marinetta said. 'We'll never get rid of them now.' And she was right. We never did.

From the moment we entered the town the next day, the children never left us alone. They followed us, chanting, clapping and even throwing stones. I heard one boy, a miniature adult in gandourah and headcloth, tell his friend, 'They are unbelievers who will surely fall into the fire.' Few tourists visited Tijikja, but there was an American Peace Corps volunteer there who had adopted a Muslim name and prayed in the mosque five times a day. This was fine by me, except that the man was a Christian who, instead of declaring, 'There is no God but God, and Mohammed is his Prophet,' as Muslims were required to do before each prayer, proclaimed, 'There is no God but God, and Jesus is his Prophet.' This was not designed to elicit much sympathy from the Moors, and perhaps it had poisoned their minds against all nsara.

We got out of the town as quickly as we could. Every minute in this crowded environment seemed a torture. We bought more dates, powdered milk for our crucial zrig and a few pounds of flour to make bread. We also bought another sack of grain for the camels, piled it all on to a donkey cart and beat a hasty retreat, still pursued by cat-calling, stone-throwing children. Their leader seemed to be the miniature adult, a boy of about twelve, who resisted all my attempts to get rid of him. When we passed the last house, he was still following determinedly. I rounded on him furiously. 'Where are you going?' I demanded.

'I'm going after you!'

'Oh no, you're not!' I said, feeling inclined to kick his backside very firmly. The other children lined up behind him. I glared at him and he glared back. To give him his due, he didn't seem afraid.

I was just wondering if I really would have to use force when a little old Haratin woman came hobbling up, shouting, 'Hey, you children! Let the strangers go in peace!' Incredibly, all of them ran away.

When we had unloaded our new acquisitions Mafoudh told me that some of his relations had visited the camp. 'They won't believe you're going to Egypt,' he said. 'They say it's impossible.' I sat down in the shade and lit my pipe. Then I took out our Michelin map and followed our planned route with my eyes. Before us lay the rest of Mauritania, Mali, Niger, the whole of Chad and most of the Sudan. 'The way is long!' Mafoudh said.

At that moment I was filled with an inexplicable sense of dread. I had the feeling that I had stepped out of the normal barriers of time and space, that I had lost touch with reality, not knowing where I had come from or where I was going. Suddenly I felt absolutely certain that I had been here before, that I had seen everything before, even that I had already reached Egypt and that time was playing backwards. I tried desperately to remember if I had dreamed this, but it danced like a shimmer of light just beyond my memory, and I walked in abject terror beyond the bounds of time, filled with images of the past, the years of struggle, the planning, the dreaming and the work it had taken to get here. And then the images passed. The terror subsided. I looked at Mafoudh and realized that only a moment had ticked by. 'Yes,' I told him, 'the way is long indeed.'

We were heading for the oasis of Tichit. It lay in the centre of the Baatin, another massive fault of rock that stretched almost the entire length of the desert between Tijikja and Walata. We were on the roof of the fault, and we had to find a route down to the valley floor. The landscape was a graveyard. The trees stood as bare as steel frames, melted, dripping molten in the sun. There were other trees, cracked and broken, bark peeling off them like fish scales, great trunk roots lying useless in the sand. The ground was littered with bleached bones of camels and goats, set hard in the flake-dry surface. There was no sign of people, no sign of rain, just twisted scrub, red sand, black dust, purple rocks and the day, hot and deathly still, going on for ever.

Once we met a nomad boy of the Kunta, and we stopped to give him water. He was a lean, gloomy youth, his face stained blue from the indigo headcloth that he wore. He squatted down and gulped the liquid from the *girba*. Mafoudh asked the boy for directions to the pass that would take us down to the floor of the Baatin. The boy explained at great length.

The way took us through a labyrinth of rock, through corridors between giant slabs of granite that were piled up on each other, creating natural dolmens and shadowed places. The rocks were everywhere – rippled rocks, melted rocks, hinged and ribbed rocks, rocks like cabbages perched on plinths. There were globules and nest-eggs and rocks folded in sutures like an enormous human brain. The camels were tired and thirsty. Our water supply was low. Even Mafoudh was heard to say, 'By God, it's hot!' By late afternoon we had come to the very edge of the cliff. We couched the camels, and Mafoudh stalked off on foot, quickly disappearing over the lip of the rocks.

Marinetta said, 'Thank God he's gone!' She had terrible stomach cramps and bad diarrhoea. She had been suffering all day but had been too embarrassed to stop while Mafoudh was there. The guide returned half an hour later, fuming. 'That Kunta boy lied to us, by God!' he raged. 'There's no way down here! God curse him, he only wanted to laugh at us! I should have stuck to the way I knew!' We had no choice but to skirt around the edge of the cliff, hoping that we would find a way down. Our water was short and night was coming on, but an hour later we were still searching. We were all exhausted and Marinetta was bent double with the cramps. As we walked Mafoudh spluttered, 'By God, if I find that youth again, I'll give him something he won't like, Shurfa or no Shurfa!'

We found a sandy place and made camp, hanging our remaining water carefully in a thorn tree. 'We'll have to leave early,' Mafoudh said. 'We've got to get down into the valley before the heat starts, or we'll run out of water.' He told Marinetta to use it sparingly for the cooking. That night the pasta tasted like chewing-gum.

We were off before first light, picking our way down a flowing dune face into the wind. All around us the cliffs were covered in a mantle of golden sand, and a hail of rasping grains spun off the dune crests like fire. The camels were tilting down the dune slopes at 50-degree angles and battling through long tunnels of deep, white sand.

There were no tracks, and we couldn't be sure even that these interlocking dunes would take us down into the valley. Then I noticed a group of camels, like black pimples in the distance, coming directly towards us up the dunes. Four dark pinpricks resolved into four Moors leading them. We ran smack into them and clasped their hands in greeting. They were travellers from the Rigaybat on their way back to Western Sahara, predatory-looking men with bullet heads, bird-thin with cavernous faces. After the greeting ritual was over Mafoudh asked about the well of Ganeb, where we were hoping to water. 'It's a long way,' one of them replied. 'You'll never make it before noon.'

Another asked where we were bound, and when I told him, 'Egypt,' he grinned and said, 'You'll never make it there either.'

'Yes, we will,' I said.

'Yes, they will,' said Mafoudh, 'and we'll make it to Ganeb before noon too!'

After they had gone Mafoudh said, 'Bah! I don't like the Rigaybat! You can't trust them.' He said that the Rigaybat had always been raiders and had stolen camels from his tribe for generations. 'Now they've got new weapons and call themselves the Polisario,' he said. 'Now they kill women and children as well!'

Within half an hour we were down on the valley floor and the Baatin was towering above us like a vast, rocky shoulder. It was even hotter down here, out of the wind. We marched over more dunes, stumbling and sinking calf-deep in the sand. Marinetta had to stop frequently to relieve her diarrhoea, and we had to halt the caravan. 'I'm sorry, Maik!' she always said, hurrying back.

'Don't worry,' I told her, wondering how she managed to keep going. She was very thirsty but she never asked for water. We all knew that the little we had left had to be saved for emergencies.

After two hours Gurfaf suddenly sat down and snapped his headrope. It was the first sign of trouble from any of the camels. I knew that he must be in pain, but we couldn't examine his back unless we unloaded. And we couldn't unload until we reached Ganeb. We forced him up with kicks and thumps and pushed the caravan on desperately. Twice more he sat down. Twice more he broke his headrope, forcing us to knot it into shorter and shorter pieces. If it got any shorter, there would be no headrope left.

The sun grew hotter, sailing up into its zenith. My throat and lips were so dry that I couldn't speak, and there was a nauseating acid feeling in my stomach. Marinetta scrambled after the caravan, her face a mask of pain and discomfort. The deep sand sucked her slim legs, making her pant with effort. A sandstorm began, drawing a veil of white dust over the valley and obscuring our view of the Baatin, so that Mafoudh could no longer lead us in a straight line. For a while I gave him directions from my compass. We went on like this for several hours.

The dunes gradually gave way to a salty grey plain, which the Moors called *sebkha*. Almost at once we collided with a herd of thirty camels being driven by two women. The camels' bellies were comfortingly bloated with water. The women told us that Ganeb was a little farther on, and a few minutes later we sighted the floating island of palms that marked the wells. 'What time is it?' Mafoudh asked. It was two minutes to noon.

Ganeb was a scene from Dante. Two Moors were digging out a shallow pit, around which stood a parade of up-ended water drums ready for filling. The well lay in the middle of a scree of stones, billions of strangely shaped grey pebbles, some of them like tiny human figures. About a hundred yards away the untended palm grove stood like an atoll, its great tresses of fronds waving in the wind. The landscape around had the crisp sheen of rock salt, the red *mirsal* that the Moors fed to their animals. The sand was snow-white but spattered with *pointilliste* nodules of black grit. Here and there were lone trees, twisted and grotesque like a vision from some ancient legend. It was still scalding-hot, and the wind brought with it a thick rain of sand that rasped in the palm trees. Through the sand-mist moved camel herds like apparitions, attended by ghostly human figures cowled in blue.

While Mafoudh took the camels off to water them at a salty well, I filled six waterbags, standing knee-deep in the shallow pit that the Moors had dug out. Marinetta made lunch among the palms and dosed herself with Intertrix. When Mafoudh returned from the wells we examined Gurfaf. There were two pustules of swollen flesh on his flanks, just below the withers, from the rubbing of the litter.

Mafoudh took out his pocket knife, and while I held the camel's nostrils, twisting his head backwards, the guide made three quick incisions on each flank until the blood streamed down. He explained that this would allow the poison to run out from the swellings. When I let go of Gurfaf's head, expecting an explosion of rage, he gave out no more than a half-hearted growl.

The following day we camped near the well of Zig with some Nmadi. I had looked forward to meeting the Nmadi for some time. They were desert-dwellers with a difference. They were said to live entirely by hunting and to despise nomadism. The only animals they kept were dogs, but they were supposed to borrow camels from the nomads in return for a supply of meat. The Nmadi we saw at Zig were very short and very spare. They were barefoot and wore shocks of wild hair instead of headcloths. Their dwellings were crude skin tents pitched among waves of sand where clumps of *halfa* grass were growing. I noticed with interest that a few goats were browsing around the tents.

After we had made camp one of the Nmadi came to greet us, bringing with him a young saluki bitch, very like a greyhound but with wide paws. The man was small and dignified. His name was Deh. There was nothing unusual about his tattered, patched gandourah. After the greetings I handed him a bowl of *zrig*. I had heard that the Nmadi despised milk as the food of nomads, but this hunter drank it with relish. I asked him about the goats, saying that I had thought the Nmadi lived only by the hunt.

'That's all finished,' he said with a bitter smile. 'Hunting is illegal, and even if it wasn't, there's not much game to hunt any more. There's only gazelle and bustard and precious few of those. We never used to bother with them in the old days. Addax was our main bag, but we used to take oryx, antelope, moufflon and even ostrich.' He told me that the game had been virtually wiped out by Polisario hunting parties, which scoured the desert in motor vehicles, hunting at night with powerful searchlights that mesmerized the animals and made them an easy kill.

'We used to track the game for weeks,' Deh said. 'We used to take the women and children with us, right into the empty quarter.' He described how they would work in three-man teams, one with a rifle, one holding the dogs and the other taking charge of the camels. 'When we found a herd of addax, the man with the rifle would drop one or two, the fattest ones, then the dogs would chase the rest. We trained them to go for the ears, nose or legs, so that the animal was alive when we got to it. Then we'd butcher the meat and wrap it in the skin. We never sold it for money. What we couldn't eat ourselves we traded in the town for sugar and tea. Some went to the tribes that lent us the camels. We never had any camels of our own.'

The drought of the previous few years had finished the work that the mass hunters had begun. Scores of Nmadi families had left the desert and drifted to the oases. A few families had remained in the ranges, but they were no longer hunters. They had become herdsmen like the Moors. 'The old life was best,' Deh sighed. 'But that won't come back. Not unless the game returns. And that won't happen, will it?' He patted the little saluki bitch, which had curled up next to him in the sand. 'You know, I used to have six dogs, all good hunters. They were worth the price of a camel each. Now all I have is this one.' As he walked back towards his camp, with the dog frollicking around his heels, I thought he had the look of a deposed monarch. I knew I was seeing one of the last hunters of the Sahara, a man whose skills could be traced back, in a direct line, to the makers of that barbed arrow head I had found on our first day out. Those hunters had lived 12,000 years ago. That made the camel, with its mere 2,000 years in the Sahara, a relative newcomer.

When the hunter had gone, Mafoudh lit a blazing fire. 'I don't trust those Nmadi,' he declared. 'They still have guns, you can be sure. We should bring the camels in tonight.'

'Why don't you trust them?'

'They're not real Muslims. They don't fast or pray, I tell you. They have spells, and magic, and magicians who tell them where to find the game. They can put the evil eye on you as quick as anything, by God!'

Later we drove the shuffling camels into our camp. A cool breeze rose, and the camels turned sideways into it, letting it massage their bulky frames. As we drove them on I thought of the Nmadi and how the era of the hunter had passed. 'Everything passes,' Mafoudh had said the first time I met him. I wondered how long it would be before the era of the camel passed away for ever. 'There will be a time when all this is over,' I said to Mafoudh.

'Yes,' he answered. 'Everyone will go by plane. It's already too hard for camels.'

My mind dwelt for a long time that night on the ages of man, the hugeness of time, the ever-changing nature of the planet. Man had bred these camels for his own use, and for hundreds of years they had been a way of life for many societies. Yet some time soon the diversity of life they had made possible would be gone.

The next day we rode across a rolling plain of stubbled grass with the hot wind chasing us. It was the hottest day of the hottest season. The land seemed burning. The wind blew in flame-thrower blasts. It was hotter than Chinguetti in June, hotter than anything I had experienced in the eastern Sahara. Everything was glaring hot – the saddle, the stick in my hands and the folds of my shirt. My hands and feet were swollen from the roasting; my throat felt like emery paper; my gums were choked with a paste of mucus. The wind rose and fell in gusts. When it hit us it was like being braised with hot, dripping fat. When it fell the stillness of the air brought beads of sweat to our heads at once. I was glad of the protection of my thick headcloth, swirling shirt and pantaloons, which allowed the circulation of cool air beneath, but nothing could ease my parched mouth or the nausea in my stomach.

As midday approached we searched vainly for a tree. In the whole of that vast landscape there was none. Instead we had to put up our tent. The sand was too hot to stand on. Even in sandals you could feel the heat cutting through. 'If you broke an egg on this, it would fry,' Marinetta said. Inside the tent it was stifling but just better than the inferno outside. Marinetta made *zrig* in two minutes. As Mafoudh drank, my eyes were riveted on the bowl. He seemed to drink and drink. I could see his Adam's apple working up and down as he swallowed. It seemed he would never pass it to me. When he did so, I thought, *He drank so much!* Then I tilted it to my lips, noticing Marinetta's suspicious, beady eyes tracking my every move. It was indescribably wonderful to feel the thick, sugary milk slip down my throat, easing the raw skin of the mouth and reinflating my shrunken stomach. I passed it to my wife. She almost snatched it from me and glared at me accusingly when she saw what was left.

Our bodies were already streaming with sweat as the liquid rehydrated our cells and was flushed out by the cooling mechanism of the sweat glands. For an instant there was an intensely pleasant sensation of coolness. But the feeling soon passed, to be replaced by the beginning of another nagging thirst. It was too hot to cook, so Mafoudh made tea. Then we just lay there in wet heaps, praying to God to take the heat away. I couldn't believe that any conditions, not those of the Poles, nor of the jungles nor of the open sea, could be worse than the Sahara in summer.

'We ought to get a medal for this,' Marinetta said.

As we lay there, riddled with perspiration, I noticed that the camels weren't eating. They had sat down without even bothering to sniff at the green clumps of *halfa* all around them. 'See!' said Mafoudh. 'The food is right under them, and they're too hot to eat it.'

'I keep seeing that advert for Sprite,' Marinetta said. 'You know, the one with the tanned woman in the tiny bikini. She plunges into the blue, blue swimming-pool and the lemonade bursts out of the bottle. And I see the big, fresh salads my mother used to make. I can even smell them.' And I laughed because as soon as she said it, I could smell them too.

It was still hot when we set off that afternoon, and it remained hot. During my research I had come across many books that waxed romantic about the 'perfect cool' of the Saharan night. That 'perfect cool' was a myth created by Westerners who had only ever seen the Sahara in winter. I wished that some of them could have been present to see the nights when the temperature hardly seemed to drop at all, when the cloud cover prevented the daytime heat from dissipating and the maddening fever stayed with you till dawn.

We moved on slowly. The plain of *halfa* clumps gave way to a barrier of sand dunes. To the north the shield-wall split into canyons and corries. The sand beneath us was ivory-white at first, changing quickly to coffee-cream, then to slate-blue. Each successive colour remained pure and unblemished, as if it had been painted. When we reached the top of the dunes we were treated to a stunning view.

The rocky wall of the fault was weathered into stumps of towers, machicolated battlements and giant blue buttresses, washed over by orange sand. Beneath it the blue-grey floor of the valley was straddled by the palm groves of Tichit.

I awoke from a deep sleep to the sound of raised voices and saw Mafoudh arguing with three policemen. They were standing over him in poses of exaggerated aggressiveness, two tall troopers in green berets and drab denims and a grizzled little sergeant wearing a peaked cap that was too small for his square head. I shut my eyes again quickly, hoping they would go away, but it was too late. The grizzled man spotted me and shouted at me in fractured French, demanding to know why we hadn't reported to the *gendarmerie* the previous night. 'We didn't arrive till late,' I lied.

'Here,' said the grizzled man, 'there are serious problems of *sûreté*.'

Tichit was the last place I would have expected security problems. It seemed half abandoned, a collection of stone shops and houses hemmed in between the cliff wall on one side and the palm groves on the other. It was tiny and isolated; there was no main road to anywhere and, from what Mafoudh told me, it was almost moribund. The sergeant explained everything on the way up to the *gendarmerie*. He said that the *préfet* was away on tour and had left him strict instructions to deal, all alone, with problems of *sûreté*.

We were shown into an enormous room that contained absolutely nothing but a tiny desk in one corner. The desk and the floor were so thick in dust that you could have tracked the progress of every beetle and cockroach that had ranged across them in the previous few weeks. The security office of Tichit was hardly a whirlpool of activity. When the sergeant placed his cap on the desk top, it left a precise mark in the shape of a cap.

He demanded our passports and scrutinized them closely. 'One British, one Italian,' he commented slowly. 'That is very strange. How come a British and an Italian travel together?'

'We are married,' I told him.

He looked at me with obvious incredulity. 'Married? How come a British and an Italian are married? That is very strange.'

'I've got the certificate if you want to see it.'

'That won't be necessary. But, tell me, why do you travel by camel? It is odd for a married couple to travel by camel with a guide. I mean, there's no *privacy*, is there? What do you do when you want to ... well, I mean, where do you all sleep? Together?'

'My wife and I sleep together, and the guide sleeps on his own.'

'It's the first time I ever saw a married couple travelling together by camel. Very strange.'

Then, apparently satisfied that we were not dangerous spies, he called to one of the troopers to scribble something in our passports. When that was done he searched about the desk, muttering about a rubber stamp. Finally he added his signature instead. Then, the effort over, he replaced his cap, leaving the precise mark in the dust as evidence of the day's work, and smiled. He invited us to take tea and dates with him.

We sat on a rug outside and went through the ritual three glasses of tea. A Hartani came up with an enormous tray of dates, and the sergeant insisted on choosing and stoning each date before handing it to us. There was a threadbare Moorish tent folded up on a rotten frame of wood and bits of old saddles straggling along the top of the wall. A scrawny desert chicken hurtled, cackling, around the yard. A Moor in a rich blue gandourah came in and sat down next to us. He was upright and clean-cut and called himself Mohammidu. He belonged to the Shurfa, he said; then he offered to accompany us as guide to Walata. When I replied that we already had a guide, he took a different tack and asked us what provisions we required. I said that we needed grain for the camels, and he beamed and said, 'I know just the place.'

Half an hour later we were inside one of the stone shops, arguing with a dark-faced shopkeeper over a sack of wheat. The man could have been a Hartani but was, in fact, a black Moor of the Masna tribe, whose oasis Tichit was. I knew that the price of the wheat should have been 1,200 ougiyyas, but the merchant adamantly and nastily refused to let it go for less than 1,700. Tired, irritated and sick with the heat, I finally agreed. When he heaved it over to us, I saw the familiar legend, 'Furnished by the People of the United States of America. Not for sale or exchange', printed clearly on the outside. 'You're a villain,' I said. 'Your country gets this stuff free from the *nsara*, and you sell it back to the *nsara* for twice what it's worth.' The shopkeeper and Mohammidu laughed uproariously.

Mohammidu explained severely that we must hire a Hartani to carry the sack to our camp. He called one over with a lordly wave of his aristocratic hand.

'I won't take it for less than 500,' the sinewy black man said.

'I'll take it myself before I pay that!' I said.

'You cannot take it yourself. You are a Christian,' Mohammidu said. Almost before he had finished I had hoisted the huge sack across my back and was staggering away with it. It was incredibly hard work, but I was still furious at having paid so much for it. The two men watched us go incredulously.

That afternoon was an inferno. Mafoudh donned his spare gandourah and sloped off to lunch with the police. No doubt they wanted to ask more questions about our sleeping arrangements. Marinetta and I lay in the shade of the palms, covering ourselves with blankets against the blast of the wind. We had been planning a two-day rest in Tichit. It was like planning a rest in Purgatory. We had already acquired the same distaste for towns that nomads feel. Towns were complicated and confusing. Only the desert was simple. We wanted to get back to its tranquillity as soon as possible.

As we lay there, a voice said, 'Peace be on you!' It was Mohammidu. He squatted next to us and asked where Mafoudh was. When I told him, he said, 'Listen! Take me as a guide to Walata instead of Mafoudh. I know the way better than him. He hasn't been there for fifteen years, and it's all changed since then. I'll go for less than you're paying him.'

'I've already agreed with Mafoudh,' I said, 'and Mafoudh is my friend. It's not very honourable to come around here when he's away, scouting for work.'

'My wish is only to help you. You wait till you see the sands of Umm Hayjiba. No God but God, you'll get lost in it!'

'Thank you and goodnight!' I said, in English.

'Don't call us: we'll call you!' Marinetta added as the Moor stalked away.

The morning was very still. Our farewell party consisted of three slim Haratin girls with cheeky faces and perky breasts. They pounced on everything we had left, squeaking gleefully as they picked up empty cans and discarded wrappings. They even collected the date stones that we had thrown away in the sand, saying that they would crush them up for the goats.

We walked across a *sebkha* of blue stones. The camels oozed strength and vitality, flowing along the flat surface like mercury. There were occasional bushes and clumps of grass cropped down to stubble like crew-cuts. As the morning wore on, the air was filled with pink sand-mist. The landscape began to radiate heat and rainbow colours. To the north I could make out the craggy line of the Baatin and, to the south, the faint glimmer of sand dunes. By afternoon we were heading towards a folded drift of sand that seemed propped up against the cliff walls.

Not long after we mounted the sky filled with a fizz of cloud. It was cumulo-nimbus: raincloud. 'Here it comes!' Mafoudh shouted, and a second later the temperature had dropped several degrees and a cold wind hit us with an alarming thump. The sky was poised for action. Over the landscape, to the south, claw-shaped fingers of fog were clutching downwards. Thunder rolled above us like a broadside. Then there was a second's silence – an eerie, expectant silence. We heard the rain slithering towards us, growing louder like some gigantic, invisible sand-worm about to attack. Then the rain surged against us in freezing droplets, lashing the camels and drenching everything in moments. The sudden shock of the cold was awesome.

'Come on!' Mafoudh yelled, slipping down from his camel. He tied on his saddle blanket frantically. 'We've got to get to that high ground,' he shouted. I jumped down and couched Marinetta's camel, helping her off. As we strung the camels together, heavy, slow drops of rain splashed around us. 'Let's go!' the guide bawled, lurching off in bare feet. The wind struck with renewed violence. I put my arm round Marinetta and we both leaned desperately into it. Rain and grit slashed against us with hurricane force.

It seemed an age before we reached the edge of the sand dunes. We climbed up the slope as far as we could and began to unload. The rain was now whipping at us with angry strokes, and there was a volley of scarlet lights in the sky. Down went the *girbas* and saddle bags. A large tin of dried milk crashed into the sand and broke open. A foam of creamy *zrig* spread out along the dune. Mafoudh grappled in the wet, milky sand to knee-hobble the camels. Marinetta was fighting to unravel the tent, which threatened to take off. Then Mafoudh began to pile wet sand around its edges, and both of us did the same. Finally, we covered it with a plastic sheet and elbowed our way inside.

An hour later I was dying to relieve myself and left the tent. The storm was almost finished; the last gloomy drizzle was shuddering out of the darkness. As I moved back to the tent I met Marinetta coming the other way. 'What is it?' I asked.

'It's Mafoudh,' she said.

'Did he touch you?'

'No.'

'Well?'

'He smiled at me. You know, like a man smiles at a woman.'

Later, when Mafoudh had taken his sodden blanket to sleep by the camels, we got out our sleeping bags for the first time. We dived into them, revelling in the few unexpected moments of privacy. 'It was nice the way you put your arm round me when the rain came,' Marinetta said.

'I'll do it again if you like,' I answered.

We watered at Akreyjit at a well among the tall stone houses there. They were windowless and looked like fortresses. A weathered little Moor at the well told us that they were very old. 'They were built six generations ago,' he said, 'but half of them are empty. So many people have gone.' He was a tiny man, almost a dwarf, one of the few white Moors left in the oasis. 'Those who had camels have taken them off to Ayoun and Tantan,' he said. 'Some of the men went to find work in Nouakchott. We still have good dates, but who wants them now?'

We climbed the hill behind the village, picking up hand axes and arrowheads that had been exposed by the rain. There were an incredible number of stone querns and acres of smashed pottery with the usual striated pattern. We had been finding these objects since entering the Aouker valley. There must have been a large population here in Stone Age times, I thought. These cliffs were once the shores of a vast lake, and the people who lived here had herded cattle. About 7,000 years ago their ways had begun to replace those of the hunters as the dominant culture in this part of the Sahara. They lived on milk and meat, supplementing them with flour made from wild grasses similar to the ones that still grew in these regions today. It was only later that the people learned to plant and cultivate their own crops and changed from nomads to farmers. The descendants of these prehistoric farmers probably lived on in the Haratin.

After we passed Akreyjit Mafoudh became increasingly moody. 'From here to Walata is the most difficult stretch,' he said. 'There are no more oases, and there won't be any nomad camps either. We're on our own from now on.' Day by day our progress was made more difficult by the sand-mist that sometimes swallowed up the entire landscape, robbing us of landmarks and reference points. We were heading for the well of Toujinit, which was east of Tichit, but Mafoudh constantly wandered south. I was afraid we would wander off the hard *sebkha* and into the soft dunes along its edge, which stretched hundreds of miles. One morning I checked my compass continually, as Mafoudh turned farther and farther south.

'What's up?' Marinetta asked me.

'He keeps going south.'

'Do you think he's lost the way?'

'You'd need to be a genius to navigate accurately in this!'

'Why don't you tell him?'

I shouted to Mafoudh to stop and explained. He regarded me almost mockingly with his big, coal-black eyes. 'I know the way, Omar,' he said calmly. 'You think I don't know my job? If we don't find Toujinit by sunset, then you take over as guide.'

When we stopped at midday, though, he disappeared into the mist on foot as soon as the camels were unloaded. 'He must be worried,' Marinetta observed. 'He hasn't even drunk his tea.' Half an hour passed, then an hour. I was tempted to go out to look for him, but Marinetta persuaded me against it. 'He knows the way back,' she said.

'I hope he does, or we're really up the creek.'

'What would we do if he didn't come back?'

'I bet I could think of something,' I said, massaging her knee.

'It might be quite nice after all,' she said.

Just then Mafoudh materialized out of nowhere and, without a word, started to make tea. He gulped down one glass like a drinker taking his first snifter of the day and was slurping his way through the second when he saw us watching him. The big hatchet face cracked into a grin. 'Don't worry,' he said. 'We'll find our well.'

Within half an hour of setting off we had blundered into the dunes. The sand-mist whisked around, performing endless veronicas in front of our small caravan. The camels wheezed and grunted as they laboured up the soft slopes and nose-dived down again, tottering on valiantly through the dust. Mafoudh ambled forward with his shuffling pace, confidently testing the sand with his stick, adjusting our direction, left and right, to find the easiest descent. The only time we halted was when Gurfaf sat down again. This time the headrope held, but the steel ring was torn out of his nostril. It took ten bloody, cud-spitting minutes to replace it. Then we were off again, up and down the wave crests, heads down into the wind.

There was no end to the dunes. The compass told me that we were going too far south. I was about to mention it to Mafoudh when the curtain of mist was swept back to reveal the solid wall of the Baatin almost on top of us. Beneath it was a grey plain of *sebkha*, and a little farther on we found grooves made by the feet of countless camels over numberless generations. Farther on still was a dead camel, a twisted fuselage of hard skin and polished bone. We found the well of Toujinit just before sunset. Mafoudh beamed at me triumphantly.

'Praise God!' was all I could say.

The well was about nine feet deep. We fashioned a hawser out of our spare ropes and lashed on our home-made well bucket. It was actually a butter-oil tin with the lid removed and two holes cut in the side. We filled all our six waterskins and carried them, bloated, over to a knot of bushes about 500 yards from the well. Mafoudh said that the bushes were *atil*, a thorny species of acacia. I collected some deadfall for the fire, but he advised me not to burn it. '*Atil* smoke can send you blind and mad,' he said. Instead we set up the little butane burner that we had brought for emergencies, and Marinetta made rice. When it was ready she poured a trickle of liquid butter over it, and we tucked in hungrily.

Next day we climbed up through the hills, crossing narrow gorges where brilliantly green *arak* trees flourished. The leaves of the *arak* were bitter and an acquired taste even for camels. Mafoudh regarded them as poor grazing, saying that they were like 'sauce on the pudding'. *Arak* stayed green when other trees withered, and this, Mafoudh said, was because of their extra-long roots.

Beyond the hills was an undulating plain where the sand was piled around billions of clusters of woody grass. The Moors, who have a name for every gradation of desert, called this type *tarha*. It stretched to the horizon, unbroken except for the faint shadow of what looked uncannily like a giant tree. The sand was criss-crossed by the stitch-like patterns of lizard tracks and the curvy indentations of snakes. We saw no snakes but plenty of long-toed lizards, leaping past with their curious sprinter's gait, and the occasional couple of white skinks that chased each other helter-skelter around the clumps. Whether they were fighting or mating I couldn't make out.

We made camp in the plain. The camels refused to eat the woody grass, so we fed them grain. Fodder was already running short, for they ate about 7 pounds of grain each every night when there was no grazing. I hoped it would last until we reached Walata. Marinetta prepared to make rice again, but Mafoudh stopped her. He announced that tonight he would make bread. 'It's the best kind of food in the desert,' he declared, 'because you waste nothing.' We watched as he added a little water to the flour and pummelled it into dough. He fashioned it lovingly into a thick oval, then fetched some of the woody grass to make a fire. When the fire had burned down to glowing spills he dug a shallow pit, laid the raw loaf inside and scooped sand back over it. He scraped together the remains of the fire and laid it carefully over the bread.

Meanwhile, following his instructions, Marinetta lit another fire and began making a gravy of onions and seasoning to go with the bread. I watched as she struggled into the camp with three heavy stones for the fireplace, hardly able to balance them in her slender arms. By now she was almost unrecognizable as the fashion-conscious mannequin I had met in Khartoum. Her skin was nearly black from the sun, and her big eyes and white teeth stood out like beacons. She had never had much spare flesh, but her body had taken on a more streamlined hardness. The muscles in her calves and arms stood out more distinctly, and her firm breasts had a new tautness. Most of all there was a greater self-confidence and alertness in her manner. She still wore the same Arab shirt and baggy pantaloons, the original colour blotted out by succeeding generations of stains and the daily instalment of sand. They were torn and ragged so that when she knelt over the cooking pot an expanse of very brown thigh showed through.

Twenty minutes later Mafoudh brushed away the ashes and sand, and out came a crusty baked loaf, nicely browned with dust. He beat it with his camel stick until most of the sand fell away, then broke it into pieces and dropped them in the gravy. The bread was magnificent.

The giant tree we had seen the previous afternoon turned out to be a huge, mushroom-shaped carbuncle of rock. It had detached itself from a massif of red granite, the base of which was so eroded into trunks and tap roots that it gave the impression of having grown out of the desert in a solid vegetable mass.

Farther on was an even stranger sight. It was a gigantic berg of granite, cut through with great oval arches, so that you could see through its belly to the other side. From afar, clothed in mist, it looked like an ogrish castle from a childhood nightmare. Close up it reminded me of the shell of a cathedral, somehow exposed to a mighty holocaust that had melted its façade, sending its noble arches out of true, crumbling its walls into fissures and crevices and distorting its high pillars and battlements.

'Fantastic!' Marinetta shouted when she saw it, and she ranged Mafoudh in front for a photograph. It was viciously hot already, but she couldn't get the shot right and forced poor Mafoudh to march back and forth with the camels in the stinging heat. He was shy of the camera and with each new shot pulled his headcloth more tightly around his face.

We spent the midday halt in a smaller natural arch farther on. In the afternoon we entered the dunes of Umm Hayjiba. As Mohammidu had warned us in Tichit, this was the most dangerous stretch of the journey to Walata. Here the wall of the Baatin was out of sight, twisting far to the north before curving back south towards Walata. Instead of following the fault line and adding an extra day to the journey, we had decided to head directly across the sands.

As we rode on that afternoon, Marinetta started telling me about a film she had once seen. 'It was the story of a woman and three handsome men who had crashed on a desert island,' she said. 'The woman was married to one of the men, but she got fed up with him. She wanted to find out which of them was the strongest, so she decided to make love to all of them.'

'And what happened?'

'She made love to all of them, and they ended up fighting each other. It reminds me of this situation. Lost in the middle of the desert, with two handsome men!'

'Steady on,' I said. 'We're not lost yet.'

There was no grazing for the camels again that night, so we fed them grain and left them sitting on the dunes near by. Quite early in the morning, before dawn, I was woken up by something large and warm crawling up my leg. I reached down instinctively to find Marinetta's hand. 'What is it?' I asked.

'That film,' she said. 'I couldn't stop thinking about it.'

'There's nothing we can do about it now,' I said.

The hand resumed its path up my leg. 'Yes, we can,' she said. 'Mafoudh's asleep.' I put both my arms around her. She felt very warm and cuddlable. I was just about to kiss her when there was a shattering clap of thunder. Mafoudh's blanket whipped back, and our guide rolled out. A gash of brilliant electricity tore across the sky. In a second I was up and we were feverishly piling everything under the cover of our plastic sheets. The wind sprayed sand across the dunes, but no rain fell. Suddenly Marinetta said, 'The camels have gone!'

Mafoudh and I looked at each other in dismay. We hadn't even noticed. 'I thought you'd knee-hobbled them!' I shouted at the guide.

'I thought you had!' he shouted back.

We scouted around the dunes with our torches. The wind had already demolished their tracks. Even in daylight the interlocking dunes limited visibility to a few yards.

At first light Mafoudh took a canteen of water and went off to search for them. While Marinetta made mugs of coffee on the butane cooker, I climbed the nearest dune and tied my blue headcloth on a pole as a sign for the guide. Below me our things looked like a tiny island in the sea of sand. The dunes rippled away for miles, all of uniform height and colour, without the least distinguishing feature. Mafoudh was already out of sight among them. I knew that in his place, without my compass, I'd have been lost inside ten minutes.

I climbed down and found Marinetta staring into the sand. 'What's up?' I asked.

'I was just thinking,' she replied, 'what I would do if you and Mafoudh were killed and I was left alone.'

'What would you do?'

'I'd head back to the last well by compass, then I'd wait there until some nomads came.'

'What would you do with our bodies?'

'I'd load you on the camel and take you with me.'

'And Mafoudh?'

'Well ... it sounds bad, but Mafoudh doesn't belong to me.'

We drank our coffee. More than an hour had passed since Mafoudh had gone off. I hardly dared think of what might happen if the camels weren't found. Suddenly there was a whistle, and I looked up to see the guide coming back over the nearest dune with the three camels in tow. He had somehow managed to tie their noses all together with his old headcloth. 'Whew!' he exclaimed. 'Thank God they didn't get too far. We'd have been dead for certain.'

By that evening the sands of Umm Hayjiba lay behind us, and we were back in the belly of the Baatin. We made camp near the well of Tinigert, in a narrow chasm full of arak trees and birds. The walls of the chasm were covered in rock pictures: cattle, camels, oryx, addax, and matchstick men. There were inscriptions in tefinagh, the Tuareg script, and other more recent ones in Arabic. I wondered if the Tuareg had once occupied this region. 'Impossible!' declared Mafoudh. 'You won't see any of those barbarians until you get to Mali. This is the country of the bidan.' My own Western culture had left its marks here too, in the form of fragments of an old motorcycle littered across the sand.

The well was no more than 6 feet deep. It stood beneath an overhanging cliff, with a deserted stone sangar on the opposite side. Clearly no one had used the well for some time because the water was thickly coated in bird lime and had a putrid taste. We brought the camels up to be watered. Marinetta was standing close by Gurfaf, trying to take a photograph of the well, when he suddenly lashed out with his rear foot, missing her by inches. The blow could easily have broken her leg. An instant later the other camels went wild, kicking out blindly right and left and stamping their hooves in the sand with crashing blows. We rushed to gather the headropes, afraid that they would roll in the sand and crush our gear. 'It's the ticks!' Mafoudh said. 'Look at the devils!' The ordure-saturated sand around the well was coming alive with thousands of steadily advancing insects. They dragged their grey, leathery bodies out of the dust, making a bee-line for anything that moved.

'They're horrible!' Marinetta shuddered as we quickly moved the camels on to stony ground. We stamped our feet so that the ticks couldn't get a hold. They had a nasty bite.

'Strange creatures,' I said to Mafoudh. 'They lie here in the sand for years just waiting for another meal of blood to come by.'

'Ah!' He shrugged. 'Just another thing God made.'

At dawn we climbed out of the chasm and across the plateau of a rocky hill called Eji. The sand-mist was on us again as thick as ever. The washed-out colours reminded me of English moorland in winter. But there was nothing remotely wintry about the heat. Near midday we were travelling along what seemed to be a narrow cul-de-sac. We were marching due east. I looked at my compass again and again. Our direction never varied. This morning we should have turned due south towards Walata. If we continued east, we would end up in the middle of the Mrayya, the empty quarter. I was reluctant to call to Mafoudh, remembering what had happened before. I felt sure that any moment he would swing south. But time passed and he never did.

At last, not long before noon, I shouted to him, 'We're going east, Mafoudh! My compass tells me that south is to the right!'

'Your compass tells you!' he scoffed. 'South is this way!' He pointed straight ahead, due east. We both looked up instinctively. The sun was almost at its highest point and was partially obscured by clouds of dust. Towards the end of the canyon was a thin rash of thorn trees. I suggested making camp there for the midday halt.

After we had unloaded and drunk our *zrig* Mafoudh said, 'Now, which way is south?' Again I took out the compass and laid it in the sand. The red needle swung to the left. South could only be to the right. 'For me, south is straight ahead,' he said, pointing along the canyon. 'I can tell by the shadows.'

'No, you can't,' I said. 'There are no shadows at midday. The compass has to be correct. It never lies. Not unless there's iron in the ground.'

'How do you know there's no iron in the ground?'

'I haven't seen any. Have you?'

'I tell you, it's the other way,' he insisted. Then he started to draw in the sand a crude sun compass in the form of a cross. 'There! North—south—east—west. Those are *my* directions,' he said, marking each direction and stabbing a twig into the ground between them. 'When the sun starts to go down in the afternoon there *will* be shadows. Then we will see who is right!'

It was a challenge. I drew a second cross next to his, marking in my version of the directions, with my south in place of his east. Then we moved into the shade to wait for the sun to sink.

Marinetta made lunch. The water we had taken from Tinigert was so foul that the evil taste permeated the food. I was very thirsty, but drinking the water was a torture. Marinetta seemed to drink it without complaint, however. 'How do you do it?' I asked her incredulously. 'It tastes like rotten eggs.'

'You know,' she said, 'the water of Rome is the best water in the world. It's so cool and fresh that we don't even bother to put it in the fridge. When I drink this horrible water I repeat to myself, "The water of Rome! The water of Rome!" over and over. Then I don't taste it.' I was amazed by this feat of auto-suggestion, and I tried it for myself. The water still tasted like rotten eggs.

We dozed off in the heat, but at about half past three Marinetta woke me up excitedly. 'Look!' she said, pointing at the sun. It was going down behind us, and the shadow marking east clearly fell across where Mafoudh had marked south. It was a hollow victory. When Mafoudh said, 'All right, you're a better guide than me,' I was so embarrassed that I almost wished I had been wrong.

This didn't end our arguments about direction, though. By late afternoon we were at it again. Mafoudh said that a teacher in Chinguetti had told him that the earth was round and that if you travelled in a straight line, you would come back to where you started from. The man had also told him that the earth went around the sun. When I said, tentatively, that this might be true, he released all the pent-up temper that he had held back from the morning. 'That's rubbish!' he said. 'Lies of communists and unbelievers! It says in the Quran, "The sun and the moon run across the sky!" — that means that it is the sun that moves, not the earth. It says so in the Quran. And nobody can argue with the Quran.'

'So what would happen if you travelled in a straight line for ever?'

'You would come to the place where the earth ends and the sky begins, and if you went on farther still, you would fall off.'

Often, when the bleak, lunar landfall disappeared abruptly into a cloud or over a sheer rock gorge, I could almost believe it myself.

Near Oujaf we found some shallow pools of rainwater, clinging to the rocks like quicksilver. This put us all in a good mood. 'The bounty of God!' said Mafoudh. 'There's nothing better than finding water in the desert when you don't expect it.' It was the last such bounty that we were to find.

The days were a battle with the moisture-devouring wind. The camels got thirsty, we got thirsty, and the waterbags got thinner from dehydration. The temperature was still in the hundreds. Every few hours we had to stop and pour out a bowl of water to ease our parched throats and bloated lips. The metallic tinkle as the water splashed into the bowl became the most welcome sound I could imagine, but the skins began to look dangerously flabby. There were no more convenient rain pools, not even traces of them. Trees were few. There were no tracks of men or goats or camels. The only movement we saw on the wind-dried earth was three gazelles. They were snow-white and skipped across the *sebkha* kicking up little puffs of dust. 'We should be like the gazelles,' Mafoudh said. 'They drink only on Fridays.'

We were searching for the well of Tagouraret over a desert floor as flat and red as a tennis court. On one side of us was the familiar frontier of the Baatin and, on the other, the chilling hugeness of the sand-sea. As the sun drifted down the colours of the earth fluctuated steadily from red to apricot, umber, brown ochre and salmon-pink. The surface was puckered with veins of granite. A seam of low dunes lay across our path, then a black *sebkha*, then dunes again. There was no sign of a well. There were no tracks or droppings, no camel bones, none of the familiar camel grooves cut into the surface rock. We scanned the horizon right and left. Nothing moved out there. By sunset Mafoudh admitted that we had missed Tagouraret. We were down to our last skin of water.

Mafoudh reckoned that there were two wells in front of us, Ayoun al Khudr and Hassi Fouini. I thought of taking bearings on them with my compass, but it was impossible, since I wasn't sure of our exact position. All we could do was preserve our water and hope we would find traces of the wells. We woke up thirsty and we stayed thirsty all day. By mid-morning we were bent over our saddles with severe kidney pains. The heat poured down like boiling oil. The dust kicked up by the camels choked us and made our eyes smart. My mouth felt swollen and shapeless, and my lips were starting to crack. Mile after weary mile the camels shuffled along, yet there was not a hint of a near-by well. I looked up once to see a man riding a camel in the desert farther south. I pointed him out to Mafoudh, thinking how slow the guide was not to have noticed.

'That's not a man. It's a tree,' said Mafoudh.

'It's a man, I tell you!'

'There are no people in this area. You find people only where there has been rain, and there hasn't been any rain here.'

'It could be a traveller.'

'No. It's a tree.'

It seemed an age before we got near to the man on the camel. It seemed strange that he never moved. When we came up to him I saw that Mafoudh had been right. It was a tree.

At midday we halted in a large wadi where there were some shreds of *atil* and a few *arak* trees. In the distance the wall of the Baatin appeared to end. Instead of cooking we made foul-tasting *zrig*. Then, for the second time on this journey, Mafoudh left the camp before taking tea. I climbed a sand bank near by and tried to identify some of the surrounding knolls on my 1-to-1-million-scale survey map. It was impossible. Mafoudh and I almost collided as we entered the camp. I saw from his face that his recce had been no more inspiring than mine. 'So what did the mighty compass tell you?' he asked.

'Nothing,' I admitted. 'Nothing at all.'

'You shouldn't interfere with the work of the guide,' he said.

'It's my life and my wife's too,' I said. 'It's not just yours, you know.'

'Then you'd better ask your wife how to find the well because that's the only way we're going to find it.'

'Why don't you both shut up and save your energy?' Marinetta snapped suddenly.

We both did.

In the late afternoon we came to the place where the cliff wall appeared to end and found instead that it angled sharply east. Mafoudh halted his camel and turned to look at me. His face expressed exhaustion and utter defeat. 'I thought the well was here, Omar,' he said, 'but I was wrong.'

'You mean we've missed Ayoun al Khudr?' I asked.

'No,' he panted. 'We've missed both of them. Ayoun al Khudr and Hassi Fouini. Both of them.'

Both of them. Now I was worried. Marinetta looked as scared as I felt. Mafoudh's knowledge had failed us. So had my compass. We had missed three wells, and the next one – ironically called Bir Nsara, the 'Christians' Well' – was a day's ride away. We had about 6 pints of water left. That would mean a drink each tonight: tomorrow there would be nothing. Our only chance was to find people, but since leaving Akreyjit we hadn't seen a single living soul. Akreyjit lay nine days behind us.

We pushed on with the thirst rasping in our throats. As the camels padded on my thoughts wandered far away, across the desert sands to the river Nile that was our goal. I thought of the deep, fast-running water, the sunlight playing over the cool ripples, the white water gurgling through the cataracts. I thought of the river people carrying pots of the stuff and laying them in the shade for passers-by. My thoughts followed the river upstream to Khartoum, where Marinetta and I had met. I thought of her sleek, tanned body plunging into the blue swimming-pool, bottles of frothing Sprite on the tables. Then I thought again of the Nile and how I desperately wanted to reach that river. It was still more than 3,000 miles away. I was jerked out of my reverie by Marinetta shouting, 'The people! The people!'

I looked up to see figures among the thornbush, women in sweeping blue and men with camels. There were donkeys hobbled in green grass and a horde of goats whose bodies glinted in the scrub. We couched our camels not far from a woollen tent. An old man with long teeth limped out and shook our hands. 'Eh? Going to Walata?' he asked. 'You're nearly there now!' Almost before we had unloaded our camels he was pressing on us a giant bowl of fresh goat's milk. As the bowl was handed to me I whispered, 'Thanks to God!' There was never a time in my life when I meant it more.

When we reached Bir Nsara the next day we found it encircled by a carpet of green grass as smooth as a billiard table. Mafoudh rode up to the well and looked inside. 'Thank God again that we found those people last night!' he said. When I joined him at the well head I understood why. Bir Nsara was dry.

We watered at a hidden *gelta* to which the nomads had directed us and rode towards Walata at a leisurely pace. 'What would you like most in the world now?' I asked Marinetta.

'I'd like a big salad, a giant ice-cream and an orange juice, and after that I'd like to lie on a clean, sandy beach with the water lapping over me,' she replied.

Walata was invisible behind a ridge, but the ground around it was churned up and covered with tracks. As we approached we heard the sound of drums and stringed instruments wafting into the desert. It was so strange after the long silence that I thought my ears were playing tricks. Just before sunset the town came into sight. Its grey, crumbling maze of stone houses hugged the torso of a rocky hill, looking down into a wadi furnished with trees like Japanese miniatures. It was dark when we made camp there, but now the sound of the instruments was flowing out of the town, a swaying, erotic rhythm. It sounded like a party.

When we had set up our tent Mafoudh made tea. Marinetta and I couldn't keep our eyes off each other. Every time she moved she seemed to brush me with her hands or feet. The touch sent a tingling sensation down my spine.

The music came solidly out of the town. 'Do you think that's a wedding?' I asked Mafoudh.

'Sounds like it,' he said.

'Don't worry about us if you feel like going to join in,' I told him.

Catching on, Marinetta said, 'Yes, it might be good. Plenty to eat and drink!'

I saw the temptation in his eyes. 'But you would be on your own,' he said.

'Don't worry about that, Mafoudh. You go and enjoy yourself.'

'Perhaps I will,' he said. A few minutes later he had washed and put on his spare robe. Then he disappeared into the night.

Marinetta watched him go. 'At last!' she said. 'We're alone!' Her eyes shone. Her brown thighs showed through the splits in her pantaloons. I put my hand on one of them. She pulled me into the tent, and in moments our stinking clothes were off and we were lying naked on the sandy floor with our arms clasped round each other.

'We've waited a long time for this!' I said.

Just then we heard the sound of footsteps and a voice called, 'Omar! Where are you?'

We scrambled frantically for our clothing, and seconds later I looked out to see Mafoudh grinning sheepishly.

'What's the matter?' I asked him.

'I couldn't go,' he said. 'I didn't think it was right to leave you. Not after all we've been through.'

Moukhtar

When the Moroccan traveller Ibn Battuta arrived in Walata he was invited to the house of the Mandingo inspector, who fed him on millet porridge and honey. 'Was it for this that the blacks invited us?' he asked his friends after the meal.

'Yes,' they said, 'and this is considered the highest form of hospitality here.'

'This convinced me that there was no good to be hoped for from these people,' he wrote, 'and I made up my mind to return to Morocco at once.'

That was in 1352, when Walata was a desert outpost of the Mandingo empire of Mali: 634 years later, when we visited the oasis, it had long ceased to be a Mandingo town. Appropriately, however, its *préfet* was of Mandingo origin. He was a gentle, friendly man who preferred to speak French rather than Arabic but lost no time in telling us, 'My people built this place.' Like the *préfet* of Chinguetti, he was one of a new generation of political appointees, installed to give the black minorities a greater role in running the country.

Like Wadan's and Tichit's, though, Walata's days were evidently numbered. The caravan trade that had made it important had finished, and the new lorry trade now went south to the thriving border town of Nema, 50 miles away, leaving the oasis stranded in the Sahara to struggle on as best it could.

Half of the houses that crawled up the granite cliffs were in ruins. The intestines hung out of them. The narrow alleys that snaked between them were so clogged with crumbled masonry that there was hardly room to walk. The walls had lost their smooth skin of orange mud, revealing their jagged underflesh of raw stone. The crowded buildings gave the impression of having mushroomed haphazardly out of the rock and, in places, were in the process of melting and merging into it again. The roofs were gone. The doorways blinked down on us like blind caverns. Piles of rubble had spread out across the hill and become indistinguishable from the native rock.

But not all the houses were dead. Along the neater corridors were magnificent doorways, decorated with intricate woven patterns like writhing maggots. Others were painted more finely with curving cross symbols coloured brown and blue. Some of the doors were left open to reveal other doors inside, also open, like an array of facing mirrors, a tunnel reaching deep into the belly of the town. Children's features looked out on us from the shadows. A little girl giggled, sitting on a decayed doorstep chewing biscuits. The disjointed head of a donkey peered down nosily from a high window.

Some Moors from the Shurfa shook hands with us and invited us inside an immaculate courtyard. There were more maggot-like paintings and a massively rotund woman sprawling on a bed of wooden laths. She looked as if she couldn't possibly get up. The young men were students, on vacation from their college in Nouak-chott, and were delighted with our Hassaniyya. They made us tea, then without warning brought us a dish of millet porridge to eat. It was delicious.

There was a square of shops beneath the hill, some of them so blocked with sand that we had to scramble over high dunes to get to them. Blue-robed men sat in huddles outside, smoking little brass pipes. A few camels with pack saddles were being loaded with sacks of American grain. No children pursued us. No one shouted 'Nsara!' In the largest and cleanest of the shops we met a merchant called Mulah Ali. He was a big bulldog of a man with drooping black jowls and a ferocious expression that made his mild manners all the more of a pleasure. He had everything in his shop, from Nescafé to tinned peaches, and he charged the correct prices. He also promised to help us find a guide to replace Mafoudh.

The first candidate arrived a little later. He had a clean-shaven, shifty face with very clear eyes; his hair was oiled and brushed. Both his gandourah and his sirwel were spotlessly white. Close up he smelt faintly of perfume. That alone should have been enough to warn me. 'So you're the Christian who wants a guide to Tombouctou,' he said, lighting a cigarette. It was a real cigarette, not one of the little brass pipes that most Moors used. I admitted that I was and he said, 'Here I am. How much do you pay?'

'Just a moment,' I said. 'We'll talk about prices when I have chosen the guide.'

'I'm the best guide in Walata,' he said. 'And I want 30,000 ougiyyas and the return fare.'

'I don't pay a return fare,' I said. 'That comes out of the guide's portion.'

'That's stupid!' he declared, his eyes flashing angrily. 'Who ever heard of a guide not getting the return fare?' He spluttered and muttered something under his breath. He seemed really annoyed, as if the job had been his by right and the conditions his to choose.

'I don't think we'll be able to agree, do you?' I said.

He dropped his cigarette, crushing it meaningfully with a heavy sandal. 'You'll regret it!' he said and marched out of the shop, glowering.

'That was Sheikh Ahmed,' the big shop-keeper said, apologetically. 'He used to live in Zourg. Now he works for the army as a guide.'

'The army is the best place for him,' Marinetta told me acidly. 'Face of vomit! You couldn't take a man who loses his temper so easily, could you?'

Later Mulah Ali introduced me to another man. His name was Moukhtar Ould Sidi, and the merchant told me that he had just walked from his tent at Meya with some goats for sale in the market. At first sight Moukhtar seemed a weak, diffident character. He was tall and very thin, and his huge, furled turban hung so low over his handsome, delicate face that it gave him the look of a simpleton. When he shook hands with me, he looked away, a trait I put down to shyness but was, in fact, good manners. Moukhtar was one of the most polite men I have ever met. When he stood up, though, you could see the lean, cable-muscled arms moving beneath the sun-bleached gandourah, the precise yet powerful gymnast's step. He must have been about thirty-five. His was the sun-drawn, elongated face of the desert aristocrat, the eyes dark and thoughtful, the body the hunting greyhound frame of the hereditary nomad.

He told us that he had started out from his camp at sunrise and had arrived in the town near sunset. When I checked my map later I saw that Meya was 30 miles away. To have done that, on foot in this heat *and* driving goats, seemed an outstanding feat. It made me feel like an amateur.

After a certain amount of pushing from Mulah Ali, who was evidently a person of some weight in Walata, Moukhtar said that he would be prepared to accompany us to Tombouctou. 'There's only one problem,' he said. 'I don't know the way – that is, I haven't done it all by camel. There's no point my lying to you. I've been as far as Ras al Ma by camel. The rest of the way I've done by car.'

I was doubly impressed by his honesty, and since honesty was always our first consideration, I invited him to visit our camp.

Mafoudh welcomed the visitor and made tea. He had staunchly refused to leave us until we had appointed a new guide, and he had promised to interview the applicants and give his opinion of their character. He evidently liked Moukhtar. He questioned him closely about his tribe and discovered that he belonged to the noble Awlad Billa, a warrior tribe based in Zourg, south of Walata. I told Moukhtar that we had missed Hassi Fouini and saw him grin for the first time. 'The water there isn't much good anyway,' he said. 'It was salty from the beginning. I should know: it was my uncle who dug it out. Fouini was one of my family, and he was the governor of Walata when the well was sunk, so they named it after him.' Mafoudh listened with eyes downcast.

When Moukhtar had gone, Mafoudh said, 'That man is one of the best. You'd be lucky to find a man more honest than that. My advice is to take him. From Ras Al Ma you can follow the shore of Lake Faguibine to Tombouctou. It won't be a problem.' Marinetta nodded in agreement. I knew we had found our second guide.

I had been promising Mafoudh a meal of fresh meat since Tijikja, when in the rush I had forgotten to buy any. It was almost a month since any of us had eaten meat, and I wanted to share some as a parting celebration. We scoured the market for a butcher but were told that meat was scarce in Walata. We were walking back disconsolately when a woman called us over to a mud house and showed us a tray of raw flesh. The woman was a Bambara from Senegal. She had the face of a witch, and her elongated earlobes hung down almost to her chin, supporting heavy, swinging pendants.

As she began to cut up the meat I noticed a young man lying on a mattress in the corner. He wore only a pair of white shorts, and one of his legs was plastered up to the groin in dung. The youth told us that he was afflicted with the 'Guinea worm'. This dreadful parasite was apparently very common in Walata and came from the polluted wells. The worm could measure two yards in length and burrowed through the body, eventually surfacing through the knee, the ankle or the eye. The youth explained miserably that he had been like this for four months. 'Haven't you been to the doctor?' Marinetta asked.

'Doctors know nothing,' he answered. 'They can't get rid of evil spirits.'

We paid for our meat and left as quickly as possible.

Mafoudh was delighted with the meat and at once began to cook it on an open fire, flipping the pieces over with my knife and pressing them so that the succulent red juice ran out. When it was ready he served it up on our plate. 'Come on!' he said. 'We've waited a month for this!'

At that moment someone said, 'Peace be on you!' We looked up to see two men from the Shurfa standing near by. They had arrived in the wadi with their camels and families a little earlier. I looked at the meat, mentally dividing it into five. There wouldn't be much for everyone.

'Welcome!' Mafoudh said, beckoning them over. But I noticed that his expression lacked enthusiasm.

That night I paid him the balance of his earnings. 'What will you do with all this money?' I asked him.

'It's already spent,' he said. 'The money you gave me in Chinguetti went on provisions for my family, and the rest will go on debts to the shops.' Then he thought for a moment and touched his faded headcloth. I remembered how he had tied the camels with it on that frightening morning in Umm Hayjiba. Already it seemed a lifetime ago. 'I think I'll buy a new headcloth,' he said. It seemed a pathetic reward for such a journey at such a time of year. Mafoudh had been like a brother to us. I was desolate to be parting from him.

*

A crowd of Moors gathered to see us off the next morning. Mafoudh was there, grinning through the waxy blue dye of his new turban, which had already spread across his face. 'Never forget to fill all your *girbas!*' was his parting advice. 'If you have water, you can do anything. God go with you, Omar and Mariam!'

Moukhtar took the lead rope. For a moment it seemed strange to see his slim form there in place of Mafoudh. 'In the name of God!' he said as the camels started off.

'The way is long!' I shouted to Mafoudh.

'Go in peace!' he shouted back.

Just before we left the wadi another figure shambled out to meet us. It was Sheikh Ahmed, the would-be guide of the previous day. All rage seemed to have drained out of him now. He was all smiles and benevolence. He laid a hand on Moukhtar's shoulder. 'Take the southern way, not the northern one,' he said. 'The northern wells are dead. Keep to the southern way and you will find water and grazing. Go in peace!'

'That's odd!' Moukhtar said as the man disappeared. 'Someone told me that the wells were open on the northern route, not the southern. Still, he is a guide. He should know.'

An hour later Walata was out of sight behind us. We tramped through sticky heat up to the head of the plateau, where a cool breeze touched our faces. Before us lay an endless vista of swelling, shallow sand hills. There were nests of withered grass stalks, and shattered trees stood grained and grey as stalagmites. The sparse vegetation had been razed to roughness and smothered in camel droppings. Prints of camels and goats covered every inch of ground, overlaying each other in billions. The earth was so compacted that nothing would grow. It was a picture of desecration, of nature spoiled and dirtied. 'There are thousands of camels and goats near Walata,' Moukhtar said in explanation. 'Too many for the grazing.'

For us these shallow, undulating hills were a new type of desert. It was called *mushla*. Moukhtar said that travel here was more difficult than in the rock-and-sand desert we had just crossed. 'You go on for days here, and nothing changes,' he said. 'Same trees, same grass, same sand hills. Rocks and mountains are good landmarks, but

there aren't any in the *mushla*. It's like this almost all the way to
Tombouctou. It's easy to get lost.'

At midday we halted as usual. We were so accustomed to loading
now that we had our saddles off in moments. Moukhtar seemed
agonizingly slow and clumsy. It was annoying that he seemed not
to know the order of things, that his ways were different from those
of Mafoudh. We had become used to a certain routine, and it had
taken on the form of a sacred law. Any variation in the routine
seemed simply wrong. Here was the natural conservatism of the
human animal, the reluctance to change, already ingrained after only
a month of travel. Already we had become as chauvinistic as the
nomads, the Moors, the Tuareg, the Toubou and the Arabs, all of
whom had different customs and all of whom insisted that their
customs were right. Such certainty helped them to survive, and if
they adopted new ways, they did so with halting reservation, until
eventually the new ways replaced the old and became as unchange-
able as the old ones had been.

Moukhtar lacked the fire of Mafoudh. He was more self-possessed.
There were no bursts of impatient cursing as he grappled with knots
in the sickening heat, looking forward to his tea. Sometimes, though,
I missed Mafoudh's endearing explosions of temper. Moukhtar and
I never argued. Sometimes I missed that too. When Marinetta passed
him the *zrig* on that first day, he shocked us both by saying, 'Thank
you.'

After we had eaten Moukhtar seemed keen to talk. He asked if it
was true that I was English, and when I said yes, commented, 'I've
heard the English ruled the world once.'

'Once,' I said. 'Not now. Now the Americans rule the world, but
they rule it with money, not by colonization.'

'It wasn't colonization that ruined us,' Moukhtar said. 'It was
independence.'

'How come?'

'The French were our bosses, but we bossed everyone else. We
had our slaves and our vassals, and they paid tribute to us in return
for protection. The French left us alone. Now we're independent you
can't call a slave a slave or a vassal a vassal. You can't even call your

camels your own because if the government wants to take them, that's the end.'

'But the government is made up of your own people, the *bidan*, isn't it? I mean, you're not the minority?'

'The government is a new tribe made up of bits of old tribes. When you join the government you forget which tribe you once belonged to.'

Moukhtar went on to say that he had personally known the country's first president, Moukhtar Ould Dadda, who was now in exile.

'Was he from your tribe too?' I asked.

'No,' he said. 'Ould Dadda was a marabout, not a warrior.' He explained that after the *coup* in which Ould Dadda had lost his power, the ex-president had been imprisoned at Nema, the only prisoner in a house of twenty-six rooms. The authorities had needed someone to keep him company, someone from a good family who was not political. One of Moukhtar's relations had been in charge of the prison and had recommended him for the job. He had been the ex-president's companion, his duties being to fetch and carry his letters, make him tea and chat to him when he felt inclined. 'They treated him well,' Moukhtar said. 'Every day they slaughtered a sheep for him. He could have any food he wanted, and his room was always full of books and papers.'

'What was he like?'

'He was a very clever man. Very well-educated. Very friendly and polite. He was married to the daughter of General de Gaulle, and they had some children. His family wasn't with him in prison, though. They escaped to Senegal before the *coup*.'

'What did you talk about?'

'Everything. Sometimes he asked about my life. He talked about politics and about different countries, things I didn't know about. I learned a lot, though. He was the most intelligent man I ever met. That's why he was president.'

I was hazy about recent Mauritanian history, but Moukhtar told me that Ould Dadd's downfall had come about over the Polisario issue. The story, as so often in Africa, had begun with a colonial power pulling out of its former colony, in this case the Spanish out of Spanish Sahara. Ould Dadda and the Moroccan King Hassan had agreed that the liberated territory would be ruled jointly by both of them. But the inhabitants of this strip of desert had thought otherwise. They had formed the popular resistance movement called the Polisario and had gone on the offensive, which had resulted in the attacks on Chinguetti and Wadan and even on Nouakchott itself. The Moors sympathized with the Polisario, and Ould Dadda lost popularity. A military *coup* by Colonel Mu'awiyya had toppled him from power.

'They let him go in the end,' Moukhtar concluded. 'He joined his family in Paris, and I went back to my goats and camels.'

I looked at our new guide with fresh respect. It was a surprising and unexpected story from a desert nomad.

When it was time to move, Moukhtar said he would fetch the camels alone. After he had gone I asked Marinetta what she thought of him. 'I think he's interesting and very handsome,' she said. 'Don't you?'

'Interesting, yes; handsome, I don't know,' I said, but it was a lie. He was handsome. He was a fine, dignified, intelligent man, as near to the myth of the noble desert Arab as any I had met, and I had met plenty. Yet his obvious attraction for my wife sent a pang of jealousy through my head. It was an unfamiliar emotion. I had never expected to feel jealous of an illiterate nomad in the middle of the Sahara.

The *mushla* went on and on. The horizon was always the same distance before us, always the same distance behind. The camels shuffled forward like robots with their monotonous, placid, unstoppable pace. They had become characters to us now: Gurfaf, greedily nipping the other camels at feeding time; Li'shal, the little camel from Adrar, whining and spitting constantly; and the noble Shigar, the best of the three, with his wide step and his patient manner. Only Gurfaf gave us trouble. The blisters on his flanks had not healed properly. Moukhtar cut them again, as Mafoudh had done, and squeezed out a good pint of pus. 'You should exchange him in Tombouctou,' he advised me. 'I doubt if these wounds will heal while he's being ridden.'

Occasionally the inflamed earth was punctuated by hollows where rain had fallen and where green shoots were nuzzling up from the sand. The trees were in leaf, and the camels moved haltingly, browsing in the luscious grazing.

There was no confrontation with Moukhtar. He soon did everything so perfectly, and with such good grace, that we could hardly recall when he had not been with us. He was never tired. He never slept in the afternoons. He was the first up and the last to go to bed. His energy seemed boundless. He performed his prayers with lingering deliberation rather than whipping through them to get to the tea. He made bread with meticulous attention to detail. In the mornings, when we set out to track the camels down, he usually found them while I was still casting around for their prints. Moreover, he possessed all the skills of the nomad. He could make hobbling hoops out of the roots of the spiny *talha* trees. He demonstrated how to make fire, twirling a pencil of hard wood on a plate of soft. He knew the names of all the constellations that indicated the change of seasons. There were twenty-eight of them, he said. He carried with him no possessions, not even a knife or a blanket, like a man who is supremely confident of being able to live off his environment. He was a superb tracker and would point out tracks as we rode, reading them like a book, saying, 'These belong to a female camel. They are one day old,' and 'This is a jackal. He passed here only moments ago.' Occasionally I grew unreasonably tired of his perfection. I suppose it made me feel inadequate. Yet I couldn't repress the feeling that he was playing 'the bright boy of the class' for the sake of Marinetta.

She was evidently fascinated by him. Often I thought I noticed her regarding him with more than a friendly interest. I couldn't blame her. I admired the man myself. Yet this interest inspired in me an instinctive urge to compete with him. I recited the names of the constellations. I tried to pick up the camels' tracks more quickly. I demonstrated the rudiments of compass navigation. I even tried to make a hobbling hoop but found my fingers too clumsy for the job. Sometimes I felt so futile that I grew cynical. Once he pointed out some camel tracks and said, 'These are three days old.'

I heard myself saying, 'Are the camels brown, red or white, and when are their birthdays?'

He looked at me seriously. 'No one can tell you that,' he said. 'Anyone who says he can is crazy.'

One day, as we sat down to drink *zrig* at midday under the spreading arms of a *talha* tree, Marinetta removed her headcloth. It was the first time she had done so in front of the guide since we had started. Her hair, cut short at the beginning of the journey, had begun to grow. Now it spread out in a glorious swirl around her pretty face. The sudden revelation was as provocative as a striptease. I hadn't until that moment fully realized how sensuously erotic hair could be. I felt angry. The anger increased as she squatted down to offer the milk to Moukhtar. It seemed a deliberate display. The guide looked away shyly, but the action only emphasized the jealousy I felt. I was about to tell her stiffly to replace the headcloth when I noticed the sweat running down her face. It was an exceptionally hot day. Perhaps, after all, she had removed it only because she was hot. Then Moukhtar distracted me, saying, 'These *talha* trees are the best trees God made. We use every part of them. We use the big roots as tent supports and the smaller ones for hobbles and ropes. Animals can eat the leaves and the carobs, and you can also make medicine from the leaves. You can eat the gum, and the wood is the best kind of wood for fires. That's what I call a useful tree!'

The only flaw in Moukhtar's perfection was that he failed to find us a live well. We had followed the southern route for four days, and the seven waterskins we had filled in Walata were down to two. Moukhtar began to show signs of uneasiness. The camels were saved from thirst by the occasional green grazing, but the situation was becoming critical for us. We were all aware that it was Sheikh Ahmed's last-minute advice that had prompted us to take this route. I couldn't forget his 'You'll regret it!' as he had stormed out of the shop that day.

On the afternoon of the fourth day we saw a thick grey wall of dust moving ominously across the horizon. It was composed of tall, spiralling columns, like whorls of smoke from a raging fire. In a moment it was upon us. The light was blotted out, and we were covered in a cindery swirl of dust. I knew that even Moukhtar could not navigate in this. We were on foot, and I told Marinetta to hang on to her camel's girth belt whatever happened. Then I ran forward with my compass and asked Moukhtar to follow me. He agreed at once, and for two hours we staggered through the blistering storm as the sand thrashed against our headcloths, stinging our eyes and choking our nostrils.

The storm had burned out by sunset, and we made camp on a convoluted plain of parched amber in a brake of spiritless thorn trees. After we had eaten we discussed the possibility of finding water the following day. 'I can't understand why Sheikh Ahmed told us this way was open,' Moukhtar commented.

'I can!' I said and related the story of how I had rejected him as a guide.

'No God but God!' Moukhtar exclaimed. 'I have heard stories about that man, but I never believed them. They say that when he lived in Zourg he used to go out into the desert and slaughter other people's goats. They say he killed fifteen before they caught him. Then they drove him out of Zourg and he got work with the army.'

'That sounds like him,' said Marinetta.

'He was trying to kill us,' Moukhtar said with slow incredulity. 'He knew how dangerous this *mushla* is! That man has the devil in him and no mistake!' It was the only time I ever saw Moukhtar angry.

Not long after we struck camp the following morning we heard the dull report of a rifle. Then a second. I suddenly felt very vulnerable, but the sight of three antelopes scuttering away in the foreground convinced me that we were not the objects of the shots. A moment later Moukhtar pointed out a solitary figure sitting under a bush and nursing a rifle. 'It looks like a Nmadi,' he said, 'but he missed those antelopes without doubt!'

When we approached him the man stood up shyly. He wore no headcloth – nothing, in fact, but a very tattered shirt of greying cloth that was only marginally decent. Moukhtar asked him if the southern route into Mali was open. The man scoffed visibly. 'The wells have been dead for months,' he said. 'And so will you be if you go that way.' He advised us to turn north to the new frontier well at Umm Murthema. 'If you ride fast, you can make it by sunset,' he said.

As we rode away, Moukhtar muttered, 'God's curse on Sheikh Ahmed! When I tell my father about this he will want to throttle the devil!'

We arrived at Umm Murthema as the sun was going down. It was in the middle of nowhere, only recently excavated by government engineers. A crowd of Haratin labourers trickled out of some ramshackle huts to greet us. They produced a rope and a giant-sized leather bucket, and Moukhtar harnessed his camel to the hawser. The well was over 250 feet deep and the water couldn't be extracted without animal power. The Haratin gathered around us ready to help us water our camels and fill our waterbags. There was a pulley mounted on a steel frame over the well. One of the Haratin slung the rope across it and dropped the bucket in. There was a faraway thwack as the leather hit the water. The Haratin jiggled the rope about until he felt the weight of the full bucket. 'Pull!' he yelled, and Moukhtar led the camel forward. The hawser went taut. The pulley creaked as the great bucket came up. Two of the Haratin grabbed it and hoisted it over to an old steel wheelbarrow, which they used as a basin. The water was muddy, but the sound of its gurgling was pleasantly familiar. The bucket went back into the well. Time and again the camel heaved on the hawser.

Marinetta and I unloaded the other camels and drove them to the wheelbarrow to drink. They gulped down the muddy water copiously. At last the seven waterbags were filled and lay like saveloys in the grey sand. The camels had drunk their fill and their bellies had swollen to bursting point. I asked one of the Haratin how much we owed them for their work. He waved the offer aside with a stumpy hand. 'This is the last well in Mauritania,' he said. 'After this you will be in Mali. The Malians are not like the Moors. There you will pay. But here, for guests, water is free.'

We spent the night in some fresh grass farther on. The camels tore at it greedily, their bellies now well lubricated. The night was moonless and very dark, but as we unloaded a brilliant orange flash lit up the darkness. For a moment it was like daylight. When it had faded Marinetta said, 'I thought someone had reconnected the electricity!'

1. The first day out: a crowd watches as we saddle the camels for the first time. Sid'Ahmed's house in the background.

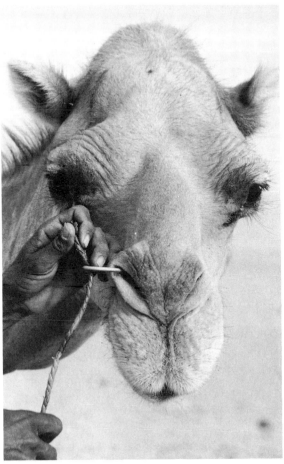

2. Threading a nose-ring: Li'shal, the small camel from the Mauritanian Adrar.

3. Handing out aspirins to the crowd at Talmoust.

4. The butterfly saddle: Mafoudh adds the finishing touches.

5. A Berabish boy, Mali.

6. A Kababish tribesman: his rosary beads hang around his neck.

7. Li'shal exhausted: Sidi Mohammed's mysterious sack is fixed behind the saddle.

8. Tombouctou: boys
playing in stagnant
waterpools.

9. Inside a Tuareg tent of
dom fibre, Tombouctou.

10. On the edge of the great Erg of Ténéré: the shark's tooth of Azzuager mountain is in the background.

11. The crumbling streets of Fachi: Christmas Day.

12. A slick of pea-green liquid: boys trawling for fish in the wadi of Umm Hajar, Chad.

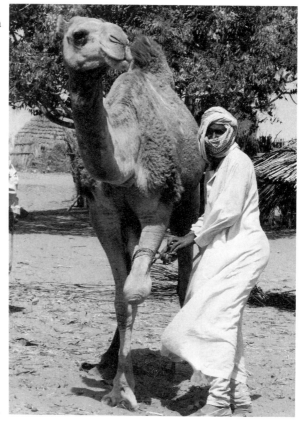

13. Gineina market: Gor'an tribesman hobbling a camel.

14. Bandit country: nearing the village of Om in Jebel Kawra, the Sudan.

15. The market in Kobkabiyya: a woman selling peanuts and dates.

16. 'Almost the end': the expanse of cracked earth that almost finished our camels.

17. Journey's end: the banks of Lake Nasser. The picture was taken by one of the Egyptian soldiers who detained us.

'It will rain tomorrow,' said Moukhtar.

The grass was full of insects and mosquitoes. Black scarab beetles scurried about everywhere. They made the call of nature an interesting experience. No sooner had you done your business than you would hear a drone like a helicopter as a scarab came skidding down to investigate. An instant later there would be another drone, then a flurry of drones as the rest of the squadron homed in. If you examined the dark pile in the light of your torch, you would see that it had come alive with dozens of beetles, heaving off fragments, splitting them and dividing them like masons and wrestling with each other as they tried to push their bits away. In seconds the pile had disintegrated and the scarabs would be removing chunks the size of golf balls with their back legs. Later they would bury them in the sand and lay their eggs in them. It was the most efficient waste-disposal system I've ever seen.

I was fascinated by the process and could watch the industrious little animals for hours. I focused on an epic battle between two well-matched contestants, a Hector and an Achilles of the beetle world (though they were probably heroines) as they struggled desperately over a fragment of dung. They grappled together, snapping powerful mandibles and flexing armour-plated legs. They sparred with excited feelers and turned somersaults over each other's chitinous trunks. Once Hector managed to escape with the dung ball, but Achilles caught him, pinning him down with his tiny claws. Again the battle wavered back and forth until, after a final thrust from Hector, Achilles took to the air and buzzed away. Triumphantly, Hector wheel-barrowed the dung towards his castle in the sand, carrying before him the seeds of his posterity, when, with devastating ferocity, a grey mouse stuck his head out of a mousehole and, in a single audible scrunch, Hector was gone.

Moukhtar's prediction proved wrong. It rained that night. In the morning we awoke to see the sky a frenzy of grey-blue cloud, coiling and billowing like a sea storm. There was no sunrise. Instead a square hatchway opened in one of the clouds, and a single golden bolt of light shot through. In that light we saw the desert transformed into bloom. The Sahara wore its richest royal livery. A million white sea-lilies had opened, as large and perfect as daffodils, and there were small yellow flowers on the stalks that criss-crossed the ground like tubers. Far across the plain the sunlight was thrown back, atomized and reflected in a billion diamonds of dripping moisture.

But the moisture brought unwelcome guests. As we loaded, the most gigantic scorpion I had ever seen dropped from under the litter. It was a horrific creature, jade-green and almost translucent. Moukhtar crushed it with his stick and it thrashed back and forth with clutching pincers and whipping tail. There was another one, almost as big, under the waterskins. Marinetta froze with horror, gasping, 'Kill it! Kill it!' as I skewered the monster.

'There's nothing worse than the sting of a scorpion,' Moukhtar said, 'but they move very slowly. Once you spot them they're easy to kill.' It was the ones we hadn't spotted that worried me. Scorpions are very fond of dark crevices, especially under *girbas* and saddlery. The threat of their presence made us doubly careful as we loaded from then on.

It was a new experience to walk through the desert and feel the wet dew on our feet. There were new signs of life wherever we looked. Many large holes had been dug in the wet sand. Moukhtar said they belonged to honey badgers. 'The honey badger has very sharp teeth,' he said. 'It will run away unless you corner it. Then it will seize hold of your leg and never let go until you kill it. And killing it is not easy, mind!' He added that the badgers were known to attach themselves to camels' legs and not to let go until they had toppled the animal. I passed their holes with greater respect after that.

There was a cool breeze blowing, drawing up the moisture from the surface and diffusing it through the air. Now and then squalls of rain hit us. Many different beasts had been lured out by the desert's new mantle. That day we spotted five jackals, alone or in pairs, loping across the damp ground and occasionally pausing to sniff the breeze. 'The jackal is a clever animal,' Moukhtar told us. 'He is always there, but often you don't see him. He hunts with his wife, and they have their own language. Just listen to it tonight. They will attack goats, sheep and even young camels.' We also found a medium-sized tortoise, scratching its way across the ground. We stopped to examine it and to take a photograph. It was light brown with a beautifully

complex shell pattern. I picked it up for a closer look. 'Careful!'
Moukhtar warned me. 'The Haratin eat tortoises. We have a saying,
"Come here, tortoise, I'll eat you! Come here, slave, I'll piss on you!"'
Right on cue, the tortoise left a spray of gluey urine on my hands.

That evening we camped in Mali. 'It's the first time I've ever
entered a country without showing a passport,' Marinetta said.

'You won't find any police or customs until you reach Tombouctou,' Moukhtar said. 'Things are much easier than they used to be.
In the past there were border posts all over. I should know: my
brothers and I used to smuggle grain from Mali. It was against the
law, of course. They said it was like stealing from the government.
But we did it anyway.' He recounted how he and his brother had
once brought a caravan of thirty-five camels from Mali, each one
loaded with five sacks of grain. His brother had gone to a village to
buy provisions and had been captured by the police. Moukhtar had
carried on alone with his thirty-five camels. He had been obliged to
travel at night but had been afraid that the camels at the rear of the
train would break away without his noticing in the darkness. 'I hung
a metal tin on the saddle of the last camel,' he said, 'and inside it I
put a metal mug. As long as I heard the tinkle of the mug, I knew
all the camels were there. But I had to pass a police post, so I took
the tin away. I was lucky. All the police were sleeping. Then I crossed
the border and I didn't have to worry.' He said that his brother had
returned after seven days.

After dark we were attacked by swarms of mosquitoes. Happily,
I had always been little affected by them, but they plagued Marinetta.
'Bloody mosquitoes!' she winced, as she slapped at her face and hands.
'I don't know why they were created.' Then, as she saw me grinning,
she snapped, 'I can't understand why they don't bite you. I'll bet you
have a bad smell or something.'

'They like some people's blood more than others,' Moukhtar said.

'They like mine most of all,' Marinetta complained. All night she
was tortured by them as she rolled over and thrashed sleeplessly.
Every half-hour her torch would go on and she would wake me up
to examine a large, angry red blotch on her skin. 'Anything is better
than this,' she moaned. 'Even the heat.'

And mosquitoes were not the only unpleasant night visitors. There were blister beetles, which could cause a violent reaction from your skin just by walking over it. There were sand flies, which could cause fever. The worst creatures of all were the camel spiders. They had 3-inch-long legs and giant mandibles that could give an excruciating bite, worse than a scorpion's sting. In the mornings Marinetta would wake up covered in stings, and even Moukhtar looked miserable while the mosquitoes were around.

Occasionally we saw people, nomads who had moved into the fresh grazing with their camels and goats and were busily erecting tents. Mostly these were the familiar pyramid-shaped tents of the Moors, but increasingly we came across the flattish, oval shelters of the Tuareg.

I was looking forward to my first encounter with the veiled people of the Sahara, but Moukhtar dampened my enthusiasm with his tales. 'You can't trust the Tuareg,' he told us. 'They are well known for cheating. They're not brave about it. They steal at night when you're not looking. The black Tuareg are the worst, but the white ones are famous cheaters too.' He related how he had once been travelling back to Mauritania on a lorry that had stopped at a remote village. A white Targui had arrived and said that his truck had run out of petrol some way out of the village. He had asked for the loan of some money to buy petrol, saying that he had grain on his truck and would sell some of it when he reached the village and pay the money back. 'Of course, I lent him the money,' Moukhtar said. 'He was a Muslim, after all. I waited for the truck to reach the village. I saw the lights coming towards us. The truck came right past the place we had stopped and I saw the Targui inside. He drove straight on and didn't even look, by God! The Tuareg are not like the Arabs. They think it's clever to cheat.'

Our first Tuareg came into the camp one day at noon. There were three of them, all quite young. The first thing that struck me, of course, was their veils. They wore indigo headcloths exactly like those of the Moors, except that the cloth was tightly bound over the lower part of their faces, exposing only the eyes. They were whippet-slim and wore yellowing shirts and black cloaks. One of them carried a shotgun and had a bandolier of cartridges around his waist. They spoke no Hassaniyya, although their extended hands and their gestures towards our tea and sugar left us in no doubt that their visit was not purely social. I felt that wearing veils like this was somehow not playing the game. You can tell so much about a man from his facial expression that to hide it seems like a deliberate attempt to disguise one's true nature. When we left them, they were examining some Lipton's teabags that we had discarded. They were holding them up to the light curiously. 'It'll take them a long time to work that one out!' Marinetta said.

All that afternoon Marinetta ran about taking shots of Moukhtar leading the caravan. She seemed spellbound by his lithe figure, and several times she asked me to get out of the way. I refused, saying that we had no time for foolishness. It was a measure of her feeling for the guide that she rarely spoke to him as she had to Mafoudh, who had evoked a more brotherly response. Her zoom lens bridged the gap created by her shyness, and she could examine his face and body closely under the pretext of photography. In turn, Moukhtar puffed up in front of the camera, aware of his attraction. He never covered his face as Mafoudh had done. 'Come on, Maik!' she told me again. 'Get out of the picture! I want to take the guide and the caravan!'

'You'll have to take the picture as it is or not at all!' I replied furiously.

'I'm sick of taking pictures of your bloody stupid face!' she yelled. A few minutes later she sulkily put her cameras away.

During our noon halt the following day Marinetta suddenly took the cameras and went off to get some shots of Moukhtar who was herding the camels 50 yards away. When I looked round I saw her pointing the camera at him as he posed proudly in front of the grazing animals. Then I noticed that she was no longer wearing her headcloth. It had fallen around her neck and she was making no attempt to replace it. Her dark halo of hair flowed freely in the breeze. Moukhtar changed position, and she angled her slim body round for another shot. The sunlight caught the supple muscles of her bronzed arms and legs. I was sure this was a deliberate revenge, and I felt livid.

When she came back to the camp, still faintly smiling, and said, 'I got some brilliant shots,' I bawled at her, 'Put that bloody headcloth on! Cover your hair up! You know that women never show their hair in Moorish culture!'

'Why should I wear that thing all the time?' she shouted back. 'You take yours off. I don't belong in this culture. I can do as I like.'

'No, you damn' well can't! You're a married woman, and you can bloody well behave in a respectable way!'

'In the Sahara?'

'Especially in the Sahara. You shouldn't go off alone with the guide.'

'Oh, so that's it,' she said. 'You're jealous!'

'I'm not jealous. I want this expedition to succeed, and you're doing everything you can to ruin it.'

'Jealous!'

'Just put your headcloth on.'

She put it on, but it was the last time she spoke to me for two days.

All afternoon she sulked silently, and even when the heat subsided she refused to talk. She spoke not a word all evening. Moukhtar commented that she must be tired. 'It's a hard journey for a woman,' he said. The next morning she dragged behind the camels as we walked. At first I made no comment. Then she got farther and farther behind until it became dangerous. I had to tell Moukhtar to stop and let her catch up. It was the first time she had ever fallen behind. She walked up with an insolent waddle, but as soon as we started she fell behind again. 'Marinetta!' I shouted at her. 'For God's sake make an effort! If you can't keep up, you'll have to ride.' She stared back at me contemptuously. A few minutes later I had to tell Moukhtar to halt again. Then I couched her camel and told her, 'Get on that camel!' She refused to budge. 'Get on that bloody camel!' I raved, really mad now. I grabbed her by the arm. Moukhtar was looking at us strangely from the front of the caravan. At last she mounted the camel. But she didn't speak all afternoon.

That night we made camp on a hillock with a flat, sandy top, like a small fortress in the rolling plain. We hobbled the camels and sent them off to graze. There was a weak sliver of moon, already waning, and the light was poor. While Moukhtar made bread, Marinetta sat on her bed and moped, silently swatting mosquitoes. Moukhtar was talking about animals again, saying, 'There used to be leopards in these parts once. The leopard is the most dangerous animal there is, by God! It's more dangerous than the lion even. It's so fast that it can kill you at once. The lion plays with you first, and that gives you a chance to pick up a weapon.' From somewhere across the *mushla* came the weird, piercing call of jackals. 'There they are!' Moukhtar said. 'See how they talk to each other!' I listened intently, then I suddenly became aware of something else. I could no longer hear the champing of the camels. It was already late. I suggested that we should go and collect them for the night, as we had done since entering Mali.

Moukhtar volunteered to go off alone and soon disappeared into the darkness. The moon had set and the night was black as pitch. Thirty minutes later he came back without the camels. 'They've gone!' he said.

'You mean they've been stolen?' I asked him, aghast.

'I don't know. They're nowhere near the camp.'

'Is it possible a thief could have taken them while we were talking?'

'It's possible. But perhaps they've gone to find better grazing. I can't find any tracks.'

Marinetta was sitting up attentively. Moukhtar asked for my torch. 'You stay here and keep the fire going,' he said. 'I'll look for them.' After he had gone I fetched some more firewood and stoked up the fire. Across the range I could see the faint glimmer of the torch, zig-zagging this way and that. I felt grim. Grimmest of all was the feeling that someone might actually have been watching us with malicious intent from out of the darkness.

Suddenly Marinetta broke her silence. 'I'm scared, Maik,' she said. 'What will we do if they've been stolen? We're in the middle of nowhere.'

'We'll be all right,' I said. 'There are some nomads about who might help us. It's better than being lost in Umm Hayjiba.'

There was a pause, and she said, 'Maik, my headcloth fell off. I didn't remove it on purpose.'

'And you don't fancy Moukhtar?'

'He's attractive. Didn't you ever look at the attractive girls in

Chinguetti? That's as far as it goes. You're my husband.' It was the first time I ever remembered her using that word.

It was more than an hour before the guide returned. 'The ground is too hard for tracks,' was all he said. 'We'll have to search in the morning.'

When I opened my eyes at sunrise, Moukhtar had gone. My first thought was, 'It is a trick!' But then I saw that he had left his sandals and gone off in bare feet. I knew he must be intending to come back. Marinetta got up and made coffee. We sat near the fire scanning the horizon. There was no movement, no trace of animals or human beings. There was nothing but desolation, and infinite emptiness, and the vacant breath of wind dragging across the wasteland. The sun rose higher. Our fire burned down. I wondered if we should ever be able to reach the Nile if we lost these camels. I wondered how we would survive. 'Whatever happens,' Marinetta said, 'we won't give up. Not now. We've endured too much already.' I felt a sudden shock of warm admiration, which spread slowly through me. It was the bravest thing I had ever heard her say. The arguments and the acrimony were forgotten. I draped my arm around her shoulder. 'Look!' she said. 'Out there!' Far away, on the edge of the plain it seemed, was a black dot. Then it became a figure leading three camels. I waited with bated breath until I made out the unmistakable form of Moukhtar.

'He got them!' I yelled. Marinetta threw her arms around me. A big tear trickled down her chin.

We reached Ras Al Ma the following day. I had been looking forward to it since we started. It was at the head of Lake Faguibine, a wedge of blue water on the map that stretched for many days east towards Tombouctou. But I was disappointed. Ras Al Ma was a bleak, grey settlement of mud houses, set among desolate thornbush. It had stood at the head of the lake once, but now the lake had gone. Faguibine, so attractively blue on the map, was completely dry. Some Tuareg who helped us get water from a well in the old bed of the lake said that there had been no surface water there for eight years.

For three days we rode across the wasteland. Where there had once been water were now acres of Sodom's Apple trees with their waxy leaves like plastic and their poisonous grapefruit-like fruit. There were low thorn trees among the mass, but the Sodom's Apples towered over them, 10 feet high and showing a craw of white roots. In places the trees formed tight corridors where our camels would hesitate, frightened by the creaking of the cactus-like leaves and the rattling of the dried, empty husks of fruit. The earth of the lake floor was grey and dusty, littered with the shells of molluscs. 'There used to be plenty of fish here,' Moukhtar told us. 'There were boats on the lake and they would catch fish with nets.' The lake shore was still lined with the huts of fisher-folk, but behind them the dunes of the Sahara rose up menacingly. Here, I thought, was the history of the Sahara in miniature. In Stone Age times this entire area, from here to Baatin, had been well watered with lakes and inhabited by fishermen-hunters. Over the ages the area had become more and more arid, and the desiccation had driven away the fishermen or turned them into nomads who left their villages, now stranded on what had been the shores of vast lakes, to die or to adapt to the new conditions.

On 16 September we saw the towers of Tombouctou on the horizon. Within an hour the whole expanse of the city lay in a great sprawl across the skyline. 'Is that really it?' Marinetta asked. 'After all this time!'

We had made it in forty-two days.

The first of my tribe ever to see Tombouctou was Alexander Gordon Laing, in 1825. Laing had never lived to tell the tale; he was murdered by his guides somewhere in the desert to the north. In the following year a young Frenchman named René Caillie had visited the place and had survived a harrowing journey back across the Sahara to tell the world of his discovery. It was 161 years since Laing had first laid eyes on Tombouctou. From where we sat now, it could have been yesterday.

We arrived among the sand dunes outside the town in the late afternoon. As we unloaded, some Arab women with lovely oriental faces came out to greet us. Moukhtar said that they belonged to the Berabish, the large Arab confederation of western Mali. The women were followed by gangs of children who slid down the dunes and shouted, 'Donnez-moi un cadeau!' The city walls looked forbidding, and we were strangely reluctant to leave the familiar safety of our camp. The desert had already become part of us. The city lay in another country, where we needed passports and visas, where we were subject to yet another set of rules.

We camped in the dunes that night. After dark the town took on the appearance of the twentieth century. We sat drinking tea and watching the squares of miraculous electric light from the new Hôtel Azalai, perched on the edge of the town. The sound of a generator drummed across the sand. From somewhere came the blare of pop music.

At first light we were saddling the camels as usual.

'Where are we going?' Marinetta asked, still fuzzy with sleep.

'To the hotel,' I said.

'With the camels?'

'Why not?' I said. 'Camels made this city.'

But as we led our tiny *azalai* towards the distant walls, it felt somehow like the walk of the condemned.

Sidi Mohammed

The Hôtel Azalai seemed appropriately named for us but was, in fact, a three-star international establishment. It was quite out of place in Tombouctou, designed exclusively for the affluent tourists coming by plane. No doubt we were the first travellers ever to arrive there by *azalai*. We marched right into the hotel forecourt with our camels, and there we unloaded our disgusting equipment: the saddle bags stained with grease and camel sweat, the broken sacks and hold-alls, the blankets smeared with the oozings of camel sores and caked with Moorish dust. The entire staff of the hotel turned out to help us move our saddles and belongings into the store. As it happened, they had little else to do. There were no other guests in the hotel.

It was a bastion of comfort on the edge of the Great Desert, set in a neatly kept garden of bougainvillaeas. Through the shuttered window, though, you could see the real Tombouctou, tall, thirsty streets, a collection of tents made of dom palm fibre, bony Tuareg camels and little boys driving donkeys. The Tuareg caretaker told us that there were no guests because the flights from the capital, Bamako, had ceased. The previous year there had been a serious aircrash in which hundreds of tourists had died. The airline no longer functioned.

After we had lugged our equipment inside, I sent Moukhtar off to graze the camels. He had already agreed to look after them for an extra daily sum. Then, without changing or taking a shower, we went off in search of the police. Our entry visas from the Paris Embassy, valid for only ten days after entry, had already expired, and we were afraid the authorities might send us to Bamako to renew them. At the dilapidated police HQ in the town square, we were received cordially by a large black officer wearing a gaily coloured cotton suit. He looked at our passports and said, 'Your visas have expired.' I was about to pour out the passionate plea for clemency we had prepared when he said, 'Don't worry. We can renew them here.' He smiled smoothly at our account of our journey and asked where we were heading for next.

'Agadez, Niger,' I told him.

'I know the best guide in Tombouctou,' he said.

Afterwards we entered the nearest shop. There was electricity. There was a fridge. There were piles and piles of tins and packets and boxes of all sizes and attractive colours. There were things we had dreamed of in the desert: chocolate, mayonnaise, evaporated milk, cheese, tinned tunny, lemonade powder. We ordered two cans of fizzy orange. As the shop-keeper opened the fridge door I felt an icy waft of air. The orange was as cold as polar water, as delicious as the most precious nectar, drinkable only in sips. After we had finished Marinetta said, 'It was worth a thousand miles just for that! Now I can feel the circulation going again.'

We wandered back to our hotel in a kind of exhausted delirium, dimly aware of the twining alleys and the flux of people: rascally Tuareg, blue-jowled Arabs, Songhai women in dresses of foaming colours. We had a meal of meat and potatoes in another flyblown hotel, where we met two American tourists. They were clean-cut college boys in neat bush shirts and khaki shorts, complete with desert boots. They were disarmingly enthusiastic about their first visit to Africa.

'There was no one else in town till you came,' one of them said. 'We had the place to ourselves. It was great! We try to take an interest in the people's lives. Betcha they don't get many tourists who ask questions about social conditions. Most American tourists just take pictures and fly out.' They were proud of having come down the Niger river on a steamer.

'The only problem is the water,' the second youth told me. 'Two doctors back home told us not to drink it. We always sterilize our water.' Each of them carried a water bottle from which they sipped, rather guiltily, now and again.

Before we left they presented me with two books. The books were Cervantes's *Don Quixote* and *The African Queen* by C. S. Forester. It was the best present I could have imagined.

Back in our hotel room I examined myself in the mirror. I was a tramp. My hair and beard were long and unkempt, my face wrinkled and leathery, beetroot-red from the sun and ravaged by dust. My body was whittled down to refugee thinness by the heat and the austerities of the journey. We peeled off our filthy clothes and turned on the shower. The water flowed out, clear, cool and abundant, swirling and eddying around the porcelain before it drained away. Stepping into it was an almost blasphemous act. It felt sinfully luxurious to stand in that endless flow for minute after minute as the accumulated muck of forty-two days was washed away. I was content with a single shower, but Marinetta went back for a second and a third after I had finished.

Afterwards we lay on a soft bed, on gleaming white sheets. It was superb luxury. Now there was no Mafoudh, no Moukhtar, no squalling children to interrupt us. At last we were alone. That evening we left our room only for dinner.

Sidi Mohammed was sitting on a wooden bench at the police HQ when we arrived there the next morning. He was a short man with a slight stoop and powerful limbs. His hands and feet were rough and as calloused as a labourer's, his movements jerky and awkward. He was dressed in a long, ragged gandourah and a blue headcloth, lapped about his face in semi-Tuareg style. The smooth-faced police officer of the previous day told us that he was an Arab of the Berabish. Hassaniyya was his mother-tongue, but he had spent some time among the Ifoghas Tuareg and spoke fluent Tamasheq. His experience had done nothing to improve his liking for the Tuareg, though. 'Only the Arabs are good,' was his opinion. 'The Tuareg are a bad lot. They're like animals when it comes to sex. They only have to see a woman and they go for her. Their women brazenly talk to men. Disgusting!'

Sidi Mohammed was one of a small elite of professional guides in Tombouctou, and one of very few who knew the route to Niger. There was little call for camel guides that way now, he said. There was a perfectly good road south to Gao and Niamey, Niger's capital, and you could easily go on the bus. Even tourists with their own vehicles wouldn't cross the country that we wanted to cross. It would

mean travelling parallel with the Niger as far as the bend, then
carrying on in the same direction across the great wadi Azouagh and
the Sakarezou hills. That country was very wild and desolate, he said,
and he hinted darkly that there were some very evil Tuareg living
there. 'Why don't you follow the road down to Gao and Niamey?'
he asked. 'It's much easier that way.'

'If we went that way, we wouldn't need a guide, would we?' I said.

Sidi Mohammed saw which way the wind was blowing and
capitulated.

Before finally agreeing to take Sidi Mohammed as our guide, I
wanted him to meet Moukhtar, who was due to return that evening
with our camels. We collected our freshly stamped passports from
the police and went in search of a bank to change our traveller's
cheques to CFA francs. There was another Westerner in the bank, a
freckle-faced Belgian girl. She wore embarrassingly tight jeans and a
shoulderless T-shirt, through which the nipples of well-proportioned
breasts were clearly discernible. Her auburn hair was splayed out in
a fiery mass. 'Can you give me a lift to Gao?' she asked us.

'Not unless you want to go by camel!' Marinetta said.

We saw her later walking through the market holding hands with
a handsome young African, while two others followed on behind.

Moukhtar arrived outside our hotel with the camels just before
sunset. We were both happy to see him. I wished suddenly that he
was travelling with us to Agadez. I asked him if he had spent the
night alone. He said that he had found an Arab camp but that the
Arabs had offered him no food and hadn't even come out to welcome
him. 'They sent a boy out with a mat,' he said. 'That's their idea of
hospitality. What a disgrace!'

Just then a young Targui appeared and offered to sell us a camel.
His Hassaniyya was poor and he spoke with some effort. 'Is the camel
fat?' asked Moukhtar.

'No, it is not fat.'

'Is it big?'

'No, it is not big.'

'Is it strong?'

'It is not very strong.'

'It's not much good then, is it?'

The Targui touched Moukhtar on the arm. 'Look,' he said, 'you are an Arab and I am Tuareg. You know camels and I know camels.'

'Yes.'

'And ... Tuareg camels are better than Arab camels!'

Moukhtar let out a delighted peal of laughter and the Targui followed suit.

At that point Sidi Mohammed arrived. He shook hands with Moukhtar, and they squatted down together in the sand. We looked on. The two Arabs were curiously different. Sidi Mohammed appeared an uncouth barbarian beside the aristocratic Moukhtar. He was as squat and powerful as Moukhtar was tall and wiry. His head seemed large and ungainly, his big eyes slightly bulging, the mouth wide with a suggestion of vulpine greed. He laughed nervously and poked Moukhtar constantly on the leg as he talked. Yet his manner was humble, almost as if he were desperate for acceptance. He was a good ten years older than Moukhtar, but their ages seemed reversed. There was, I decided, something faintly tragic about Sidi Mohammed.

After he had gone Moukhtar said, 'He's very experienced, there's no doubt. He knows camels. He's been to Mauritania, Niger, Libya, Algeria and Morocco, all by camel. I don't see any harm in the man, but you can't tell until you get into the desert.'

I knew, as always, that taking on a fresh guide was a gamble. Marinetta commented, 'He's experienced, but he's not what you call an attractive type, is he?' Perhaps it was for that reason that I decided to hire Sidi Mohammed.

We stayed in Tombouctou long enough to buy provisions and to exchange the ailing Gurfaf. Meanwhile, I had promised myself a pilgrimage to the houses of Alexander Gordon Laing and René Caillie. Gordon Laing's house was almost derelict, but his forty-day stay there in 1825 was recorded on a plaque. I asked our guide, a Soninke lad called Sanaa, why Gordon Laing had been murdered. 'He came dressed as a soldier,' the boy said. 'And the Tuareg thought he had come for war. So they followed him and killed him. They strangled him with a headcloth.'

Caillie had fared a little better – perhaps because he had disguised himself as an Arab. On arriving in Tombouctou in 1826 he had been sorely disappointed that the place bore no resemblance to the legendary 'Golden City' of European imagination. He had travelled north to Morocco with a caravan of 1,400 camels carrying ostrich feathers and, after many privations and narrow escapes, had made his way back to France.

None of the West's first visitors to Tombouctou had met with a hospitable reception. It seemed ironical to me that these houses, like shrines, should become important tourist attractions, a source of revenue for the descendants of those who had treated their first tourists so badly. As we re-entered the hotel that evening a gigantic poster beamed down on us: 'Mali, Land of Welcome'.

Sidi Mohammed told us that there were still Tuareg in Mali who were as forbidding as they had been in Gordon Laing's day. Only the previous year a French couple had been murdered in the Adrar-n-Ifoghas. They had been travelling by Land-Rover and had stopped to talk to some nomads. The Tuareg had seized the man and murdered him. The woman had locked herself in the car and had managed to write a description of the killers, then she too had been taken. 'How were they murdered?' Marinetta asked.

'They were strangled with a headcloth,' Sidi Mohammed said.

He tried to persuade me to buy a shotgun, saying that there were bands of Tuareg on our route who were in opposition to the government and who would attack strangers. 'I'm not afraid of thieves,' he said, 'but these people are different. They will follow you into a lonely place and then murder you.' He said that there were often battles between the Arabs and the Tuareg in Mali. Both of them were nomadic races, but while the Tuareg herded cattle and goats and a few camels, the Arabs were principally camel herders and ranged farther afield. Just the week before, he said, there had been a fight between them, quite near Tombouctou, in which five Tuareg had been injured and two Arabs killed. The Tuareg still languished in Tombouctou hospital.

Tombouctou may never have been the golden place of European legend, but at sunset the streets and the tall stone houses took on a rich aura of gold. The streets were an arabesque of wynds and alleys feeding into each other like tributaries and merging with the wide avenues that had their confluence in the central square. The avenues were uneven and littered with the bones of slaughtered animals and sherds of pot. The potsherds might have been there hours or centuries. I saw an old lady dump a cracked pot in the street; it was used as a football by a gang of children and quickly smashed to bits. Over the years the fragments would get smaller, mashed and ground under the feet of people and the hooves of donkeys, stamped into the grey dust until they merged with the fabric of the place. Dust to dust. From the square the oily blue snake of a road ran out past the new power palaces of the city, the headquarters of UNICEF, USAID, CARE and OXFAM, each with its radio antenna like an imperial flag and its stable of four-wheel-drive vehicles. Beyond them and interspersed with them were the elongated domes of Tuareg tents, matting skins of palm fibre stretched over timber frames. They too might have been there for centuries.

Far from being the predatory bandits of Sidi Mohammed's stories, the Tuareg of Tombouctou seemed cowed and vanquished. Many of them were refugees from the desert, driven into the city by the Great Drought. If they made a living at all, it was by selling daggers, swords or silver rings to tourists. Like the Moors in Chinguetti and Nouakchott, many of them were kept alive by American grain. Just before starting our journey I had read an article about the Tuareg of Mali entitled 'Sons of the Wind'. For the Tuareg we met in Tombouctou, at least, it seemed the wind had changed.

After only a few days we began to feel a sense of oppression in the town. It was awkward being the only guests in the hotel, and the staff were unhelpful now and even hostile. Adolescent youths followed us in the streets, silently watching from doorways and street corners, always hovering in the background like a bad conscience. Our room was no longer the refuge it had seemed on the first day. Once they got to know it, groups of Tuareg took to standing outside our window, knocking on the shutter and offering us miscellaneous items for sale. The caretaker did nothing to stop them.

The old argument reappeared between Marinetta and me. Her dress seemed to get more blasé each day. She no longer wore her headcloth, and her Arab clothes had been replaced by a figure-hugging salopette. Youths whistled at her, and children whispered obscenities that they looked too young to understand. I noticed that Sidi Mohammed's greedy eyes followed her and remembered the look of surprise on Moukhtar's face when he had first seen her dressed like a Westerner. The day before we were due to leave I advised her to wear the headcloth in the market. 'At least it will spare us the whistling and leering,' I said.

'Why should I?' she answered. 'This isn't the desert. Tourists don't wear headcloths. What about that Belgian girl?'

'Exactly,' I said. 'Some Western women come here only for male attention. They think that they can behave as they like because they are free of the restrictions of their own countries. They don't realize that African societies are even stricter than their own.'

She refused to change, and in a rage I left without her, taking the Soninke boy Sanaa to help carry the provisions.

We had been in the market only a few minutes when a clot of angry red cumulus formed over the buildings, turning into a claw of black dust. The market erupted. Women picked up their babies and wrapped up their meagre wares. 'We've got five minutes before it hits us!' Sanaa said. Everywhere people were leaping for the shelter of mud walls in apparent terror. I saw one woman, with a baby on her back and carrying a bowl of milk on her head, knock down a little boy in her hurry to get away. Instead of picking him up, she cursed him, then charged onwards, all without spilling a drop of milk. Sanaa and I ran back to the hotel. We had almost reached it when the rain began. A crowd of youths sheltering under the gate told me that Marinetta had left the place a few minutes earlier, heading for the market. I knew I had to find her.

As I turned back, the rain hit me with the surging crash of a waterfall. In the winding alleys it was boiling in grey bubbles. It swept off the roofs through the spouting, gushing in a torrential stream through the market. The stalls were deserted. Every doorway, arch or covered passage held a scrum of people. Faces stared at me from behind the bars of windows or from shop entrances. Marinetta's face was not among them. The dark stream was up to my calves. Bits of wood, paper and excrement floated in it. Filthy water from the roofs poured down my back. The dark cloud hovered over the canyons of the streets, the thunder seeming to shake the stone walls.

My sandals turned soggy and made me slip and slither in the mud
beneath the torrent. I staggered into the large covered market, and
there was Marinetta. She smiled at me, sitting calmly among some
Soninke women. Every time the lightning crackled and thunder
boomed, half of them dived under their blankets and screamed.
Marinetta pointed to a pretty Soninke girl next to her. The girl was
about eighteen, her hair coiled and braided into intricate ringlets. Like
Marinetta, she was not wearing a headcloth. I asked the girl what
this exotic hairstyle was called. 'Rasta,' she replied.

'What?' I asked.

'You must have heard of Bob Marley!' she said.

All traces of the storm had disappeared when Moukhtar brought the
camels back the following day. This time he had with him an Arab
who had for sale a magnificent white camel belonging to the prestigious *mayneg* breed. The Arab agreed to take the injured Gurfaf in
part exchange. The new camel was called Seb'i, 'the Seventh'. As the
Arab led Gurfaf away I felt as if I had parted with an old and faithful
friend.

We removed all our equipment and the new sacks of provisions
from the hotel store and annoyed the manager by filling our waterbags from the hotel kitchens. Moukhtar told me that he had arranged
to buy a she-camel with the money I had paid him. 'She's not very
pretty,' he admitted, 'but she'll make a profit in Walata.' I asked him
if he wasn't worried about riding back alone. 'No,' he said. 'I've
bought a special charm from a marabout. No bandits will see me.'

When Sidi Mohammed arrived Moukhtar harangued him mercilessly about his duties. The older man listened with slightly bowed
head. Then we loaded the camels together and led our caravan out
of the town, going east.

Rain had fallen along the valley of the Niger river. Thousands of
nomads were moving back into the fresh pastures with what remained
of their herds after many years of drought. Wells that had been
abandoned were being dug out and used again. The ropes creaked
again, the pulleys trundling round as the heavy buckets swung up to
the well-head. Camels, goats, donkeys, sheep and even oxen were
pawing thirstily in the dust around the watering troughs. The rolling

plains were scattered with the camps of Arabs and Tuareg, their
goatskin tents like giant tortoise shells. Their camps looked pitifully
poor, and Sidi Mohammed said that most of these nomads had lost
much of their livestock in the drought. 'They stay here only because
they're used to it,' he said. 'It's just habit, that's all.'

Sidi Mohammed himself had once lived in these ranges. 'I used to
live in a leather tent just like these,' he said, 'and I used to have some
camels and goats. But then there was independence and the drought.
It went bad for the Arabs. I lost everything and moved to the town.'

'Did you get any help from international aid?' Marinetta asked
him.

'Gah!' he said. 'We got a bit, right at the beginning, but after that
nothing. The government took most of it and sold it to the big
merchants. That's why you see it all in the shops, Italian oil, Japanese
sardines, grain from the United States. The government are all flying
to Switzerland in aeroplanes – *whooooosh!* Or they're driving cars
and sitting in air-conditioned houses with the fans going *swiiiishsh,*
swiiiishsh. It's a story everyone knows, by God!'

Sidi Mohammed was a camel man by experience but a labourer
by training. He had taken caravans as far as Morocco, trading camels
with the Rigaybat in Spanish Sahara and bringing back copper and
blankets from Goulimime. He had worked in Morocco four times,
the last time as a labourer constructing a road. 'The Moroccans are
the best people in North Africa,' he said. 'They ask no questions.
They don't bother you as long as you give them no problems. But
if you cause trouble, gah! Then you *have* trouble!' He said he would
like to return there but that the caravan route was now blocked. 'The
Polisario messed it up,' he said. 'I don't blame the Polisario. The
Rigaybat are good people, but no one can cross that border easily
now.'

He seemed to have an instinctive feel for the camels, always
selecting a camping site that would afford them the best grazing. He
pointed out several mistakes in our loading technique, adjusting my
pack saddle to make it more comfortable. He lapped the leather neck
straps with cloth so that they wouldn't rub on the camel's skin and
showed us how to place the litter farther forward so that it would
not cause swellings on the flanks. He tut-tutted over the state of our

girbas and oiled them thoroughly inside with butter. If we had hobbled the camels near the camp at night, he would always be up before dawn to loose them and let them graze a little before we loaded. He never cooked but within minutes of unloading would produce a large enough pile of wood, of the right size and type, for that night and the morning. He would inquire solicitously of Marinetta where she would like the fire to be placed. As a guide he was confident and unerring. He would make a point of stopping anyone we passed and eliciting current information. Was such-and-such a well open or closed? Had rain fallen here or here? Was there trouble from bandits ahead? He would go out of his way to visit a camp or talk to a traveller, often sprinting off on foot and catching us up later.

On the other hand, there was a darker, more mysterious side to Sidi Mohammed. He was sulky and would often refuse to answer my questions, saying, 'Even a child knows that!' And why, for instance, did he always disappear for half an hour every morning, just after we set off? Why did he do the same in the afternoon? At first I thought he must be answering the call of nature and was suffering from some stomach complaint that he was reluctant to tell us about. But when I offered him some medicine, he replied, 'Gah! There's nothing wrong with my stomach!' Every day he would absent himself at the same time and would catch us up, panting breathlessly, without a word of explanation. Once or twice I looked back to see him squatting behind a bush.

Then there was the mystery of his sack. He had with him a bulky fibre sack, which he opened rarely. When he did so it was with great circumspection, always carrying it well away from us and turning his back. He opened it with nervous deliberation and retied it at once. We were never able to see what he took out of it.

Once when we were riding, I noticed a slight protrusion in the back of his gandourah. When the breeze blew the garment up I saw that it was a vicious little stiletto in a bronze sheath, designed to be hidden in the waistband. Many nomads carried knives, but the nature of the weapon and its concealment seemed characteristic of Sidi Mohammed. He was a man who harboured secrets.

When we fed he would grab the food with his big, calloused hands before Marinetta and I were even seated. He would shovel the rice or couscous into his mouth, swilling it down with water. He kept the water bowl in his left hand while pawing at the food with his right. He would continue to shovel until every grain was finished, then he would push the plate away sullenly, muttering, 'There wasn't enough butter, Mariam!' or 'That rice wasn't cooked properly!' Then he would pick up the water bowl again, hawk and spit into the sand in front of us, burp and belch loudly in our faces, pick his teeth, hiccup, swill the water round and gargle it and, finally, throw the water bowl down contemptuously. Then he would deliver another instalment of burping and spitting. The only rude sound his repertoire lacked was a fart.

He complained long and continuously about the food. He hated sardines. The diet was monotonous. There was no fresh meat. The dates weren't of the best type. In Tombouctou he had assured us that he ate everything, including sardines. He would wait till Marinetta was obviously preparing rice and say, 'Why don't you make couscous today, Mariam?'

Then she would go red and answer, 'Get lost! The rice is already prepared.'

'But you don't cook it properly.'

'If you don't like it, make it yourself!'

Now it was Marinetta's turn to be disgusted by the guide's manners. She detested his spitting and burping. 'Do you think he does it on purpose?' she often asked me. It was a difficult question. Sidi Mohammed was an intelligent man, but the circumstances of his life seemed to have made him bitter, uncouth and resentful. Marinetta hated the way he would brush her backside with his hand when taking the water bowl from behind her litter, and the manner in which he stared at the arm-slits in her shirt, though which her bra was clearly visible. She mostly avoided taking photos of Sidi Mohammed and answered his criticism with shrewish rejoinders.

Sidi Mohammed's main complaint was the lack of fresh meat. Once in the first few days we met an Arab boy leading a goat, which he intended to sell in the market. He offered it to us at a reasonable price, and Sidi Mohammed implored me to buy it. I told him frankly that I had only a small amount of cash to last us to Agadez, nearly 1,000 miles away. I considered fresh meat a bad investment this early in the journey. Sidi Mohammed muttered, 'It's just like prison. No fresh meat!'

'When were you in prison?' I asked him.

'Last year, in Libya,' he said. 'The Libyans caught me crossing the border by camel and threw me into jail.' I was intrigued and, over the next few days, managed to extract the full story from him. When the Moroccan route had closed, Sidi Mohammed had found employment in Libya, first as a shepherd, then as a caretaker. Things had gone well until he had returned to Tombouctou on vacation. During that time the Libyans had tightened the entry regulations, as their country was swamped with 7 million foreign workers, when the native population was a mere 2 million. Unable to enter the country legally, he had crossed the desert border from Algeria by camel and had been stopped by Libyan border guards. 'I did it three times,' he said. 'The first time they just sent me back to Algeria, and the second. The third time I went with twelve others. We had only one camel between us, and each of us had two jerrycans of water. We must have been 200 miles inside the country when the helicopter spotted us. We knew it was the end. Some soldiers came to arrest us, and the border guards remembered my face. They threw me into prison.'

'How was it?'

'How do you expect a prison to be? It was tough, that's how it was! They gave us only bread and coffee and some macaroni and rice. You had to work all day on the roads. If you slowed down, they beat you with a rubber pipe. It was no joke, I can tell you!'

'Were you convicted by a judge?'

'Judge! In Libya! Don't make me laugh! I was just thrown into jail. No one asked questions. I told them, "I'm not a criminal." And they said, "You're a thief of the route." That's what they call you if you enter illegally.'

'How did it end?'

'I escaped, by God! I ran away from the work party, and they didn't see me. The prison was in Ghat, near the Algerian border, and once I crossed the border they couldn't do anything. Then I got a truck back to Tombouctou. Now I can't go back to Libya. Perhaps they'd shoot me next time.'

Often he would recite bitterly, 'I'm forty-eight years old, and my life has been nothing but fatigue. I had eight years knowing nothing and forty years of fatigue. It never ends, by God! Nothing but fatigue, that's my life.'

'At least you're getting paid for it this time,' Marinetta said.

'Gah!' he replied. 'Half the money you gave me in Tombouctou was taken by that policeman who introduced us. He said he had to have a cut for bringing me the work. If I had refused, he'd never have given me the transit pass for Niger. That's Mali now. Corruption and thievery, by God!' So intense was the mask of tragedy on his face that I almost laughed.

'You can understand why he's such a miserable old sod,' Marinetta commented later.

Sidi Mohammed was one of the strange, hybrid characters created by a combination of drought and political changes in the Sahara. Born a nomad, an expert in desert ways, he had been forced to take refuge in the town, where he possessed none of the skills required for survival. 'You can't get anywhere in the town unless you can read and write,' he said. 'And even if you can read and write, they won't give a job to a white man. When did you see a white working in an office in Tombouctou? If you did, he was only the caretaker.'

It was an aspect of his ambivalent attitude that he wouldn't hear of the idea of sending his children to school. 'What's the point?' he said. 'They'll never get a job. And, anyway, it's not right when the government tries to take your children away. I've seen how they do it in Libya. By force. I don't want my children to grow up not knowing who their father is.'

At the same time he had acquired a taste for some of the benefits that modern town life bestowed. He had become addicted to the radio. 'The Bee-Bee-Cee Arabic Service,' he said. 'I never miss it. "This is London ... and here is the news ... and here are the chimes of Beeg Beyn for eight hours Greenidge Meentaym. Dong! Dong! DOOONG!" I know all the announcers by their voices, by God! "This is London ... Boosh Hawse, London doobel-yew-cee-too!"' I was touched by the revelation. I thought of how Marinetta and I had been interviewed at Bush House before leaving to Nouakchott. The mention of it by this illiterate camel man made it seem suddenly very near.

It took us eight days to cross the Niger valley. The rains had ceased, and we were stuck in the meteorological no-man's-land between the Saharan wet season and winter, when there is a resurgence of summer heat. For the first time we began to feel the effects of the immense distances both before us and behind. The landscape was dreary — spiky trees, spiky grass, spiky rocks, grey stones, grey sand, undulating hills. Soon there were no more tents or people to relieve the monotony. The sun blazed down. Our lives became a mindless cybernaut routine: get up, load, walk, ride, unload, eat, load, walk, ride, on and on like an invariable musical tone. It seemed that we were getting nowhere, marking time in the same spot. We were travelling through time but going forward not at all. Sidi Mohammed muttered and hummed to himself, always the same 10 yards ahead. Marinetta rode close behind me, disinclined to talk, silently lapsing into the dreams that whiled away the featureless hours. The pacing camels lulled us half into sleep. The journey became an illusion. We began to forget who we were and what we were doing there. The strands that connected us to our own society had ceased to exist. It was as if we were under a spell.

My mind plunged into lotus-eating dreams, a flux of past, present and future. An endless movie played backwards inside my head. The plane was touching down in Nouakchott, the plane was touching down in Paris. We were sitting on the Spanish Steps in Rome. We were sitting in Marinetta's home in Rome with General Peru looking stern and uncompromising. We were diving into the swimming-pool at the Sudan Club in Khartoum. I was walking into a classroom in Dongola, nervously self-conscious before fifty black heads. I was sitting in a plain car in Belfast, and five crisp gunshots cracked over my head. Somebody screamed, 'Black bastard!' and then I was standing at the tail door of a C130 with the wind and fumes whistling through, one of sixty men with parachutes set to jump. The blood pumping like fire behind bleach-white skin, the red light flashing and the dispatcher shouting, 'RED ON!' The silent four seconds before the green light says, 'GO!' The aircraft behind me. The drone of the engine dies away. The canopy develops with a snap. I am floating down to earth like a poppy seed. I am floating across the desert on a camel, but where am I going? What is the future I am travelling towards? Sidi Mohammed is still 10 yards in front of me. Perhaps five minutes have passed. Patience. That's all we need. Eat well. Walk a little. Ride your camel. Maintain your health. Fill your *girbas*. Don't overstrain. Don't try to be clever. Keep going on, bit by bit. On and on, load, walk, ride, load, each camping place a conquest, each night a tiny victory.

We watered in the Tilemsi valley, where many Tuareg had pitched their camps. The plain was dotted with white-skinned *mayneg* camels. We saw men collecting wild yellow grasses and placing them in a basket, just as their hunter-gatherer ancestors had done 7,000 years before. Once we saw a Targui leading a young girl by a rope tied round her leg. The girl was stunningly pretty and totally naked. As we came nearer I noticed that she walked with a limp and had the vacant look of the sub-normal.

When we passed these encampments few people came to greet us. Those who did looked at us with hostility and whispered together menacingly. They never failed to ask for tea, sugar or tobacco, and we never failed to refuse. Often I grew tired of Tuareg ways, their hostility and their lack of hospitality. Sidi Mohammed told me, 'There is a darkness in them. They have always been like this. I first came into this region when I was a boy, with a slave. Two Tuareg youths came into my camp and pointed at me. "Is that an Arab or a human being?" they asked. I took my gun and sat under a bush. I told the slave to move all our baggage. If they had touched him, I would have blasted them, by God! Then an old man turned up and ordered them to leave us alone. I had no trouble with them after that.'

'Is it their custom to demand things from travellers?' I asked.

Sidi Mohammed laughed. 'In their own language they call themselves *Amahaq* – you know what that means? It means "Those who take". That's all their nobility is – taking. Before the *nsara* came they lived by robbing trade caravans. The *nsara* finished that. Now they pester you for tea and sugar instead.' He said that in the past the Tuareg had claimed tribute from his people, the Berabish. For four years they had paid. The fifth year they had invited the Tuareg for a great banquet and afterwards had slaughtered them all, throwing their bodies into a well. 'The Tuareg are nothing now!' Sidi Mohammed said.

Once, near sunset, we passed through a camp under the brow of a hill. The Tuareg there looked wild. They were unveiled and wore wiry crops of hair; their swords were hung across their shoulders in leather baldrics. They followed us on foot as we rode, asking questions and demanding tobacco. After we got rid of them Sidi Mohammed said, 'Those were Tuareg vassals – they have warriors, marabouts and vassals just like the Moors. They are thieves, without doubt. They will find our camp tonight if we aren't careful. Omar, you should have bought a gun.'

We camped in a dry wadi near some low, rocky hills. There was no moon, and we hobbled the camels tightly. While dinner was cooking, one of us watched them constantly. We had few weapons at our disposal if we were attacked. We had our survival knives, camel sticks, a rather bent hatchet and our emergency flares. After we had eaten we drove the camels into the camp. We sat awake for hours, listening to their belching and gurgling. A slight breeze whispered across the stony ground. Nothing else disturbed the tranquillity of the desert night.

On 15 October we descended into the valley of Asakrei. There were some leather tents scattered about, and as we made lunch in the bushes a group of six men came to visit us. They looked dangerous, dressed in their long, dark gandourahs, their faces hidden by veils. They carried daggers and axes and wore thick skin sandals. They were inscrutable under their headcloths and came on with the dreadful steadiness of an army. Suddenly Sidi Mohammed said, 'Don't worry: these aren't Tuareg. They are Iddao Ishaak. They are of Jewish origin. They are rich in camels, but they aren't warlike.'

The men sat around us in a circle, and several of them relaxed by removing their veils. Two of them began to make a fire a few yards away, and Sidi Mohammed grew very excited. He told us in Hassaniyya, 'They're going to slaughter a goat for us!' He was disappointed, however. The men let the fire burn down to ash, then mixed the ash with chewing tobacco, which they masticated with relish. They told us that until the previous year the drought had been terrible here. Thousands of head of livestock had perished, they said, and hundreds of Tuareg families had moved south as far as Nigeria and as far north as Tamanrasset. '*They* won't be back!' Sidi Mohammed commented drily. 'They lost everything. I saw plenty of them in Tamanrasset last year, selling off their goats and camels. They'll never be back, by the Prophet!'

One of the Ishaak told us that the *nsara* had given them oil and grain. 'The only thing that saved us was God and the Christians,' he said. 'The government gave us no help. They still take from us the animal tax for animals we haven't got!'

Sidi Mohammed suggested that we should offer to buy a goat, and at last I agreed. The men fetched us a white kid, which I bought for about £10. Sidi Mohammed looked as happy as a child at Christmas. 'Shall we slaughter it now?' he asked eagerly.

'No,' I told him. 'We'll slaughter it tonight. I'll carry it on my camel.'

'You can't do that!' he protested, his face falling. 'It will die and then it won't be *hillul*. We won't be able to eat it.'

I showed him how it could be slung from a canvas sheet, a trick I had learned from my nomads in the Sudan, but Sidi Mohammed remained doubtful.

That afternoon we climbed up the valley, along rolling hillsides where spires of blue rock pushed out of wedges of purple and the path twisted between egg-shaped white boulders like a waterless river. All afternoon Sidi Mohammed fretted about the goat. Regularly on the half-hour he would ask, 'Is it all right, Omar?' 'Isn't it tied too tightly?' 'Isn't its head drooping too low?' When I offered to tie up its head with string he cried, 'No! No! You'll break its neck!'

We were travelling towards the wells at In Telli, where we hoped to rest for a day. It would be the first rest we had enjoyed since leaving Tombouctou, and we were all looking forward to it. At about four o'clock Sidi Mohammed could stand the tension no longer. 'Come on, Omar,' he said. 'Let's kill it!'

'No,' I repeated, unable to suppress a slightly truculent satisfaction, 'we'll slaughter the goat when we get to In Telli. Not before.'

Sunset came and In Telli did not appear. We stopped for sunset prayers. 'Why don't we make camp here?' Sidi Mohammed said.

'No, we agreed to go on to In Telli.'

'But this is a good place for the camels. There's good grazing here.'

'We go on!'

'I'm only thinking of the camels.'

We carried on, descending slowly into the valley of In Telli, where we made camp. As soon as we had unloaded, Sidi Mohammed grabbed the goat, sighing audibly with relief that it was still alive. He slit its throat with his knife and a splash of crimson stained the sand. In moments he had skinned it neatly and expertly. He cut out the liver, kidneys, heart and lungs and began to roast them on the fire. When the organs were roasted he laid them out on a sack and began to cut them up carefully. The discarded intestines and skin were already obliterated by scarab beetles, hundreds of them squabbling over tiny pieces of carcass. Sidi Mohammed divided the meat into equal portions. Ours were considerably more equal than his. 'In the name of God,' he said, grinning wolfishly, 'let's eat!'

In Telli lay in a natural depression encircled by black cliffs, with higher blue mountains in the background. Near the wells was a single mud house, but it was deserted. Two tents, covered in canvas, were rolled up on frames outside. Next to the house was a corral where goats had been kept. The wells were shallow and all contained water, though it seemed to be polluted with algae of some kind. Not far off, below an overhanging rock, we discovered damp sand; water lay 18 inches below it. We dug out a pit and watered our camels, then set them off, hobbled, among the green trees in the wadi.

We put up the tent, Arab-style, near some bushes. Sidi Mohammed returned from driving the camels away and began to cook another leg of goat, roasting it on a low fire. The rest he cut into strips, which he laid out to dry on a thorn tree. As he was cooking a young Targui appeared, carrying an axe. 'They can smell fresh meat from 5 miles away!' Sidi Mohammed commented, but he was obliged out of custom to give the man some meat. After he had gone we stuffed ourselves again. Sidi Mohammed ate most of Marinetta's share as well as his own, even picking up the pieces I had discarded and declaring, 'There is still meat on that!' He picked at the bones with his knife, smashing them open on a rock and slurping at the delicious marrow-bone jelly inside. After this performance he belched, rather more loudly than usual, and said, 'Why don't we stay here two days? One is not enough, by God!'

Later he went to chase the camels, and I wandered off to search for sweet melons, which grew in places around the wells. They grew on creepers, about forty melons to a plant, but were far rarer than the bitter melons, from which they were distinguished by a slightly different skin pattern. I had just discovered a plump little fruit when I heard Marinetta shouting, 'Maik! Maik!' I ran back, clutching the hilt of my knife. Two Tuareg were standing over Marinetta, looking quite menacing. She had stepped behind the tent to wash herself and was desperately clutching a towel around her legs. 'Go away!' she was shouting at the men, but in Hassaniyya. Either they didn't understand or they were pretending not to.

'Here not good!' I told them in my pidgin Tamasheq. 'Over there good!' I pointed to a tree about 20 yards away. In any culture what they had done would be considered extremely rude. Reluctantly the men followed my directions. They sat down in the shade.

'Are you all right?' I asked Marinetta.

'Yes, but I had just got my knickers off when I saw them coming. It was so embarrassing.'

'What do you think they want?'

'They were pointing at the meat.'

Later I took them some of our meat on a plate. They ate it quickly, then strode away.

When Sidi Mohammed returned and heard the story, he muttered, 'We shall have nothing left at this rate!' We were distracted, however, by the curious appearance of his hair. He had tried to cut it short with his knife, and now it stood out in odd crowns and tufts all over his head. The effect was horrific, but Sidi Mohammed seemed quite unaware of it. On the contrary, he repeatedly ran his hand over the uneven surface, smiling proudly like a man in a hair-oil advertisement and saying, 'Eh, Omar, what do you think? I made a good job, didn't I?'

'Beautiful!' I grinned back, and Marinetta collapsed with giggles.

We watered the camels again in the afternoon and filled all our waterbags. After sunset we cooked the remaining leg of goat and Sidi Mohammed divided the meat into portions once more, this time evidently according to age, not beauty. Sidi Mohammed, being the oldest, got the most. Again we were treated to a repertoire of sucking, cracking, slurping and belching, and afterwards he placed a large portion of uneaten meat in a tree. The meat made him expansive. 'Ah!' he said. 'I remember when I was in Libya, I had a friend who was a police chief. He employed me to hunt gazelles. I went by car, and I never got less than sixteen in a day. The meat was so tender, by God!'

'But surely the meat isn't *hillal* when you shoot it?' I said, remembering what a fuss he had made over the goat.

'It is when you bless the bullets!' he said. 'The Libyans are good people, you know. It's only the government that is bad. At least the Libyans are pure-blooded Arabs. Why, there are tribes in Mali that are more like apes than men. They're not human beings at all. But there are slaves everywhere, even in Libya. Once, when I was a caretaker, I borrowed the company car. I got it stuck in the sand and had to abandon it. There was a lot of trouble about it. I wasn't supposed to have taken the car at all. My supervisor was a slave, and he had the nerve to tell me that I would be finished. "You're just a slave, that's all!" says I. "You're nothing!" And I kept my job. He was afraid, you see.' He described how another supervisor, this time an Egyptian, had ordered him to move a bench first to one place, then to another, then back again. 'I knew he was doing it to be clever!' Sidi Mohammed said. 'So I told him, "If you don't make your mind up, I'll break your neck!" He never spoke to me after that! Ha! Ha! But half the Egyptians I met in Libya were queers, you know. They liked other men. I once had to share a room with an Egyptian who was queer. He touched my leg, so I got my knife out. "If you touch me again, I'll slit your throat!" says I.' Before his stories got any more hair-raising we decided to retire.

When we awoke the next morning I noticed that the package of meat that had been put in the tree was gone. It should have been shared between us. 'I bet he ate it in the night!' Marinetta said, incensed. We still had the dried meat, which I kept carefully tied in one of my saddle bags.

We left the wadi of In Telli behind and climbed up through a
chasm just wide enough for the camels to pass. The walls were screes
of black stone, shattered into pieces like lumps of asphalt. Along the
canyon sweet melons grew. We picked them and peeled off the skin,
handing the slices out and cramming the succulent flesh into our
mouths till the sugary juice ran down our chins. We emerged on to
a plateau, where the camels padded across the smooth, silver bed of
what might once have been a tarn. The hardpan mud still shone
dazzlingly with sodium salts. Around its rim lay trees, moribund and
skeletal, and hundreds of castle-like termitaries, 6 feet high and solid
as granite. We descended over some red dunes, where the sand was
splashed with the green of melon plants. Far to the east we saw a
line of hills, deep blue in the morning sun. They were the Sakarezou
range, which we should have to cross before reaching Niger. To the
north and east lay endless acres of *rag*, black stones and gravel, dotted
with broken islands of trees and tufts of coarse grass.

We came into a wide, sandy wadi, which meandered out of the
plateau, and made camp under a shady *talha* tree. Sidi Mohammed
was unusually quiet as we unloaded, and afterwards took a little
water and stalked off to a bush near by. A moment later came the
unmistakable sound of bad diarrhoea. He walked back clutching his
stomach and sulked moodily until it was time to eat. After lunch he
clutched his stomach and lurched off again towards the bush.

In the afternoon we broke out of the wadi and entered a plain of
great, oscillating wave crests. In places there were patches of thistle-
like *heskanit* grass, the spiky seeds of which attach themselves to
anything that passes. An enormous jackal, wolf-grey and as muscular
as a racing dog, dashed in front of us and disappeared into the range.
After that we saw two Tuareg riding north on fast camels. Sidi
Mohammed went off to greet them and returned a while later saying
that we must turn south to reach the waterpool at Ouritoufolout,
where we would water the camels before crossing the hills of
Sakarezou.

Sunset came. The sun was a huge glob of orange going down on
our right. At the same instant the moon rose directly to the east. It
was full, but it looked as if someone had taken a bite out of the upper
edge. When we stopped to unload the bite appeared to get bigger

as the silver light diminished. I suddenly realized that I was seeing the earth's shadow cast on the screen of her satellite. It was an eclipse. I stood there, spellbound, as the moonlight drained away, leaving only a thin sliver on the lower rim. After months in the Sahara, travelling so close to the earth, I had started to acquire an intuitive feel for the size of the planet, its vastness and its smallness, in a way I could never have done in a distance-shrinking motor vehicle. Now I was reminded of the endless clockwork motion of the universe, circular, a cycle of endings and beginnings, births and deaths, the beginning of the journey no more than a point on the way to its end. The motion ticked on to infinity, our tiny, vast journey a minute part of the gigantic works.

My metaphysical musings were brought abruptly to a halt by the sound of bad diarrhoea. Soon, Sidi Mohammed limped out of the darkness and asked for medicine for his stomach. 'It's that powdered milk,' he moaned. 'I drank too much of it. It doesn't agree with me.'

'It's not the milk,' Marinetta said. 'It's all that meat you stuffed yourself with. It's a fitting punishment, by God!'

The waterpool was in a deep cleft between the sand hills, screened by trees and thick undergrowth. There were pied crows and ibis in the branches, and the nests of weaver-birds hung down from them like fruit. A Targui youth was watering about fifteen camels there when we arrived, and he told us that the water was good. Our camels seemed nervous and edgy, leaping up and shying as we loaded the *girbas*, throwing off blankets and saddle bags. I hadn't seen them behave like this since they had been attacked by ticks at Tinigert and wondered if they were being eaten by flies. 'They're afraid of something,' Sidi Mohammed said. 'It's not the flies. But when they behave like this they've got another three months' work left in them at least.' It seemed a marvel. They had already covered a phenomenal distance, in the hot season, and were still going strong. No wonder the Arabs called this animal 'the gift of God', I thought.

The Targui boy pointed out the best route towards the mountains, and we rode on through the ruins of the rainy season. The *heskanit* had changed colour from mellow green to yellow, its portable thistles hanging ready on the tips of swollen ears. The tribulus, so green and succulent a few weeks before, had dried into grey rats' tails like rotten string, the bright yellow flowers fading into the cruel caltraps of thorns that would remain in the sand long after any trace of the plant had disappeared. There were brakes of salt-bush, the waxy leaves frayed and nibbled by locusts, and white butterflies that still played around in their shadows.

Sidi Mohammed announced that his stomach had recovered from 'the milk', and at lunchtime he asked, 'Where's the dried meat? I'll cut it up for you.'

'No, you won't,' Marinetta told him curtly, 'because you'll eat more than you cut.'

Several pieces of meat were writhing with maggots. When Marinetta made a disgusted face Sidi Mohammed said, 'I'll eat them! There's nothing wrong with a few maggots. You just clean them out with your knife!' He ate the maggoty bits raw and then a large helping of rice and cooked meat. Afterwards he burped loudly.

The afternoon wound on; the unchanged and unchanging landscape drifted by. 'How good it would be to be clean, well dressed and comfortable,' Marinetta said wistfully. It seemed an attractive proposition, but I knew it was false. No matter how bright the life of comfort seemed when you were deprived of it, the reality was an illusion that faded like fairy gold as soon as you left the desert. Then you would dream restlessly of being back there. I thought of Wilfred Thesiger's words: 'He will have within him the yearning to return, weak or insistent according to his nature. For this cruel land can cast a spell no temperate clime can match.' Marinetta had read those words, but she didn't yet feel their meaning. One day, I thought, when all this was over, she would. Meanwhile our lives were caught up in a cycle of movement, a machine-like routine. Nothing could be achieved without that routine, not writing a book, nor running an empire, nor crossing a desert. I remembered again how I had first seen the Sahara from the banks of the Nile and how I had longed to find out what the land looked like beyond that horizon, how all my life had spread out before me then like a premonition, and my heart had thumped with a mysterious excitement. That had been more than seven long years ago. I wondered, as all men have wondered, about the bigness of time and the smallness of human beings. The desert seemed to spring these thoughts on you constantly. How did it all fit together in the eternal jigsaw, man with woman, woman with man, mankind with earth, earth with space? The sunset caught me still wondering.

We made camp on a platform of hard *rag*. Sidi Mohammed was his talkative self again. 'All the Arabs need is green grazing, water and a beautiful face,' he said. Then he stared at Marinetta. 'Ah, God, there's none of that here!' he said. This, I thought, was revenge for Marinetta's remarks about the meat. In case she hadn't caught on he pressed the point. 'I heard a discussion on the radio about who were the world's most beautiful women,' he said. 'They said it was between the Indians, the Sudanese and the Arabs. I reckon the Arabs are the most beautiful.'

'It's a pity there wasn't a discussion about the world's most impolite people,' Marinetta said acidly. 'The Arabs would easily have won *that!*' In the rice that evening there were two bones covered with flesh. Sidi Mohammed grabbed them both.

The following morning we crossed the wadi Azouagh. It was the largest watercourse in the southern Sahara, draining water from the mountain massifs of Hoggar and Aïr. Now it was waterless, but the bed was cut into a series of deep troughs where the mud had dried rock-solid and had cracked into deep, brittle blocks. It took an hour to negotiate a route through the channels. On the opposite bank we found the skeleton of a Tuareg camp, abandoned quite recently. Beyond it lay a featureless plain extending to the foot of the mountains. Before we mounted our camels we discovered a ripe growth of sweet melons and sucked their moisture gratefully.

We crossed the plain and clambered into the hills. The hillsides were a rubble of tarry blocks, but the guide found a sandy path through them, leading us up to another shady wadi, where we halted for midday. Marinetta prepared rice, and Sidi Mohammed went off down the wadi to relieve himself. After he had gone Marinetta grinned at me and said, 'He'll get a shock when he grabs for the bones today!' She took three joints out of the stock of dried meat. One was large and the other two much smaller. 'Which one will he go for first?' she asked.

'The biggest, of course,' I said.

'Right!' she said, and began to scrape all the meat off the largest joint. She had them all in the pot by the time Sidi Mohammed returned. When she served the plate I saw she had cleverly disguised the meatless large joint so that a very tempting edge showed above the rice.

We sat down to eat. Sidi Mohammed's eyes lighted at once on the promising joint. His big hand shot out and seized it. As he lifted it out Marinetta and I casually took the smaller joints, leaving Sidi Mohammed staring wistfully at the polished white surface of a bone devoid of the smallest fragment of meat. His face was almost painful to behold. He threw the bone viciously into the sand, muttering with disgust, then looked enviously at the meaty joints we were now chewing with great relish. 'What's up?' I asked innocently.

'The meat's gone!' he said, eyeing our joints murderously and pawing round in the rice with his hand. The hand came up with rice only. When he went off to fetch the camels later, we collapsed and rolled about clutching our sides. It was the funniest thing I had seen since leaving Chinguetti.

It took us two days to cross the mountains. Afterwards we came down into sweeping prairies of dried *heskanit* grass. Walking through it was a nightmare. The prickly burrs sprang off the plant as soon as you touched it and embedded themselves firmly in any soft surface. Within moments our sandals and *sirwel* would be so heavy with burrs that we would have to stop to remove them. But this was also a delicate operation because the burrs then stuck in your hands, leaving tiny spines which could be removed only with tweezers. At the end of the day our hands would be raw and red and swollen from the embedded spines. One morning, after half an hour of *heskanit*, Sidi Mohammed stopped and rolled up his *sirwel*, right to the groin, revealing for the first time a pair of legs that were hairless, white and very bandy. He looked a comical figure, holding up his pantaloons with one hand and the headrope with the other, cursing as he tried vainly to find a path through the seams of vicious grass.

The *heskanit* did not prevent Sidi Mohammed's regular absences. They were becoming longer now, and for several days we had been forced to wait for him to catch up. He never offered any explanation for his departures, and it tortured us to know what he might be doing. If I asked him, he would mutter and snatch the headrope, stalking off in an obvious bad temper. Once, while we were waiting for him to catch up, Shigar's nose-ring got caught up in a thorn tree and was ripped out. The ring tumbled into the sand, and while I was desperately searching for it, the camel started to wander off. I rushed after the beast, not knowing how I could possibly control him without ring or headrope. Marinetta held the other camels and watched me getting farther and farther away. It took me many minutes to herd the animal back to the thorn tree. When I arrived Sidi Mohammed was back, grinning and saying, 'There's no problem, is there?'

I felt the anger boiling through me. 'I hired you as a guide,' I said. 'And you mentioned nothing about these disappearances. Now you tell us where you get to every morning and afternoon or we don't shift from this spot!'

He looked at me challengingly, uncowed. I thought for a moment that he would ignore the threat. Then he shrugged and said, 'It's not your business, but I'm a Tijani.'

A Tijani! I knew the word at once. Tijanis were a secret fraternity, a kind of Freemasonry of the Islamic world. Founded in Algeria in the eighteenth century, membership had burgeoned throughout the Sahara and into the Sudanic lands beyond. It included heads of state, holy men, respected teachers as well as wandering dervishes. 'But what do you do?' I asked him.

'I have to do my meditations twice a day,' he said. 'We repeat holy words and count them on our rosaries.' It struck me suddenly that I had seen him putting away his beads on several occasions after his absences.

'But you already say your prayers five times a day,' Marinetta said. 'Isn't that enough?'

'No.' Sidi Mohammed smirked. 'You see, those prayers are said by every Muslim. It's laid down in the Quran. Those prayers are your capital. The extra meditations are like your interest on the capital. The more you do, the better your chance in the afterlife. That's why I do it. I've got little enough in this world. I want to make sure I have plenty in the next.'

*

There was no easing of the heat. A hot wind blew almost constantly. We found no waterpools and no people, and the border seemed deserted. We were hoping to hit the wadi Tillia, which I thought marked the Mali–Niger frontier. My Michelin map and my 1-to-1-million survey showed the border in different places. The strip along its eastern side had recently been claimed by Mali, and the frontier had been redrawn. Water was short, and the camels seemed as tired and spiritless as we were. Once when we stopped at midday Sidi Mohammed said, 'I'm worried about the water. The camels are thirsty, and there's no one around. This wind can kill us too.' I had never heard him sound so gloomy.

It was impossible to travel in a straight line. We were climbing interlocking sand hills, one after the other, up and down like a roller-coaster. As we staggered up to the summit of one hill, expecting the plains of Niger to unfold beneath us, we would be met with the sight of yet another hill obscuring the horizon. A grey, salty mist hung in the air and made eye navigation difficult. We were forced to ride more often to avoid the terrible *heskanit*, and the camels became exhausted. I could think only of reaching Agadez now. The Nile was a hazy dream, somewhere beyond the bounds of the world. Rest and good food were what I craved, an asylum from the endless heat and the vicious *heskanit*.

Time passed but we came to no wadi. The folds of sand that we were crossing opened like the riffling pages of a book. The tiny watercourses between them were steep and bone-dry. Then, one afternoon while we were still on foot, the mist cleared. We saw below us a sandy hillside falling away to a plain of purple *rag* that cut between the hills. 'That's our wadi!' I said.

In moments the *heskanit* had disappeared, and we were making our way across a hard carapace of rock. We saw that the wadi was alive with hundreds of goats, the white parts of their skins reflecting the sunlight brilliantly.

'Thanks to God!' Sidi Mohammed said. 'Where there are goats there are people!'

The sky was pure blue now, with wisps of cloud. As we descended into the valley a school of about twenty ibis careened above us, wheeling and banking like aeronauts. A few minutes later they landed in the wadi and presented themselves like a welcoming guard of honour as we approached. We sighted a herdsman. He was a black Targui, wearing an old shirt of faded red, black pantaloons and home-made sandals. He carried only a stick and an old skin bag and had a fat she-donkey without a saddle. Sidi Mohammed spoke to him in Tamasheq, and the man replied in a soft drawl. 'I can't make out his Tamasheq,' Sidi Mohammed said. 'He calls it Tamajegh.' But he understood enough to take directions to the nearest well, In Ghouma. We followed the procession of goats and reddish sheep out of the wadi, crossing an elbow of sand. There were suddenly many signs of life. There were human figures collecting wild grasses. There were the small, faraway forms of white camels. A troop of jet-black cattle came tromping over the hillside, quite unlike the humped cattle we had seen previously. They had great silver-white horns, 4 or 5 feet in span, which they carried like heavy crowns as they moved. They were the ancient long-horn stock of the Sahara, beasts whose ancestors had lived here before any camel.

Four skin tents were perched on the hillside. They were inhabited by black men in ragged clothes. The nomads were friendly. Their manner held no trace of hostility or aggression. One of them, a tall, gentle-mannered man, led us to the wells. There were many shallow, hand-dug pits, which yielded water very slowly. Some young children were filling *girbas* and slinging them under the bellies of their donkeys. After the suspicion we had grown used to, there was a palpable sense of peace here. I guessed we had already crossed the border.

As we moved towards the border post at Tillia, Sidi Mohammed grew visibly nervous. He advised us not to enter the village. 'They'll think we're Polisario for sure,' he said. 'Look at these foreign saddles.' He told us that the Nigérien police were far stricter than those in Mali. 'They'll prevent us from going on,' he said. He seemed really scared, and I imagined he was remembering his capture by the Libyan police the year before.

His fear set off a nagging doubt in my own head. We had no permission to travel in Niger by camel. Over a year before, I had written to the Nigérien Embassy in Brussels to apply for it but had never received a reply. I had no idea what kind of reception we would get in Tillia; I knew only that if they stopped us here, it would be a humiliating end to our journey, which was only in its second stage. Finally we agreed with Sidi Mohammed that we would bypass the border post and present our crossing of the western plains in Agadez as a *fait accompli*.

We worked our way around the settlement, keeping it just below the horizon. No sooner had we left it behind than we spotted four Moorish-style tents on the brow of a dune. Sidi Mohammed grew excited, saying, 'Those are Arabs for sure!' He insisted on visiting them. 'I haven't spoken to my own people for weeks,' he complained. I hesitated, thinking that the camp was too near the village for comfort. 'They might slaughter a goat for us!' Sidi Mohammed said. I knew then that there would be no stopping him.

As we approached, a crowd of men and boys came out to greet us. They looked like Tuareg, but they wore no veils and spoke Hassaniyya. They were Kunta Arabs, and their chief was a man called Sid'Amer, a sullen-looking man with a shaven head, a goatee beard and a very dark skin. They pressed us to stay, shouting, 'Welcome! Welcome to the guests! Couch your camels and unload!' Sidi Mohammed had couched before I could stop him and was smiling and shaking hands. The Arabs were pointing at our saddles and saying, 'These people have come a long way!'

Sidi Mohammed's eyes were already alight with the thought of meat when I took him aside to show him something I had noticed before we couched. It was the fresh imprint of a Land-Rover track going through the camp. I guessed that the only people who had Land-Rovers in this area were the police. 'They will tell the police we were here,' I said.

'Nonsense,' he replied. 'These are good people. Arabs. They won't let us down.'

We made camp on a dune near the Arab tents. Sid'Amer and some servants took our camels off to graze farther down the dunes. Once we were separated from our animals, the manner of the Arabs changed. They crowded round us, staring coldly instead of smiling. They began to ask pointed questions of Sidi Mohammed. Who were we? What did we want here? Then came the clincher. Sid'Amer let slip that the authorities in Tillia had asked him to stop any strangers or travellers who passed that way. 'They don't like "thieves of the route",' he said, staring hard at Marinetta and me. 'You have to report to the *gendarmerie* in Tillia tomorrow morning.'

'And if we decide not to?' I asked.

'I will have to tell them that you were here.'

'I thought so.'

'Life is hard here,' Sid'Amer whined guiltily. 'The government gives whites like us a hard time.' This sounded extremely comical from Sid'Amer, whose skin was charcoal-black. The Arabs left us sitting there.

Sidi Mohammed had almost begun to quake when he heard the words 'thieves of the route', and now he looked miserable. He made tea and sat staring into the fire, saying, 'At least we won't eat sardines tonight. They are Arabs, and Arabs will bring us meat.' A boy appeared with a tray and set it down in front of us. A savoury smell rose from beneath a wickerwork cover. Sidi Mohammed sat up and licked his lips. He lifted the cover reverently. Then his face dropped. Inside was a sticky, half-raw mass of porridge sprinkled with dust.

'Ha!' scoffed Marinetta. 'So much for your meat!'

'Rubbish!' said Sidi Mohammed, gulping hard and smiling weakly. 'This porridge is just as good. This porridge is my favourite dish!'

The *gendarmerie* was a clean, well-kept building, recently painted and with the tricolour of Niger fluttering on a pole outside. We couched the camels in some mesquite trees near by. A green-bereted trooper came out to greet us and asked for our passports. Sidi Mohammed handed over his identity card tremulously, saying, 'I'll stay here,' as we were shown inside.

The adjutant was a studious-looking man with spectacles and a brand-new combat suit. He put down a book on African history as we entered and told us to sit down. Just then the treacherous Sid'Amer of the previous night came in and began whining obsequiously in Hausa. The officer listened for a moment, then sent him out with a gesture. I wasn't sorry to see him go. The adjutant looked at us silently. Then he said, 'I have seen tourists come in vehicles. I have seen them come in planes. I have even seen a tourist who came on a bicycle. But I have never seen tourists who have come all the way from Mauritania *by camel*!' I almost thought he was about to congratulate us, but instead he said, 'What will you Westerners think of next?'

He relapsed into silence and scrutinized our documents. He examined Sidi Mohammed's ID card with extra vigilance, even removing several prescriptions for pills that were folded up inside. 'And where is this person . . . this Mali person?' he asked. I told him that our guide was outside. He frowned. 'Employing a foreign guide in Niger is very irregular,' he said. 'So is entering the country by camel. I will have to send a radio message to our *préfet* in Tahoua. There won't be a message back until at least tomorrow.' When he noticed our expressions he added that we were welcome to use one of the empty houses in the village until a reply came through. Then he sighed and said, 'Ah, tourism! It is good for the country, but it is so *tiring*.'

After we had unloaded the camels at the mud house, Sidi Mohammed took them off to graze outside the village. When he returned he asked us anxiously, 'You didn't tell them I worked in Libya, did you? They don't like the Libyans. Never mention them here.' I said that there had been some doubt about our employing a foreign guide, and his face dropped again into a mask of misery. 'I'm forty-eight years old and I've had forty years of fatigue,' he said. 'That's all my life is, by God! Nothing but fatigue.'

In the afternoon Marinetta and I explored the place. There were sixty or so oblong houses of mud brick laid like boxes on the sloping, golden sand that rose up from the wadi. The wadi was filled with Sodom's Apples and giant acacias, each of them hanging in the azure sky like a nimbus of green smoke. Beyond them the land rose again to the foot of a cliff with the colour and texture of a crusty loaf. There was a well in the basin of the wadi, where a crush of longhorn and shorthorn cattle stamped and bellowed. Wedges of white camels mixed in with them and ranks of goats and sheep. The well rope was being lifted by a bony she-donkey, which staggered forward, driven on by the sticks of some narrow-faced Arabs. They carried swords like Tuareg, and their faces were ghastly blue.

When we returned to the house we found Sidi Mohammed serving tea to half a dozen Arabs, one of whom was Sid'Amer, who had compounded his disgrace by inviting us to eat at his town house and conveniently 'forgetting' about it. After they had gone I told Sidi Mohammed, 'Don't make tea for anyone and especially not for Sid'Amer. He's done us no favours.' Our tea and sugar were already short, and I had no more than £20 to last us to Agadez. Here in the village we had to pay for everything, even water and firewood. The longer we were obliged to stay here, the more of that small sum would be eaten away.

When I examined our supplies later the sugar seemed surprisingly short. I found myself wondering how much tea Sidi Mohammed could have made while we were away. 'Have you seen his sack?' Marinetta asked. 'It looks fatter than it was.'

I looked at the sack as it stood in the corner of the room. It *did* seem fatter. 'You really think he'd steal the sugar?' I inquired.

'Why not? What happened to that meat?'

We both looked at the sack. He was out checking the camels. 'Why don't you look inside?' Marinetta suggested. It was very tempting. The sack and its contents had nagged at us for so long. But I couldn't bring myself to open it. Instead I squeezed it from the outside. I could feel a packet of powdery stuff, which might well have been sugar. But it could have been there from the beginning, I thought. Just then Marinetta hissed, 'He's coming!' and a moment later Sidi Mohammed walked into the room.

We hardly slept that night, disturbed by the barking of dogs and the unfamiliar sound of strident voices. The following morning there was no word from Tahoua. We were told that the *préfet* was away at a meeting and couldn't be contacted. Only he could grant us permission to go on. It was gloomy news. We walked around the village restlessly, practising some simple Hausa on the traders in the market and taking photos. There were many skin tents pitched on the slopes and even inside the mud-walled yards. They were the homes of both Arabs and Tuareg.

Already the village seemed like a prison. I began to have serious doubts that we would be allowed to continue. There was little alternative to crossing Niger unless we went through Libya, a route that seemed impossible given the present political circumstances. 'It doesn't look as if we'll get our medal after all,' Marinetta said. Then she laughed.

There was no one about. I put both my arms around her. 'Do you still think that getting married was a mistake?' I asked her.

'I can't believe I ever said it,' she answered. 'I think we're made for each other. When did I say otherwise?'

I thought of those dreadful scenes in Chinguetti. It was a staggering six months since the day we had landed in Nouakchott. It was three months since we had left Chinguetti with Mafoudh. I no longer had any doubts about Marinetta's ability to reach the Nile. She had already made a unique journey. Moreover something had happened in those six months that I couldn't quite describe. It was almost as if we had started as two people and slowly melted into each other. 'I think I've sort of got *attached* to you,' Marinetta said.

There was still no news from Tahoua the next day. The tedium began to obscure all other feelings. Sidi Mohammed made things worse by complaining: 'No other guide would have to put up with this. I never thought I'd run into these problems again.' I was worried that our food would be finished before we even got out of the place. We were down to a few kilos of rice and one of macaroni, some lumps of dried meat and some tins of sardines. 'I can't eat those sardines any more,' Sidi Mohammed groaned at dinner. 'I can't even force them down.'

'We can't afford meat,' I told him.

'They give me a pain in the heart,' he said.

'And he gives me a pain somewhere else!' said Marinetta. 'Talk about hardy desert nomads!'

We had been in Tillia six days and still no message had arrived from Tahoua. Then, one afternoon, a very solemn *gendarme* arrived to escort us to the *gendarmerie*. The adjutant was sitting on a chair outside, and he was smiling. He told us that authorization had been granted both for us and for Sidi Mohammed and handed me a stamped *laissez-passer* with our names on.

I could hardly wait to saddle the camels, but Sidi Mohammed seemed reluctant to leave. 'Can't we go tomorrow?' he asked.

'No,' I said. 'We've wasted enough time. From now on we'll travel ten hours a day at least.'

'The camels won't do ten hours a day.'

'Yes, they will,' I said. Then I noticed that he was no longer wearing his gandourah. He was clad in his shorter undershirt and *sirwel*. I asked where it was. 'I agreed to sell it to a soldier,' he said, sheepishly, 'and he can't pay me till tomorrow. I wanted to get some meat.'

I was adamant and sent him off to retrieve the garment and to fetch the camels. Meanwhile I filled six waterskins at the local pump, and Marinetta went to the market to buy provisions. She returned with twenty-four tins of Italian sardines.

We camped for the night on a dune not far from the village. To please Sidi Mohammed, now complete with gandourah, we dined on rice and meat. It was to be our last taste of meat before we reached Agadez. In the morning I awoke to find that a dog had carried off our meat supply. The well-gnawed sack was lying a few yards away, empty. When I showed it to Sidi Mohammed he shook his head in misery.

The days were the longest we had experienced. We were travelling for almost the entire day, with only a brief halt for lunch. Our food was running out. Gone were the handy supplies of peanuts, biscuits and dates that had taken the edge off our hunger previously. Soon the macaroni was finished and all that remained was the rice and sardines. Sidi Mohammed would mutter and grumble about the food all day. 'By God, those sardines make my ears whistle!' he complained. 'There are people with hot stomachs and people with cold ones. My stomach is hot. Sardines are only good in a cold climate, by the Prophet's life!'

He muttered too about the fishy smell and how it was always with us, grouching that he had no toothpaste to remove the odour from his mouth. 'You're supposed to be a nomad,' Marinetta told him. 'I never heard of a nomad using toothpaste!' But even Marinetta and I were fed up with sardines. As the days passed our portions grew smaller, and we were constantly hungry. A hollow feeling gnawed at my stomach acidly all day. Marinetta lapsed into food fantasies. 'Just a piece of fresh bread and cheese!' she would say. 'Or some fruit — grapes, red apples or mandarins!' She told me about the rich Milanese cake that would be in the shops in Rome and the thick nougat made in Sardinia at Christmas.

Once, just before we ate, I joked with Sidi Mohammed. 'After we get to Agadez none of us will have to eat sardines ever again.'

'And I will never go with a tourist who makes me eat them,' he said, nastily. 'It's not right, by God! I will protest!' He had often told me stories about his trips with other tourists, usually by motorcar. 'I never ate with any of them!' he claimed proudly. 'You are the only *nsara* I've eaten with. But the car is the only way to travel now. The camel is nothing but fatigue. That's all my life is, all fatigue, God knows! I'm like a beast with a rope round my neck, slaving away for money.'

'Money's not everything,' I suggested.

'There's nothing that can't be bought for money,' he insisted. 'The man who has money is king, by God!'

'Money doesn't buy courage.'

'It buys you people who have it,' he said. 'Money is everything. I pray God every day to bring me plenty of it. Money is power, Omar, and if you don't believe that, you're a fool.'

The days were as hot as those of summer. Ribs of cirrus cloud formed in arches across the sky, giving the illusion that we were travelling inside the body of an enormous animal. We were exhausted, and each instalment of loading tired us more. At midday Sidi Mohammed would complain that his head was spinning from the heat. Marinetta and I no longer thought about sex. The idea of it had long since passed behind us as our bodies weakened. Marinetta walked less and rode more. She no longer looked attractive. Her body was skeletal, her face an overdone reddish-purple from the sun. Her spectacles were broken and she wore a pad of cotton wool on the bridge of her nose. Her features had taken on the savage look of constant ill-temper. Insects still bothered her at nights, and in the mornings she would slap calamine lotion on her skin, which dried in pink pats. She would search the baggage obsessively for scorpions. She looked a pitiful figure now. I imagine I did too. She would wish she was in Rome or Sardinia, somewhere far away from the desert. 'It's all blank,' she told me once. 'It's all depression.' I sensed that she had begun to lose touch with her identity. She could no longer recognize herself as that desirable jet-set girl, the frequenter of fashion shops, the diplomatic passport holder, the flier first-class. Instead here was a savage, primitive, ragged woman, able only to snarl and fight to survive.

On 1 November we left the sandy country behind us and entered a desert of grey and black *rag*. Black knolls of rock appeared to the north, and cracked slabs of granite stretched for mile upon mile. The camels winced as their worn-down soles touched the sharp stones, and Sidi Mohammed pulled a wry face. 'I hate those rocks,' he said. 'They hurt the camels' feet, and anything the camels feel, I feel myself.' He was stopping frequently now to urinate and told me there was blood in his urine. I gave him some rehydration salts and a handful of antibiotics. The new infirmity robbed him of his strength and energy. In spite of his complaints, he had always been an indefatigable worker. Now I had to collect the camels alone each morning, fumbling with their nose-rings in the dark. I had to saddle almost alone, and often the loads were badly balanced and had to be adjusted later. At nights there was the added effort of finding fire-wood, which sometimes took up to an hour on this naked plain. As soon as we had eaten, one of us would have to go off to make sure that the camels hadn't wandered too far and bring them to graze near the camp. We would let them off their hobbles at four in the morning, which gave them an hour of grazing before we started at five.

One evening we camped in a place where there were the tracks of many jerboas. The Arabs ate these fluffy desert rats, roasting them, fur and all, on an open fire. Sidi Mohammed said that he would bag some of them with his stick. He was away an hour but came back empty-handed. 'You didn't get one?' I asked.

'I got one, Omar,' he replied mournfully. 'I hit it with my stick. But when I went to slit its throat, it was already dead. It wasn't *hillal*, so we couldn't eat it.'

We crossed a vast plain of powder-grey with the bronze chunks of a hill in the background. There were seams of golden grass like trickles of liquid across the dark wilderness. I wondered if the hill was the edge of the Tiguidit fault in which Agadez was situated. We camped on the plain for a night, and in the morning Sidi Mohammed announced that he felt better. We hitched our camels up wearily and shuffled across the void in darkness. As we moved, the night's black shell split open in cracks, which formed the giant letters of a strange alphabet. The cracks widened into fissures, and the fissures filled with sea-blue liquid. Yellow gashes appeared in the sky, and the dark night clouds peeled away to reveal a fiery undercoat of crimson. The yellow furrows melted back to smoky-grey, and the sun sneaked up under a bulge in the veil of cloud, puncturing it with two thick rays, which spread out like the arms of a starfish. Day. The desert appeared, supreme, primitive, beautiful and naked, nothing but featureless *rag* and rugged rock stretching to the base of the hills.

By mid-morning we had come to an island of green where some Tuareg were camping. They were friendly and begged us to stop. They brought us a bowl of salty camel's milk and told us that the wells we were searching for, Ighazer Meqqoren, were near by.

Two Tuareg boys rode with us to the wells. One rode a russet gelding and the other a white bull-camel, but both the animals looked thin and underfed. The boys rode on the odd-looking Tuareg saddles, no more than an L-shaped seat with a long backrest and an extended front horn, which terminated in a three-pronged metal claw. The saddles looked flashy, but I knew that they would be useless for carrying heavy baggage like ours. Both the Tuareg carried swords, slung over the back of their saddles. 'You're going to Egypt!' one of them exclaimed. 'But from Agadez you are going by plane, no?' They didn't seem to believe that we had come by camel from Mauritania. Tombouctou was far enough away for them. Soon a procession of donkeys was following us. Little boys and girls rode them, and they carried waterbags made out of the rubber inner tubes of motor tyres, slung beneath the belly in the peculiar manner of Tuareg here.

We arrived at the wells at midday, and Sidi Mohammed went off to fill our waterskins alone. 'You can't say he's bad at his job,' Marinetta commented after he had gone. This was true. As a guide and as a worker, Sidi Mohammed was the best we'd had. When he returned he told us that he had tried to exchange his gandourah for a goat with some Tuareg at the well. No one had been interested. 'Can't you just be patient?' Marinetta asked him, pityingly.

'I need meat so much,' he groaned. 'All the tourists I've been with have eaten out of tins like you. But I never expected to eat sardines every day!'

The following day we met a cocky Tuareg youth on a pure-white camel. He was dressed in spotless white and wore dark glasses. On his camel was slung a transistor radio in a decorated cloth bag. As he came near I noticed the smell of perfume. 'Mon patron,' he began, 'give me some tea and sugar.' When I refused he asked me rudely, 'Why not?' and added, 'There is plenty in the market ahead.'

'Then why didn't you buy some?' Marinetta cut in. 'We're the ones coming out of the desert.'

Before sunset we had arrived at the foot of the Teguidit cliffs, and in the morning we sighted the unearthly structure of a TV relay mast. It looked strange here in the desert, but in a way I was glad to see it. It spelled rest. By midday we sighted the village of In Gall with its grey buildings and two massive growths of palm trees. Agadez lay east of us, 70 miles away along an asphalt track. We entered In Gall in the afternoon and were halted at the gendarmerie by three smart policemen, who examined our laissez-passer. The chief was a heavily jowled Soninke who looked uncompromising. I felt very glad that we had an official paper. He looked us both up and down very slowly. I realized suddenly what an odd sight we must be, ragged and unkempt and dirty, dressed anyway in Arab clothes that belonged to Mauritania. 'How long have you been married?' he started to ask us.

'Not one of those!' groaned Marinetta.

'How is it possible for a woman to travel with two men? You know ... isn't it difficult for sex?'

We were glad to escape from him and filled our girbas at some shallow pits beyond the town. From there we could see a new road of shining asphalt crossing a metal bridge and, beyond it, a signpost saying 'Agadez 119 KM'.

For three days we followed the road, moving fast and stopping little. The signs of civilization burgeoned around us. There were strips of burned-off tyres and pieces of engines lying along the hard shoulder. We were still hungry and thirsty, and the empty Sprite and Pepsi cans we saw tortured us with thirst as the discarded meat cans tormented us with hunger. Occasionally cars passed us: a road-construction team in a tipper-truck and once a Westerner driving a vehicle marked 'Paris–Algiers–Dakar'. 'That's where we should be, Omar,' Sidi Mohammed said. 'In a comfortable car like that, not riding these camels. Why tire yourself and little Mariam out on camels? I'll never understand.'

'It'll all be in a book some day,' I said.

'Gah!' he said. 'Books! The only book worth reading is the Quran. The knowledge in books is very fine, but it's no good to you in the afterlife, is it?'

We moved along the roadside past Tuareg camps of palm-frond huts and herds of piebald camels with brilliant white eyes, which Sidi Mohammed said were from the Aïr mountains farther north. We passed wells where Tuareg were watering thin horses and once saw in the distance some Fulani tribesmen in broad-brimmed hats, leading a parade of black-and-white cattle and carrying spears. In the evening of 6 November, just before sunset, we saw Agadez, or at least the glitter of its petrol-storage tanks, on the brow of a rocky hill. We made camp as far away from the road as possible, but all evening we were disturbed by the roaring engines of great trucks going to Niamey and the smell of their fumes.

As we sat down to our last evening meal together, I felt numb. 'I'm looking forward to getting back to Mali,' Sidi Mohammed said. 'It's the best country on earth, by God! The only problem is that it has no economy and it's ruled by slaves. But if there were schemes like there are in Libya, every man working on his own farm, that would be so good. I hate living in the city. Your children die because the mothers can't feed them. In the desert there is always milk. Oh, yes, there's milk in the city if you can afford it, but not for the likes of us. Certainly not if you're white. I hate the city, but what can I do? All my life I've had nothing but fatigue, by God!'

Just then Marinetta announced that the sugar had finally run out. 'There'll be no sugar for coffee tomorrow morning,' she said.

Sidi Mohammed hesitated for a moment, then edged over to his sack. I remembered, guiltily, how I had squeezed it in Tillia. 'It happens I've got some sugar here,' he said, grinning and showing his vulpine teeth 'I brought it from Tombouctou. I thought it would come in useful before we finished.'

It took us three hours to reach the town the following morning, hiking along the shoulder of the highway, where juggernaut trucks juddered past, blind as moles. It was difficult to adjust to the power and speed of these vehicles after our slow-coach camels' pace. The animals were terrified of the fume-spitting monsters and shied away, straining on the headropes. Once Shigar's nose-ring was ripped out and had to be re-inserted.

We crossed the asphalt road, Sidi Mohammed directing like a policeman on point duty, and came to a hill from where the town sprawled out beneath us. It looked as big as Nouakchott. There were rings of new buildings across the outer skin and, in the centre, a pattern of streets circling the famous red mosque that stood out above them like a disjointed leg. We entered the back streets and came into a bustling market square. There was life here in plenty. The zinc roofed stalls were piled high with cheap, gaudy goods, clothes and colourful blankets. The streets were awash with milling bodies, black, brown and coffee-coloured. It was a confusion after the quiet of the desert. Several Tuareg youths attached themselves to our caravan as we dodged through the traffic and wove a winding course in and out of the crowds.

We found a small hotel tucked away down a side street, next to a filling station. The manager was a polite young Targui dressed in Western clothes, who brought us bottles of lemonade from the fridge. We looked on incredulously as a real frost formed on the outside of our glasses. We drank the lemonade and went out to unload our camels for the last time.

As we couched them, an enormous camper drew up at the filling station next door. There was a middle-aged Swiss couple in the front seat. Evidently they had come across the Sahara, but the desert had left little mark on them. Their dress was spotless and their coiffeured hair immaculate. I watched the sequence of expressions that played across their faces as they noticed us, beginning with 'Camels! How interesting!' and ending with 'Hippies! How disgusting!' as their eyes fell on our filthy clothes. After that they looked away.

We unloaded and moved our gear into the hotel store. The manager was very helpful and friendly. He told me confidentially, 'These youths who have followed you are all well known for robbing tourists. Don't trust any of them. I say this only for your *sûreté.*' I thanked him and went out to find Sidi Mohammed being hustled by a tough-looking Tuareg youth with a mop of spiky hair who was wearing a faded blue-denim suit. A few more diffident boys hung around behind him. Before I could speak the youth said in French, 'I will take your camels to the market. My uncle is the market manager. I will get good price for you!'

'*Merci,*' I answered. 'We don't need any help selling the camels. We know how much they're worth.'

The Targui looked belligerent, standing with his feet firmly apart, his hands thrust deep into his waistband. 'You know nothing here!' he said. 'We know everything!'

The aggressive posture somehow ignited a rocket of fury in my mind. 'If you don't clear off,' I told him, 'I'll wrap this stick around your neck, and *then* I'll call the *gendarmes!*' I felt the veins standing out on my forehead. My muscles were as tense as iron. I couldn't believe how vicious I felt. It was as if six months of the accumulated effects of living on the edge of survival were pouring out of me at once. Scoffing to himself, the youth called to his friends, and they strutted away.

Sidi Mohammed looked at me approvingly. 'Thieves and criminals!' he said.

As we approached the camel market, a toothless old man in an invalid chair came hurtling towards us and attacked us verbally. The sale of camels wasn't till that afternoon, he said, and there was a commission charged on animals brought into the market, whether they were sold or not. Finally, he allowed us to lash them to some hitching-posts and to wait until the appointed hour in the shade of his straw shelter. We spent our last few francs on bread and sat there enjoying the fresh texture of the stuff and watching the world go by like a film on a ciné-screen.

The Tuareg here looked different from those in Mali. They wore flowing robes in voluminous cotton, their swords always dangling from their left side, their headcloths and their veils, the famous *tagelmoust*, covering most of their faces. Their headcloths were arranged into elaborate crowns, twisted around the head in a halo or piled up into a spiralling column and held in place by a sash or belt. The Fulani we saw among them might have belonged to a different planet. They were darker, with odd, bony faces and hair gouged into short locks. They were very lean. They wore tight-fitting pantaloons of garish colours, leopard-skin and vermilion, and wide-brimmed sombreros of straw. Their women went bareheaded and wore scores of concentric earrings, which rattled as they walked. There were Arabs here too, merchants of Moorish origin who, as usual, dominated the camel trade. One of them, a stern-looking man called Najim, expressed some interest in our camels. 'They're very weak,' was his opinion.

'So would you be if you'd come as far as they have!' I told him.

Najim laughed. He agreed to buy all three.

As he led them away later, I felt miserable. I had become attached to all of them but especially to the patient Shigar, who had carried me from Chinguetti. I doubted that we should find such enduring desert camels here in Niger. Marinetta and I had already made a record-breaking trek, and we had done it during the most difficult time of the year. Yet I knew that more than half of any victory we had achieved belonged to those camels.

Sidi Mohammed was already packing away his gear. He intended to stay with a relative in Agadez for a day or two before catching the bus to Niamey and another to Gao and Tombouctou. I paid him the balance of his earnings out of the money I had just received from Najim and added a small bonus to buy new clothes or meat. I handed over the remains of the rice and powdered milk. I grinned. 'I don't suppose you want the sardines?'

'Gah!' he said. 'I'm going to eat meat tonight!' He put the food away and tied up his sack. 'If you come back next year, Omar,

I'll take you to Taudenni,' he said, 'but next time we'll go by car.'

'God willing,' I said, and we shook hands. Then he turned and walked away, as happy as he probably ever would be but still a lonely, tragic figure, slightly bowed and moving into the distance with the shuffling gait that had become so familiar to us.

We were back in our hotel before sunset. I sat down at our small table and unfolded the Michelin map. It was an antique now, coming apart along the folds and almost yellow where my fingers had scrabbled at it. I had marked the line of our march in red felt-tip. I looked at that line now, half way across the continent of Africa at its widest point. I stared and stared at it, trying to measure our achievement, but the coloured tracks and roads and settlements kept swimming out of focus, merging together and defying my attempts to separate them. I couldn't even remember having crossed that vast landscape. All I could remember now was the exhaustion and the torturing heat. We had covered almost 2,000 miles in the Sahara in the hot season. Now our journey was no more than a line on the map.

Sidi Mohammed was shouting, 'Omar! Omar! This is London! This is the chimes of Beeg Beyn, Boosh Hawse, London doobel-yew-cee-too! Dong! Dong! Dooong!' I awoke and found the sun streaming into the room and someone knocking at the door. I remembered hazily that we had arrived in Agadez the previous day. Wrapping a towel around me, I opened the door. It was Sidi Mohammed. I told him to give me a few minutes and I would meet him in the hotel courtyard. As I shut the door, Marinetta groaned, 'It's like the story of Mustapha's old shoes,' she said. 'Every time you think you've got rid of them, they turn up again.'

Sidi Mohammed explained nervously that his relative had advised him to report his presence here to the police, and asked if we could go to the police HQ together, since I had our *laissez-passer*. I told him to steady on and ordered breakfast. Some elderly French tourists entered and sat down, wishing us a hearty *'Bonjour.'* The men were stout, and their wide buttocks were encased in large pairs of shorts. The women wore expensive cotton dresses from Paris. Sidi Mohammed's eyes followed them distrustfully. 'I wouldn't have anything to do with the likes of *them*,' he said. 'Not even if they wanted a guide, I wouldn't. I prefer the young, open-minded types.' As we walked to the police HQ afterwards I asked if he had eaten meat the previous night. 'Yes, by God!' he said. 'I ate till I could eat no more.'

'You'll never have to eat sardines again,' said Marinetta.

'Gah!' he said.

We parted from him for the last time at the police HQ. Afterwards we explored the town. It was thriving now in the height of the tourist season. Most of the tourists drove down the Saharan highway from Tamanrasset, which they referred to as 'Tam'. Many of them were heading for Ouagadougou, capital of Burkina-Faso, which they called 'Wogga'. To me this seemed like calling New York 'New' or London 'Lon'. They looked as exotic as the locals, with their fluffy, tinted hair, their skin-tight jeans and their incongruous boots. They rode in Toyotas and Land-Rovers painted with legends such as 'Afrique '86' and 'Beyond the Sahara'. Their vehicles were equipped with rock-blaring stereos, freezers, cookers and water-sterilization units. To me they seemed more unapproachable than the Tuareg.

Near the red mosque we discovered a real Italian ice-cream parlour. It was owned by a bearded man called Vittorio. His hair was thin and white, and he wore a Moroccan caftan and a pair of jeans. Marinetta asked him how he liked working in Agadez. 'I don't work here. I *live* here!' he replied, anxious to stake his claim. He had once been a bank clerk in Rome and had arrived in Agadez with another Italian fifteen years before. They had run a flourishing tourist business with a fleet of vehicles, but the other man had died and business had dwindled. Now he was reduced to running an ice-cream parlour. 'Trade's not much good now, and winter's coming on,' he mourned. 'No one eats ice-cream in winter.' Vittorio was married to a Tuareg woman and they had several children. When I asked him if he spoke Tamasheq, he replied, '*Sono insabbiato* – I have got stuck here!' He wasn't a Muslim. His ambiguous dress, neither Western nor native, did not speak of great contentment in this environment, I thought.

Vittorio told us that if we wanted to go farther, we would have to consult the tourist office. It was the body that could give us permission to continue. When we visited the office that afternoon we came up against our first hurdle: a puffy-faced Tuareg in traditional dress, who was the office manager. His *tagelmoust* was drawn so tight that only a circle of brown flesh showed like a single giant eye. Marinetta christened him Polyphemus.

He asked where we wanted to go and shook his head at once when I said we intended to cross the Ténéré Erg as far as the oasis of Bilma. From there we would turn south across the Grand Erg of Bilma as far as Lake Chad. Polyphemus shifted in his chair. How many camels would we take? How much would we pay our guide? He doubted if we would be allowed to cross the Grand Erg, which was too near the fighting between the Libyans and Chadians in Tibesti. Had we any proof that we had come all the way from Mauritania? The Ténéré Erg was a dangerous place for foreigners. Even for locals it was a dangerous place. Polyphemus um-ed and ah-ed for an hour, saying, 'I have to think of your *sûreté*.' I felt like telling him that if we had had as much trouble from threats to our *sûreté* as we had had from petty officials talking about it, we should never have got past Nouakchott. In the end he sent us to Niamey to obtain official permission from the Interior Minister.

It was December before we got everything arranged. We returned from Niamey with a busload of tourists, armed with a formidable battery of documents. We had letters from the British and the Italian honorary vice-consuls to Niger, a letter from the Minister of the Interior giving us permission to cross both Ténéré and the Grand Erg and another authorizing us to enter Chad from the border post of N'Guigmi. The French Embassy had issued us with entry visas on behalf of Hissein Habri's Chadian government in N'Jamena. We had even obtained permission to take photographs. The wad of papers had taken us days to compile, days of dreadful waits in corridors and offices. During that time I concluded that governments fear wilderness. They are happier with towns and villages, where people are easier to control. That fear brought us constantly into conflict with the very bureaucracy from which we were trying to escape.

After we had presented our credentials to Polyphemus, we made a bee-line for the camel market. To our surprise there was another Westerner there buying camels. With him was a beaming little black Targui in Western clothes, who introduced himself as Musa. He said that he worked for the tourist office. 'Any trek you want, I can fix it up!' he said. 'My name is mentioned in *Africa on the Cheap*.' Musa's current charge was an Englishman. He was a red-faced man, a little younger than I, short and stocky, with very stony eyes. In three clipped, upper-class sentences he told us that he would be taking the same route as we were by camel, through Niger, Chad and the Sudan. He already knew about us, he said, through an organization called Friends of the Sahara in London. I told him I had never heard of it.

'In Africa,' our new acquaintance declared, 'one always has to work through an intermediary. That's why I'm employing the Musa chap. Always helps to make friends with the natives, you know.' I asked how long he had been in Africa. 'Arrived last week,' he said. He explained that his love of the desert had begun some years before, when he had made a camel journey in Morocco. Ever since then he had been planning to return. He suggested that as we were all travelling the same way, it would be a good idea to travel together.

'Do you speak Arabic?' I asked him.

'No,' he said. 'But I *have* got a satellite navigation unit.' And he was a Friend of the Sahara.

'Oh, Jesus Christ!' said Marinetta.

We had dinner with him that night. His conversation was punctuated by pauses during which he would drift off, his eyes focusing somewhere in the middle distance. He talked about the Tuareg, saying, 'They're the *real* desert people.'

'Sons of the Wind,' said Marinetta, smirking. I kicked her under the table.

'Quite,' he said. 'Take yesterday, when I arrived from Niamey. A Targui came to meet me on a motorbike and took me to see Musa. He was so friendly and hospitable, and he didn't charge me a penny.'

Before we had finished the conversation, the Targui who had collected him on his arrival entered and loudly demanded money for his petrol. In an attempt not to seem flustered, the Englishman said, 'May I introduce you to ...?'

'Don't bother,' I told him. 'We've already met.' The hospitable Targui was the youth I had threatened to assault outside our hotel on the day of our own arrival.

The next day I told our acquaintance that we would go on alone.

*

Bilma lay more than 300 miles north of east across the hyper-arid wasteland of the Ténéré Erg. For centuries salt caravans had traversed those sands, bringing salt from Bilma and the smaller oasis of Fachi. Once the caravans had travelled together for fear of raids. Nowadays they went piecemeal, only a hundred or so animals at a time. We had already decided that we would need five camels for this arid stretch. Two animals would be needed just to carry fodder for the others, for in these ergs there was very little grazing. It took us another week to assemble our caravan.

Each day we were in the market early, examining every camel for sale. We were helped by Najim, the Arab merchant who had bought our other camels. He told us they were now grazing in the Aïr plateau but that the two Moorish camels were still weak. Most nights, just before sunset, we would lead yet another camel to the local compound, where it would be looked after by an honest Hausa shepherd called Abu Bakri. In the mornings we acquired piles of provisions: cones of sugar, sheets of dried meat, tins of sardines and corned beef, rice, macaroni, couscous and biscuits, dates from Algeria and butter-oil from the USA. We bought six new waterbags to replace the worn-out ones we had brought from Chinguetti and ordered two new pack saddles, which were inexpertly made by Tuareg smiths. We also bought a sharp machete for cutting wood. The stores, increasing daily, were soon cramming the hotel's spare room.

By the end of the week we had our five camels and lacked only our new guide. We had often speculated about who he might be. Each guide was an adventure in himself, a unique chance for insight into the nature of Saharan people. Each of our three Moorish guides had been symbolic of some desert quality — Mafoudh was brotherhood, Moukhtar nobility, Sidi Mohammed tragedy. What would our next guide represent?

It turned out to be ripe old age. He was a Targui called Udungu Ag Ibrahim, a man of about sixty from Aïr. He was like everyone's grandfather, his face as bald and cherubic as a baby's under the *tagelmoust*. He had lived in Algeria and spoke Arabic as well as a little French. He was quiet, dignified and friendly, and he was quite used to Westerners. 'I went with *nsara* twice to Tamanrasset,' he said.

'But they drank so much wine! God help us, they were out of their wits most of the time!'

'There won't be any wine on our trip to Bilma,' I said.

'Good,' the old man replied, 'because Bilma is the hardest trek of all. I shouldn't really go there. I'm an old man now. I should stay home at night. But I've still got young children to look after. So I go.' I had no doubts about his strength. His limbs were massively powerful despite his age. He examined our camels and pronounced them good. Then he advised us to buy four plastic jerrycans to supplement our *girbas*. We arranged to leave Agadez on 13 December.

Udungu was waiting for us at the camel compound when we trundled our baggage up on a hired handcart. Together we walked to the market and bought two sacks of sorghum for the camels and five bales of the best hay, which we rearranged into two loads. Then Udungu bought a cheap woollen sweater. It was the only cold-weather clothing he possessed.

Marinetta and I had already taken our warm gear out from where it had remained sealed in the bottom of our saddle bags. I had an old nylon anorak, a heavy-duty pullover, tracksuit trousers and socks. Marinetta had brought a new down-filled jacket, warm trousers and a balaclava. Both of us had a pair of Gore-tex desert boots supplied for us by Asolo.

When all was ready the shepherd, Abu Bakri, brought the camels out of the compound and helped us to load. The compacted hay was the greatest problem, and the Tuareg pack saddles, poorly made by comparison with the Moorish one, were ill-fitting and inadequate. I was pleased with the camels, though. They seemed strong, patient animals for the most part, all of them geldings with well-padded humps. One was a very old animal, as strong as an elephant but missing several teeth. He was a veteran of the Bilma salt run, and we named him Shaybani, meaning 'the Old Chap'. Udungu chose to ride a youngish red camel, which Marinetta named Pepper, and I chose a sand-coloured animal with some unsightly but harmless swellings on his neck. We called him Abu Wirim, 'Father of the Swellings'. Marinetta rode a snowy-white camel, which we referred to as Abu Nakkas, or 'Father of the Quarrel', because he was the most troublesome of the group, yet also the strongest. The fifth camel had a hump so bulky that he could never have been ridden. We called him Abu Sanam, 'Father of the Hump'.

We tied the loaded camels into two strings. I took one headrope and the guide took the other. The two hay-carrying camels in Udungu's string looked very like haystacks with legs. 'It's a long time since I've been to Bilma by camel,' Udungu announced, pulling up his veil for a dignified departure, 'but I used to go there all the time when I was a boy. Once you've been, you never forget.'

'Didn't Mafoudh say that?' I asked Marinetta.

'How long is it since you went to Bilma by camel?' Marinetta asked the guide.

'About twenty years,' he replied.

'God help us!' she said.

We passed the market, where people jeered and cheered at us, and skirted around the edge of the town, past the petrol-storage tanks shining bright as silver, past cohorts of donkeys piled with firewood from the hills. We passed rocks and trees and grass and more rocks. When we were out of the city Udungu let his veil drop. This was like addressing someone as *tu* in French. It meant we could be friends. It was comical to see the wrinkled face tanned and brown about the mouth and pink below, where the *tagelmoust* usually covered it. Noble Tuareg were supposed to keep their mouths covered at all times, even while eating.

We camped on an island of grass and coarse bush pricking out of the rocky plain. Marinetta made rice, and we sat down to eat in the shelter of our hay bales, turned against the cold night wind from the north. Udungu produced from his saddle bag a very large wooden spoon like a serving spoon. 'Eh!' he said. 'We Tuareg don't eat with our hands as the Arabs do.' Udungu ate little, and he ate with consummate grace. There was no hint of a rude noise to be heard.

We spent the first hour of the morning rearranging our loads to make them more comfortable for the camels and easier for the three of us to shift. Then Marinetta and I went to fetch the animals. We managed to bridle four of them with only minor snuffling and snorting, but as I approached the last one, the red camel called Pepper, he took one look at the headrope and skipped away. His front legs were hobbled, but he had evidently mastered the technique of running with the back legs and hopping with the front. In moments he was many yards away.

I called Udungu and we made a concerted pincer movement, but the camel seemed to anticipate us and gambolled off out of reach. I cursed myself for not fixing the hobble tighter on a camel whose character I did not yet know. In desperation Udungu saddled Abu Wirim and went in pursuit. He worked his way around Pepper cunningly and carefully drove him back towards our camp. He inched closer and closer to the runaway. Suddenly the old man rose up out of the saddle, let go of the headrope and launched himself through the air like a free-faller, landing heavily on the red camel's back. For a moment he clung on desperately to the tufts of hair sprouting from his hump. Then the animal roared angrily and kicked out like a horse, charging forward on his hobbled legs. Udungu wobbled, then fell. He hit the ground with an audible crunch and lay there winded. The camel halted a hundred yards away and turned to watch.

I ran over to the old Targui, hoping desperately that he wasn't seriously injured. He sat up and rubbed his left wrist. It was badly bruised but not broken. I sat him down among the baggage and rubbed some analgesic balm into the sprain, then wrapped it in a bandage. He was a brave old man, I thought. I would never have dared to chance what he had just done. 'It's too late now,' he said. 'The camel knows both of us, and he won't let us get near him. If someone else tried . . .' We both looked at Marinetta.

'No!' she gasped. 'I'm too small! I can't do it!'

A few moments later I watched her walk up to the camel and bridle him as if she had done it every day for years.

We lost three hours over the red camel. It took us another hour to load. Udungu's sprained wrist hampered him, and the pain made him wince as we grappled with the hay. We lifted the two sacks of sorghum together, and Udungu grunted, 'I could lift that weight on my own once. Now look at me, by God! That's what old age does to you!' The provision sacks, crammed with enough food for weeks, were equally heavy. So were the large jerrycans, which had to be balanced over the bales of hay. The camels rose, complaining, to their feet. Within half an hour a headrope twanged. It was Abu Sanam's, at the back of Udungu's string. He sat down at once, and we only just prevented him from rolling on the hay. We clove the broken rope together, and while Udungu and I strained to lift the bales, Marinetta pulled on the bridle and encouraged the animal to his feet.

Things went smoothly for a time. Then Abu Sanam started bellowing again. *Twang!* went the headrope. *Waaaah! Waaaah! Waaaah!* went the camel. Rushing back, we saw that the hay had toppled forward and was threatening to pin the poor beast's neck to the ground. We removed the bales painfully, reset the saddle, then reloaded. So the morning passed, a string of disasters. Headropes broke, jerrycans tilted and leaked water, *drap, drap, drap,* into the sand. At noon halt the cooking pan collapsed and spewed rice and corned beef across the ground just as the food was ready. We had to build another fire and start again, while the camels shifted restlessly under their loads.

Things were worse in the afternoon, when we rode our new camels for the first time. We plodded along in silence until the cold set in, and Marinetta decided to put on her socks. She leaned hard across the litter to get at her feet. The saddle, dislocated suddenly by the shift of weight, tilted ominously. 'I'm falling, Maik!' she yelled. I slid down but was too slow to catch her as the litter keeled over and dropped her with a crash under the camel's feet. The girth was still caught round his legs, and as I pulled her clear he went berserk, kicking out and thrashing savagely at the weight dragging on his leg. I seized the headrope, but it was all I could do to keep him from bolting. He roared and spat and flailed like a drunken horse, dropping green vomit, his eyes ablaze with terrible madness. He stamped and beat at the litter until it cracked into matchwood splinters. He wasn't still until he had smashed it beyond repair. 'God Almighty!' Marinetta said, staring at the pathetic remains of the saddle that had carried her from Chinguetti. 'Just imagine if I hadn't got out of the way in time.' She was still shaking from the shock.

Bits of luggage were scattered about. Among them were the cameras, still in their padded holdall. Marinetta examined them with trepidation but found them intact except for a broken lens cap. The only spare saddle we had was one of those spiky Tuareg riding saddles, which I had brought along in case we needed to do any fast, light riding. As soon as I had fitted it into place and pulled the girth tight, the saddle split. I looked at it in exasperation, muttering, 'Those bloody useless Tuareg smiths!' We had no choice but to walk until we could rig up an alternative. I was relieved that Marinetta was unhurt. Bowling along later by the caravan, in her thick jacket and balaclava, she looked like a yellow teddy-bear. I took her hand for a while. It was very cold but as small and soft and delicate as a child's. A nice hand, I thought.

We walked until after sunset and made camp in the moonlight. A chilling wind cut down on us from the north. Marinetta shivered in her anorak. Her period was approaching and she felt feverish. I gave her an aspirin and told her to rest in her sleeping-bag. Udungu's wrist was hurting him, and as I re-dressed it, I noticed it was badly swollen. When I went to relieve myself later, I found that I had liquid diarrhoea, the worst I had suffered since leaving Chinguetti.

I awoke to a freezing dawn and saw the moon bathed in orange flame and, beyond it, the flamingo-pink essence of the sunrise. I lit a fire and woke old Udungu. He crouched over the flames, warming his ancient bones, and rolled a cigarette with rough tobacco and the type of brown paper used for wrapping parcels. He nursed his wrist and blew his nose loudly two or three times. It was like the bugle call of reveille. Marinetta, woken up by the trumpet blasts, immediately nicknamed him Tromboney.

As we moved down from the Aïr plateau over the next few days, the weather got progressively colder. We wore our jackets and boots constantly, and old Tromboney limped on with his threadbare blanket clutched around him. It was far colder when we were riding, so we walked longer hours. This arrangement didn't suit our guide. After two hours of walking, he would say, 'It's tiring, by God!' Then he would add, 'I'm an old man now. I can't walk all day as I used to.'

'You ride when you feel like it, uncle,' I told him, but he always felt it necessary to make some apologetic remark before hoisting himself into the saddle.

Gone were the days of rests and midday shelters. Now we halted for no more than a few minutes at noon, dipping into a meal cooked the previous evening, followed up by a handful of dates. Udungu would eat only the soft dates. 'I can't eat the hard ones,' he told me. 'I haven't got the teeth for it. I'm like old Shaybani, the camel. He's an old man, and so am I. The Ténéré has worn us both out.' His lack of teeth gave him problems with the macaroni too. I watched him chewing it in vain with his soft gums. 'Can't you cook it longer?' I asked Marinetta. 'The poor old boy can't eat it.'

'I cook it as it's supposed to be cooked,' she said. 'It's *al dente*. Don't try to tell an Italian how to cook pasta!'

Udungu had been a regular rider across Ténéré as a youth. He had made his first journey to Bilma by camel at the age of fourteen. That must have been in about 1926. Since then he had travelled all over the Sahara, first as a caravaneer and later as a guide. One experience that he shared with Sidi Mohammed was having seen the inside of a prison. In his case, though, the prison had been Algerian. He had taken some camels for sale in Libya and, having sold them in Tripoli, had recrossed the Algerian frontier. He had been arrested in Djanet. 'They took me before the judge,' he said, 'and he asked me, "Where is your passport?" "I don't know passports," I said. "Do you know prison?" he asked me. "Because that's where you're going!" And that's where I went.'

'How was it?'

'It wasn't so bad. We got food. We got tobacco. We didn't have to do anything but sit all day. I was there for three months. There were all kinds of people there – men, women and children, Arabs and Tuareg, and even Christians.'

He had once been a guide for caravans smuggling cigarettes and other goods north and south across the Sahara. 'The cars get searched,' he said, 'but no one sees the caravans.' He told us that he had once brought a caravan of forty camels from Tindouf to Agadez, heavily laden with copper. There had been little grazing on the way, and when they reached Agadez thirty of the forty camels had dropped dead. '*Shshshok!*' he said. 'Dropped dead just like that, poor things. And the ones that didn't were never the same again. Ha! Ha!'

Recently, though, he had retired to Agadez. He had remarried late and had six young children. He had taken out a licence as a registered guide and travelled often with tourists, generally by motor vehicle. It was several years since he had ridden a camel, he said. 'I shouldn't really be here,' he told me. 'It's a hardship for an old man. But when you've got young children, that's the price you have to pay. You have to keep working if you need the money.' Udungu had once owned camels and goats and had pitched his tents in the Aïr mountains. I asked him if he had any camels left. 'Only one,' he said, 'and he's got the mange.'

After four days we watered in the wadi Borghat, in a pit about 6 feet deep. There was no one about but a Tuareg woman with some goats. She had a broad, primeval, elemental face, like an embodiment of the Sahara. It was neither black nor white: there was a touch of nobility in it, a touch of earthy ignorance, a pinch of joy and sadness. She giggled at us when we attached our saucepan to a rope to use it as a well bucket and spread out our plastic sheets as a watering trough. She was justified. After two fills the saucepan sploshed into the well and floated cheekily on the water. I was about to tie myself to a rope and go down for it, when Udungu clambered into the pit using an old frame of wood lying along its side. He climbed out, grinning, with the pan in his sprained hand.

The woman went off with a long staff and began knocking carobs down from the *talha* trees as the goats clustered around her feet. She saw Marinetta pointing the camera at her and giggled again. Later she came back with a leather well bucket and helped us to fill our jerrycans. A razor-edged wind blew across the great erg and dashed itself among the thorn trees. When the watering was finished I gave the woman a block of sugar and some tea, which she screwed up in a square of faded cloth. I offered her some *zrig*, but she tasted it and wrinkled her face into a grimace. I wondered what she must think of us.

It was late afternoon before we got moving. Tromboney was for remaining in the wadi the night to let the camels graze, but as usual I wanted to push on. 'When I go by car I just sit back and do nothing,' he grumbled. 'With the camel there is too much work, by God!'

The sun was going down behind us in pink dragons rampant. Moonrise came like a fiery eye. Coolness spilled out of the moonlight and washed across the flagstone desert floor. There was silence but for the percussion of camels' feet and the creaking of saddles. Often I looked behind to check that they were all there. The monster-insect

ruins of a camel skeleton gaped at us insanely out of the shadows.
A little farther on was a dead camel, still intact except for vacant eye
sockets, smelling of decay. Udungu said that it must have fallen out
of a salt caravan quite recently. That night we halted in a rocky creek
where a few barbed-wire trees were fodder for the camels. They were
the last trees we saw until Fachi.

We awoke to the noise of a high wind licking out of the night,
sucking at the eardrums and scourging us with sand. It was icy. There
was nothing to be seen beyond the capsule of our creek. The camels
had wandered far down the wadi in search of food and were huddled
together against the cold. They sniffed resentfully as we offered the
headropes, jumping up and snapping when we reached for their nose-
rings. By the time we had heaved on the baggage the sun was up in
a flurry of red and grey. We trudged on across a fractured land of
peaks and ridges, while the sand-rasping gale tore at us, soughing
and sighing through the desert, drawing mournfully across the sharp
rocks like a violin bow on a lank string. The wall of sound slammed
at our heads, drugging us dumb, whispering in tongues, drowning
our senses under a tuneless bagpipe haw. It was too cold to sit for
long in the saddle, but when we walked the sand-blown grit was
worse. We bandaged our heads like mummies and turned, crab-like,
away from the lacerating sand.

Soon the texture of the earth changed. The rocks fell away, and
we advanced on rippled flats of sand. The wind wheezed out of the
erg with its hollow entrails. The camels stopped, sullenly leaning
away from the whipping dust. Abu Wirim sat down and cast his
load. Udungu and I teetered in the thrashing hail, grunting with the
weight of the grain sacks. Once the camel was up, we noticed the
jerrycans leaking. We couched Abu Sanam and readjusted the balance.
If we looked directly into the wind, needles of sand stung our eyes
sharply. We were on our way again when the oilcan sprang a leak
and had to be plugged. Next the hayloads slipped forward, first on
one camel, then on the other. 'Damn this hay!' I cursed through the
wind. 'It's the cause of all our problems.'

'Hay is better than money in Ténéré!' Udungu shouted back. 'You'll
see! You'll see!'

We kicked and thumped at the camels until they got up and staggered into the eye of the storm.

We walked for hours. My legs trembled with weakness. The day got no warmer. Udungu stomped on with his poor piece of blanket. Sometimes he would sit down with his back to the wind, ducking under his covering to light a wretched cigarette from his glueless brown paper. In two puffs it would be finished. His eyes were full of sand. Once he sat down and clawed at them feverishly. 'I can't see *anything*! I can't see *anything*!' he repeated. He took from his pocket a phial of antimony and applied it delicately to his eyelids with a make-up brush. The black-circled lids gave him a momentary trans-vestite look. Then the sand began to stick to the antimony, building up into bushy growths like goggles on his face. Marinetta forgot the cold and laughed for ten minutes.

The sabre edge of the wind soon slashed away her humour. The earth was flailing at us with elemental anger, trying to obliterate us from its face. The cold penetrated right to the marrow. Had we really run the gauntlet of that terrible heat only weeks ago? This desert was desolate, too desolate for human beings. We were on one of the most famous caravan routes of the Sahara, yet it was difficult to imagine anyone else being in this primeval land before us. But other Westerners had endured conditions even worse than this. In 1815, for instance, there had been the British sea captain James Riley. He had set out with a caravan of 4,000 camels and 1,000 men when a storm like this had attacked them. Hundreds of men and animals had simply disappeared. Desperate for water, the guide had ordered his servants to slaughter some of the camels so that the survivors could drink their blood. But no one had wanted his own camels butchered, and the cameleers had struck back viciously at the servants, killing them and the guide. Then they had drunk the blood of corpses and camels. One of the drinkers had been Riley, who had thrust his head up to the shoulders in a camel's open belly and swallowed the nauseating liquid. He was among the twenty-one men who survived.

The camels were gasping with the cold. Dragging behind them, Marinetta was sobbing. 'Shut up!' I told her. 'This is the challenge we came for. Crying won't get you anywhere. When the going gets tough, the tough get going!'

'You're just a robot!' she squealed at me. 'You have no feelings for anyone!'

'You can't afford feelings when you're dead!' I said.

That day we marched eleven hours without a break. By evening we were dropping with exhaustion. We made camp in a sandy crack beneath the shark's tooth of Azzuager mountain. As soon as we unloaded, the camels pressed themselves together, shuddering. Udungu was shivering too, and he quickly got into the shelter of the hay bales. I laid out some hay for the camels, while Marinetta piled the equipment into a windbreak. We cooked the evening meal with our legs stuffed into our sleeping-bags. The wind and sand eddied out of the emptiness.

Marinetta grumbled about my heartlessness and sulked. Unable to sympathize, I told her, 'This is the challenge you wanted. Crying's a disgrace. Where's your stiff upper lip?'

'That's just your bloody British crap!' she said. 'You British think it's wrong to show your feelings. I don't feel any different from you, but to us Italians it's not a disgrace to show it. Stiff upper lip! What rubbish!'

I reminded her that if it hadn't been for my insistence, she would be wearing the wafer-thin ski jacket she had brought with her for the Saharan winter. Only my advice had made her send to Rome from Nouakchott for the mountain jacket she now wore constantly. 'Where did you think you were going?' I asked her. 'To a fashion show?'

'If I was, you would be the last person I'd take with me!' she stormed. 'You look more like a dockworker than a gentleman!' Then she turned over in her sleeping-bag and refused to speak again till morning.

When we awoke we were half buried in sand. As I climbed out of my sleeping-bag a bitter chill gripped me. I trembled violently, desperately trying to hold a match still enough to light the fire. Udungu's face was a caved-in pelt of suffering. He looked a hundred years old. He had no down-filled sleeping-bag to protect him; he had no more protection, in fact, than the ragged old blanket that covered his bones by day. He had no socks either, and his feet were almost blue inside their plastic moccasins. I gave him my spare socks and he pulled them on gratefully. But afterwards he sat in front of the dying fire, mesmerized, half paralysed by the crippling wind. Marinetta stood watching me, shivering and unable to move. Even the camels were wretched, braying miserably as I attached the headropes. 'Come on!' I urged the others. 'Let's get moving! If we don't move now, we'll die here!'

We loaded and set off into the freezing wind. Marinetta, warmed by a mug of scalding coffee, slung her cameras around her shoulder, hoping to get some unusual shots of the caravan in the sandstorm. I was glad her pang of apathy had passed. Old Tromboney took the headrope and stamped on doggedly right into the heart of the storm. The desert was electric and alive, sobbing and wailing like a banshee demon. The cursing chorus of the wind was hypnotic. Water spilled, and the jerrycans had to be balanced. The hay slid forward. The walking haystacks sat down and turned out of the wind. The rest of the camels crowded round, chewing hungrily at the precious grass as we strained to lift it. Marinetta fought them off with a stick.

Later she lost another lens cap and ambled off into the dust to retrieve it. I turned to find her gone and was petrified with sudden terror. I glimpsed the puffy yellow pads of her jacket through the swirls of sand, and I told Udungu to stop while I fetched her back. I ran across the sand until I found her. 'I've got to find that lens cap!' she shouted.

'To hell with the lens cap!' I shouted back, dragging her forcibly to the caravan.

That afternoon we passed a mace-shaped marker of black steel, which showed that we had entered the great erg of Ténéré. An hour later, when the wind had already begun to thrash itself out, we saw our first salt caravan. There were 100 camels in two coiling silver strings like centipedes. Their tentacle-like legs seemed to flow out like sea plants in a current. Three men came dashing towards us across the sand. They asked for nothing but to shake hands. I understood their need for human contact in this dreadful void.

At sunset we made camp by the hulk of a burned-out car. As we unloaded the wind stopped suddenly. Now the silence lay on us, heavy and unnatural after the searing noise of the sand. I could hear a phantom *shooooosh, shoooooosh*, like the sea sound in shells. The stillness was complete. It was broken only by old Tromboney who sat down and groaned, 'Aaaah! God! These shoes are killing me!' The cheap plastic shoes had brought up red blisters on his ankles beneath the socks. They were too small for his calloused feet. He borrowed my knife and slit the plastic on the heel and the uppers. Then he tried them on and beamed with satisfaction.

After dinner I asked him if he had any idea what had happened to the occupants of the car. 'God knows!' he said. 'There are plenty like this in Ténéré.' He said the word carefully, with reverence almost. 'People have died here, oh, many people. Many die in Ténéré! The Ténéré is the worst desert in the Sahara. The government won't let anyone go without a guide. They don't let any car go alone, not after what happened to the *préfet*'s wife.' Udungu related how, two years before, the wife of the *préfet* of Agadez had set off across the Ténéré in a Land-Rover. With her had been a driver, her three children and the best guide in the area. None of them was ever seen alive again. 'Every guide in Agadez was called out to search,' he said. 'I was one of them. There were planes; there were army and police. It was nine days before they found the bodies – all dead. They had turned off the main route after passing Fachi: no one knew why. The Land-Rover was *kaput*, and their water was finished. They found the guide's body miles away. He must have gone off to look for water and died before he found any. The wife had written notes. She said she saw the planes passing, but they didn't see her. That's Ténéré – it's wild, by God!'

The story was awful, and I was glad suddenly for the low temperatures. In summer this place would have been doubly terrifying. Udungu said that there had been similar deaths every year until the government had erected a series of markers, like the one we had seen earlier that day. Without them, he said, it was almost impossible to travel in a straight line.

I soon understood the need for the markers. The desert we walked out into the next day was utterly featureless. It was a vast, endless sand-sea, the largest in the central Sahara, larger even than the fabled 'Empty Quarter' of Arabia. The emptiness of it was suffocating. There was nothing at all to attract the eye but the metal flags spaced out every kilometre. It was like walking on a cloud, an unreal nebula that might cave in at any moment. Sometimes its dappling ripples looked like water, a still, untided ocean undulating to every horizon. In all that vastness there was not a tree, not a rock, not a single blade of grass.

In the afternoon we passed another salt caravan. There were perhaps 200 camels this time. From afar the columns of animals seemed to stand still. They appeared to remain motionless until we came abreast of them, then they sprang out suddenly into three dimensions. It was a strange phenomenon caused by the lack of anything to mark the distance between us. Tuareg in white robes rode among the laden camels. They looked like scanning machines, welded to their camels' backs and periscoping out into the emptiness through the embrasures in their veils. Udungu called out something to them in Tamasheq, but the words fell back lifeless on the sterile sands, and the caravan flowed on unstoppably until it was swallowed by the maw of the Ténéré.

We saw nothing else moving until sunset was near. Then we heard the boom of engines and pinpointed two trucks in the sand. Like the salt caravan earlier, they appeared not to be moving. Not until we passed them did they seem to accelerate into action, roaring by a mile away. Or was it 2 miles? Or even 10? There was no way to judge distance or scale in Ténéré. I remember only the grating gears ricocheting over the dark sand, the trucks creeping like caterpillars and the spirals of smoke from their exhaust. I recall old Udungu saying, 'Trucks are no good in the Ténéré. Camels are better, by God!' I remembered having read somewhere that goods could be moved by camel here at one-seventh the cost of motor transport. That was why the great caravans still existed.

We walked on in the deep sand, and the shadows of our camels spread out before us, horrific crane-fly shapes on the unblemished surface. Far away was an object bigger than a marker but unidentifiable in the vastness. We plodded towards it for hours. Udungu said, 'I can't walk any more. I'm an old man.'

'Ride, uncle,' I told him.

Stalking up on her slim legs, Marinetta muttered, 'Sons of the Wind! More like Gone with the Wind!' Poor Udungu must have wondered what we were laughing at.

I quickened my step towards the object, but it was not until I was right beside it that I realized it was a curious metal structure. It looked like a science-fiction robot, a column of iron growing out of some oil drums, with lamp-post-like branches and two huge crystal eyes that gazed vacantly across the erg. Marinetta said it looked like a totem pole. There was a mud-brick wall near it and beyond it a hut of Sodom's Apple stalks. Udungu told us that this was l'*Arbre de Ténéré* – 'the Tree of Ténéré'. On this spot had grown the only tree in the whole vast erg until it had died in 1975. One story, probably apocryphal, was that it was hit by a truck. For generations the tree had guided caravans to a brackish well near by, now hidden by a mound of ordure. The steel monument stood as a tribute to the last ancient life of this sand-sea and as a marker of the place where the old Bilma caravan track met the new route to Libya.

It was bitterly cold again that night, but Marinetta stole some pieces of Sodom's Apple wood from the hut as we passed it and picked up some ends of *talha* wood left by a lorry crew. In the morning it was frosty but clear. It seemed to take old Udungu longer to get his old bones cranked up now that the cold had set in. He would make his own tiny fire and sit staring into the flicker of flame, his leathery face reflecting the orange firelight until the sun, leaping up from behind, stirred him into action. The camels would be blubbering in a knot 5 yards away, and we would spread out a few sheaves of hay among them as an early-morning snack. They refused to eat the grain we had brought. As the guide had predicted, I felt very grateful for the hay.

All day we saw not a single feature. The effects of the lack of scale were curious. I watched Marinetta once as she ran away from our caravan trying to get a shot of us from the front. She zig-zagged crazily over the sand, looking so ridiculous that I laughed. When I tried it myself I realized that without anything to fix on, it was impossible to run in a direct line. Any ripples or shadows on the surface gave the impression of relief. We found ourselves moving towards what appeared to be a mass of dunes only to find them dissolving into sandy waves a few inches high. A piece of discarded firewood could be mistaken for a camel or a tent, a blackened sardine can for an abandoned car. Once that afternoon Udungu said, 'There's a campfire ahead of us, by God!' We moved towards a red-gold spot some distance away. It was the sun's reflection on the surface of a rusty marker.

Early the next morning we came to the beginning of the great dune chain that stretched unbroken as far as the oasis of Fachi. The colour of the dunes was insubstantial, made fuzzy by a fine drift of sand over them, producing a shiny effect of silver, gold and metallic blue. They shimmered like the colours of a Persian carpet, altering constantly with the sun, a dynamo of change, a mobile display of shape, shade and texture. All the dunes were formed parallel with the prevailing north-east wind, which meant that we were travelling along with them and rarely crossing them. The sand looked like an ice-cream dressing: the dunes were perfectly made icing-sugar scallops. The sand was sensuous, undulating, curving voluptuously like smooth, creamy female flesh. The sand hills were like Reubens models, full-bodied beauties stretching naked on an endless beach.

The stillness brought harmony. The camels floated along with effortless grace. The fear had gone with the savagery of the storm, and we were no longer numbed or frightened by this vista of emptiness. 'The sand makes you feel free,' Marinetta said. 'It gives you a strange feeling – you want to throw your clothes off and run through it naked, then lie down in the middle of it and make love. It would be really fun to lie in the sand and roll down the dunes and to feel the softness of the sand all over my body.' I caught her feelings instinctively. The void of sand touched off something deeply sensual, set something very ancient stirring in your loins. It *was* a kind of freedom, the liberation of an essence repressed and savage, the beast at bay in the shadows, the tiger burning vicious, bursting, beneath the skin. It was the reptile left behind us in the water, the dog-shark basking in the deeps, the slinking wolf-bitch lurking in the forest, all beckoned and drawn here now to the shadowed surface by this savage wilderness of Ténéré.

That evening, as we were making camp, Marinetta said, 'Let's put the tent up tonight.'

'It's not so cold,' I said. 'It's no colder than usual.'

She removed her glasses and looked at me steadily, challengingly, with her big, child's eyes. 'Who mentioned anything about the cold?'

After we had eaten, Udungu went off to his shelter of blankets and hay bales, and I doused the fire. A few minutes later Marinetta called me from inside the tent, and I crawled in to find her curled up with her sleeping-bag pulled up to her chin. She wore neither glasses nor headcloth, and in the darkness her white teeth shone faintly. 'Now I *am* cold,' she said. I slid my hand into the downy warmth of the sleeping-bag. Inside she was totally naked. 'Have you forgotten?' she asked, as I looked at her in surprise. 'This is our honeymoon.'

The next day we topped a rise and saw a Cessna aircraft in the sand. For an instant I thought it had just landed. Then I noticed that its doors had been flung off, and the creeping sands had coiled into its belly. I wondered how long ago it had fallen out of the sky. Had its passengers died or survived? 'That's been here eight years,' Udungu said. 'Sandstorm.' It was amazing. The hull was so shiny that it might have been there only a day. I guessed that the abrasive desert sand had polished it and kept alive its colours. 'When it's your time, down you go,' Udungu said. 'Camel, car or plane, it's all the same.'

'It makes you feel humble,' Marinetta said. 'All the most advanced machines we've made can't stand against a desert storm. People always talk about conquering nature, but it can't be conquered. We're part of it, aren't we? How can you conquer something that you're a part of? It's all so well balanced, life and death, famine and plenty, rain and drought, that there must be a guiding mind behind it. It's all too perfect. You can see it so clearly in the desert. The desert is really the place to find God.'

I remembered Mafoudh saying, 'Anyone who thinks there is no God must be blind! Who do they think made all *this*?'

Time's passage was marked only by the wax and wane of the sun. It was universal time, whole and unfragmented. Dunes overlapped dunes. Sand washed like water over camel tracks, camel dung, human tracks, tyre tracks, the litter of engine parts, hulks of vehicles, the shell of an aeroplane: ice-cream sand, unblemished sand, sand with sulphur-yellow beneath it, sand of crimson-red. We followed our markers, travelling on the side of a slope where the valley was hidden by the chiffon veil of sand. It was like travelling on the edge of the world. Was this Mafoudh's place where the earth ended and you stepped off into the abyss?

Suddenly there was no marker ahead. The sand-sea seemed at once more threatening without the familiar black flag. Udungu forced his camels down into the low ground without a word. I felt sure the marker must be farther up and did not follow him. I had followed our guides for thousands of miles: why this sudden obstinacy filled me I shall never know. An instant later Udungu was out of sight behind the dunes. I carried on with Marinetta behind me. Then the headrope broke. Old Shaybani refused to go any farther up the slope. Perhaps the old camel sensed that something was amiss. I had to dismount and grab his jaw with one hand while hanging on to the rope with the other. My own camel wouldn't keep still, and finally I had to unhitch the rope and retie it. When I remounted Udungu was still nowhere in sight. We shuffled on for a few more minutes. A faint sound, vaguely human, drifted across the desolation. A nag of worry crossed my forehead. It had been wrong to split up. I had no choice now but to keep on going, with Marinetta following on silently. The next ten minutes were a lifetime: then I noticed some camel droppings in the sand. They must have come from a salt caravan, which meant there must be a route here. I followed them for a few moments and cleared a low dune. From there I saw the next marker, standing out like a monolith, magnified by the emptiness. Old Udungu was moving towards it on his camel. He was waiting for us when we reached it.

'Omar!' the old man croaked. 'Do you know the way? Are you a guide? What were you thinking of to split up like that? Listen, it's splitting up that makes all the trouble in Ténéré. Splitting up kills people in Ténéré. There are jinns in Ténéré, Omar, bad spirits. If a jinn gets into your head, you don't know east from west. The jinn spins your head around. They make you think you know the way when you don't. Why did the *préfet*'s wife die? Jinns! Why did her guide leave the road he knew? Jinns! Why have so many died here? Jinns! The jinn was inside you today, Omar. Don't laugh at the jinns. You can't see them, but they're there. They can kill you easily, the jinns!' He looked at me over his veil with unsmiling, ancient eyes. 'This Ténéré is the worst desert in the Sahara, Omar,' he said. 'The Ténéré is wild!' I didn't argue. However you expressed it, the jinn had been in me all right.

On 24 December two big black crows settled in the sand as we struck camp, waiting to pick at our discarded tins and grains of spilt rice. A little later we saw the smudge of pencil-black along the horizon that marked the cliffs of Fachi. We dawdled on, lulled by the sound of the camels' pads. Marker after marker went by. Suddenly one of the markers read 'Fachi'. At almost the same moment I saw a smoky line of palm trees like a dark parade of Zulus by the cliffs. We descended out of the sand-sheet towards a cluster of buildings on a mound. The green of palms and acacias and gardens was miraculous in this sterility. The contrast was complete. We made camp on the tilting slope, and a uniformed *gendarme* came out to welcome us. Our departure from Agadez had been announced on the radio, he said.

The *gendarme* settled down with Udungu to drink tea. Darkness closed in. It was Christmas Eve, a night linking other times in my life, the parts left behind and the parts yet to come. Christmas. It had a homely ring. But I knew that more than anywhere else I would rather be here, with my wife, with this old Targui, in this miraculous green island in the earth's greatest desert.

Camels woke us, grumping and keening, hundreds of camels. A salt caravan had crept up on us in the night, and its camels were couched 500 yards above us on the sand-sheet. Another caravan, an outward-bound one, lay couched by the palm trees below us, amid a Himalayan range of salt packs, pack saddles and hay bales.

As I opened my eyes I found a bulky stocking lying across my sleeping-bag. It was an instant reminder of all those Christmases past. It was a childish, yet touching, symbol of Western culture. Inside the stocking were biscuits and dates, a new toothbrush, a tiny notebook, the rounded cap of a sugar cone and a piece of soap in a box, saved from the far-off Hôtel Azalai in Tombouctou. At the very bottom my fingers closed on some pieces of charcoal. Marinetta laughed as I brought them out. 'In Italy Papa Noel brings charcoal for the badly behaved children!' she said.

I kissed her and said, 'Happy Christmas.' Then old Udungu surfaced, a beardless, nut-brown Santa Claus. We gave him a bag of tobacco, and he beamed at us. I wished that I could have given him a box of Rizla cigarette papers.

Fachi was the best present of all. It was the jewel of the sands. For centuries its diffident Beriberi inhabitants had been plagued by the rapacious camel men of the Sahara. They had been pillaged by hawk-faced Tuareg from Aïr and Arabs from the Fezzan. Toubou raiders, the black terror of the eastern Sahara, had come striding out of their stronghold in Tibesti to besiege the place. Little wonder Fachi was built like a fortress. Its houses were very close together along febrile, winding alleys, twisting and snaking left and right, opening suddenly into an unseen courtyard shaded by a green tree, then closing up again and jerking out of sight. The houses were entered by very tight slit-openings, too narrow for a man to pass through without turning sideways. Little Beriberi women stood at them as we passed, wearing many-coloured blankets. The fortified labyrinth of streets was crumbling and dissolving, the palm beams standing out through cracks in the clay. The great bastion that stood over the town was crumbling too, and blocks of masonry littered the passageways beneath it. Beyond the honeycomb of buildings lay the screen of the palm groves, and through openings in them was visible the vast yellow erg of Ténéré, rearing up like a tidal wave.

After we had inspected the old town we walked down to watch the salt caravan loading. There were about 200 camels, formed into squads, among which men rushed about tightening ropes, balancing salt packs and stringing camels together. Each animal carried several pillars of salt wrapped carefully in sheets of woven palm fibre. The salt packs hung high on the camels' backs, and above each saddle was a cylinder of tightly packed hay, which would feed the animals on the return journey. The camels were slung together in tens or dozens, and most of them were muzzled with straw masks to prevent them from eating the hay. Scores of Beriberi women from the oasis were bustling about the caravan with bowls and trays. They were collecting the tons of fresh camel droppings that were valuable for making bricks and for fuel. We stood and watched the caravan as it moved out into the erg on its way back to Agadez, section after section, column after column, like a great legion, until laden camels and walking men seemed to fill the landscape. I wondered what the old salt caravans must have looked like. Here there were 200 animals. In 1908 there were supposed to have been 20,000 in a single caravan. Once, in the Sudan, I had travelled with a herd of almost 1,000 camels, which had dominated the desert for miles. Twenty times that number seemed unimaginable.

We bought a new load of hay from the incoming caravan, and some firewood. Some Toubou tribesmen sold us two of their saddles with wide wooden frames and tails of wood. I was familiar with this type of saddle from my days in the Sudan and knew it was far superior to anything used in the western Sahara. The presence of these Toubou, short, slim, black-featured men, reminded me that in a few days we should be out of the world of the Tuareg and into the bleaker, wilder and more dangerous region of the eastern Sahara.

Before leaving we had to refill our water set. The only water available was in a palm garden, at the base of a steep incline that our camels were unable to descend. The garden belonged to a Beriberi who was using a sweep well, a weighted mast of wood on a pivot, which drew up the water from a shallow pit. These sweep wells were very ancient, dating back at least to the time of Pharaonic Egypt. I had to carry the four jerrycans up the steep slope, collapsing breathlessly as I reached the top each time. Udungu was fussing over the saddles, and Marinetta kneeled down to take shots of my agonized features as I battled with the slope. 'Brilliant shots!' she said.

'Thanks a bloody million!' I gasped.

We led our camels off through the palm trees and past the white crusts of salines, where the newly arrived caravan was filtering in. We turned through a pass in the cliffs, and a few hours later we were out once again in the unsullied sands of Ténéré, passing into dunes like whipped cream. The grey massif of rocks fell far behind, veiled in a wash of dust. Fachi was no more than a green memory, but that Christmas had been one that would stay with me always.

The next morning two cars growled quietly past like shining, mechanical spiders crawling along the raw crust of the sand. One of them stopped ahead, and a man and a woman got out. They were German tourists who were visiting Bilma for Christmas. They were dressed in shorts and T-shirts, though we were muffled in our turbans and jackets. The door of their Toyota fell open, and the smell of cosy Christmas warmth drifted out. As we rode away the man took some shots of us with a video-camera. 'Plenty of Christians come to Bilma at Noel,' Udungu said. 'The people in Agadez and Bilma make plenty money from the Christians at Noel. I used to travel with the Christians in their cars. You do nothing but say, "Go right!" "Go left" and "Straight on." There's no cold in a car. This cold is getting too much for an old man like me.'

I smiled at him, but I knew that for me this journey would have been meaningless in a car. I would have watched the desert go past as if on a TV screen, living within the safety of an artificial environment and separated from the desert by speed and tremendous range. I knew that motor travel was not without its risks, and I appreciated the expeditions of pioneers to whom vehicles presented technical problems that were challenging and interesting to an enthusiast. But vehicles cut one off from that sense of unity with the earth that was almost a religious sacrament for me. The slow march of our camels allowed us to see and feel everything around us. We saw the tiny sand-skippers that hollowed out minute crevices in the surface, and the small burial mounds of jerboas. We saw the tracks and spoor of caravans, which told the detailed story of their progress. We saw the power, beauty and primitive sensuality of the sands, felt the fluctuations of heat and cold, experienced the cycle of day and night unhindered by the presence of artificial light. A car could cross Ténéré in two days, when it took us seventeen, but after two days the magnificent sand-sea would be no more than a blur in your memory. For us there was no contact with the outside world, no easy route to safety. We were in the Sahara and of it, as we had always wished to be.

For two days we ploughed on through a freezing wind. It cut across the erg like a scythe, droning from sunrise to sunset with the deep notes of an engine. Often we looked behind, thinking a vehicle was coming, and realized it was only the wind. The sky remained blue and cloudless, yet the wind whipped at us with freezing breath. It blew in gusting oscillations lasting two or three seconds. Between bursts you could feel the steaming heat of the sun scourging down. Then the heat would be obliterated by a reprise of the freezing air. We were crossing through an expanse of dunes like a ladder in the smooth nylon of the erg. Marinetta wore two blankets and two pairs of trousers, and still she shivered with cold. The camels took every opportunity to turn away from the avenging fury, sitting down and shaking so violently that several times I was almost flung out of the saddle. Their eyes dripped mucus tears as we forced them on into the cold.

When we sat down to eat now we would gobble enormous amounts of rice and couscous, shovelling the food into our mouths like starvelings. 'The cold isn't so bad,' Udungu said once, 'as long as you have plenty of food. In the winter it's food you need, not water.' I felt hungry almost constantly. There was a nagging ache in my stomach all morning, and often I would look at my watch, saying to myself, 'Not long now till we eat!'

The relief came when the wind dropped. Then we would roll up our jackets, and Udungu would break out of the cocoon of his blanket and beam again through his broken teeth and his big, warm eyes in the wrinkled walnut face. At those moments he would talk about his life smuggling camels to Libya and about his experiences with the different peoples of the Sahara. 'The Arabs and the Christians are brothers,' he said, 'but the Tuareg are different. They are an old people, who were here before the Arabs and the *nsara*. But the Tuareg are better than the Toubou. The Toubou are devils. They don't fear God. They kill without mercy. Don't take a Toubou guide from Bilma, Omar. Take a Beriberi. The Beriberi are honest people.'

On 29 December we crossed a ridge and saw the grey tip of the Kawar cliffs with the oasis of Bilma standing beneath them. In the old days the people of Bilma had learned of the approach of a salt caravan by the 'singing' of a nearby mountain peak, which reverberated whenever a caravan was within two days of the place. Nobody listened to the peak any more. Now they had the radio.

The oasis announced its presence to us in subtle ways as we traversed doldrums of sand. There was a rusty bollard from a previous generation of markers, toppled over and lying in the dust like an unexploded bomb. There were clumps of grass, the occasional palm tree. Then the whole grey-green vista of the oasis leapt into perspective below us, with those same steel signposts that had led us across the erg ushering us down to the well-defined track. It led into the belly of the settlement like a drawbridge. We passed a rusted tower that might once have been a lighthouse but was now covered in graffiti. Then the walls of mud brick and salt slabs closed in on us. The erg was out of view behind us. The icy wind from the north was blocked out. The streets were wide and still and lined with nim trees. We had crossed the great Ténéré. We had made it to Bilma. The *gendarmerie* loomed up like an ancient citadel among the pattern of mud brick. Outside its broken gates a vehicle was parked, and three Westerners in swimming trunks were being searched by police.

Mu'min

The Westerners were Italians who had arrived the previous day from Djanet in Algeria, coming across the desert on a forbidden *piste*. One of them was a surgeon from Genoa, a man who might have looked dignified wearing anything else but swimming trunks. He was slim and streaky-blond, with an even poolside tan. The other two were engineers, both dark and bearded with pasta paunches overhanging their trunks. The surgeon paced up and down like an expectant father, smoking cigarettes and fuming to himself. The others unloaded mounds of cardboard boxes under the supervision of a *gendarme*. The boxes were labelled 'mayonnaise', 'tinned salmon', 'tinned pineapple', 'chocolate' and other things I would rather not have thought about.

The Italians sniggered at our awkward jackets and turbans. One of the engineers laughed outright. Old Udungu glanced at them once, then pulled his veil up to his nose. The chief of the *gendarmes* came out to welcome us, saying that he had expected us two days earlier.

Before we left the surgeon complained that the police had kept them there a whole day. 'These Africans don't understand what time means to a Westerner,' he said. He looked miserable when I said that we had been held for six days in Tillia. Six days was all it had taken them to drive from Genoa, he told us. They only had ten days left in which to motor across the Ténéré and back through Algeria to Italy. Udungu asked me to inquire if they wanted a guide to Agadez. 'We don't need a guide,' the surgeon said. 'We'll cross Ténéré without a guide, you'll see.'

We made camp in some thornscrub outside the village. The day warmed up, and the camels stretched and shook their humps, shuffling about and nibbling among the thorn trees. A young Toubou called Abba Kelle arrived and offered to be our guide as far as N'Guigmi.

He was very clean-cut and earnest and spoke fluent French, yet I sensed something insincere beneath the simpering smile. 'I've taken plenty of tourists to N'Guigmu,' he said. 'I like the tourists, the men *and* the women.' He smiled charmingly at Marinetta. 'The route to N'Guigmi is no problem. I can even tell you how many sand dunes there are.'

'I don't want to know how many sand dunes there are,' I said, irritated by his know-it-all manner. 'Have you taken tourists by camel or by car?'

'Mostly by car,' he admitted, 'but it's no problem. Camels and cars are all the same.'

That night I dreamed about Abba Kelle. I dreamed that we were sitting by a campfire under a brilliant full moon. As I watched, the young man's features dissolved and decomposed. Steadily they changed into the features of a wolf. 'It's no problem,' the wolf told me mildly. 'I like tourists!'

'I'm sorry,' I said, 'but we really can't take anyone who changes into a wolf!'

A man called Mu'min was waiting for us at the *gendarmerie* the next morning. The chief said that he had been recommended as a guide by the town's headman, the *sarki*. Mu'min was a Beriberi, one of the settled people of the oasis. He was a lanky, lonely, silent man who seemed reluctant to talk. His face was as scored and weathered as salt brick, and mahogany-black. His mouth was a nest of broken teeth. He wore a coil of white turban and a long black cloak, and his eyes were shaded by dark glasses. When he did speak it was in snatches, between puffs at the fat rolls of Gauloises cigarettes and coughs and vicious spitting. The young Abba Kelle was there too, sitting some distance away and looking quite normal this morning. I asked the chief which of the two guides was the better, and he told me, 'Mu'min is more serious than the other one.' I would rather not have taken either, but the chief said it was forbidden to go without a guide. In the end I took Mu'min.

While the new guide collected his belongings, I sat down with Udungu. He had been to the market and showed me a bag of Bilma dates he had bought for his children. 'They didn't want me to come,' he said. 'They cried when I left. They said, "It's too cold, father!"'

They were right. It's too cold for an old man like me. I won't come to Bilma again by camel – not this year anyway.' I paid him his due and a small bonus, and his old eyes beamed over the *tagelmoust*. The walnut-hued skin puckered into a million wrinkles, like a dried-up *girba*.

'It's like parting from your grandfather,' Marinetta said.

In the afternoon Mu'min arrived with a mattress, four thick blankets, two canvas windbreaks, a radio, a flashlight, a Tuareg sword and a huge sack of dates. I told him that the dates were too heavy for the camels, but he protested that they would be useful to us. 'We will give them to the Toubou we meet on the way,' he said. 'It will help us to get through.' I made him cut the sack down by half. In the twelve days it took us to reach N'Guigmi he never gave anybody one of those dates.

As we loaded the camels, a car went by. The Italians from Genoa were moving on, but they weren't crossing Ténéré. We learned later that they had been sent back to Djanet. Perhaps that was why they drove past staring in front of them. They didn't even wave goodbye.

Before leaving the oasis we had been told to report to the chief of *gendarmes*, who wanted to check our agreement with the guide and to note down our official departure time. In his narrow office Mu'min and I stood before his desk while he read the contract out loud. Suddenly Mu'min scowled and said, 'What about my return fare?'

'I don't pay return fares,' I answered him.

The sour, broken-toothed face screwed up as he glared at me. 'That's not right! A guide should always have the return fare!'

'You should have mentioned it sooner,' I said.

'Yes,' the chief agreed. 'You should have mentioned it when you made the contract.'

'If you've changed your mind, I'll have the money back,' I told Mu'min.

He felt in his pocket and brought out the wad of francs I had paid him as an advance. As I put out my hand to take them, a more thoughtful expression came over his face. He looked at the notes, then stuffed them back into his pocket. 'Let's go!' he said.

We camped an hour outside Bilma, on the edge of the oasis.

Mu'min told me to watch the camels carefully when they grazed. 'If they get into any cultivation, there's a fine of 5,000 francs to pay,' he said.

In the dusk he erected a neat little shelter from his windbreaks and retired into it, cloaked and blanketed like a queen ant. After we had eaten he told me that this would be the nineteenth time he had been to N'Guigmi by camel. In the past he had worked as a caravaneer, taking salt and dates as far as Yoruba in Nigeria, a thirty-day trek. 'That trade finished ten years ago,' he said. 'It all goes by lorry now.' He didn't much like the Yoruba anyway. He didn't like the Tuareg either. He spoke Toubou, but he hated the Toubou. And he had worked in Libya and learned Arabic, but he had no sympathy with the Arabs. You could tell that if we hadn't been there, the list would have included Westerners as well. Mu'min didn't like anyone but the Beriberi. They were a minority in the desert, tending palm trees and digging salt. They were neither slaves nor Haratin, he told me; they had once been a famous warrior tribe. Properly called the Kanouri, they were closely related to the Bornu of Lake Chad, who had once ruled all this region. In N'Guigmi there were plenty of Beriberi, Mu'min said. Mu'min seemed to like N'Guigmi.

Later he went back into his shelter and switched on the radio. It was the first time we had heard a radio in the Sahara. The voice of a far-off stranger, drifting unseen into our camp, seemed an intrusion. After a few moments, Mu'min said, 'There's big fighting over in Chad. Habri's men are driving the Libyans out of Tibesti. Oh, there's big trouble in Tibesti now!' For a short time we mulled over the news, not knowing if it was good or bad for us. The machinations of the greater world outside our tiny camp seemed suddenly awesome and incomprehensible. Then our thoughts turned to the next day's journey and our next source of water. Only when I came to write up my diary did I realize that it was New Year's Eve.

We had been in the Sahara eight months. We had been married two-thirds of a year. It seemed only yesterday that we had left Chinguetti with Mafoudh. It seemed a century ago. The desert distorted time. Time was day into night, sunrise, sunset, the passing of the planets, the silent theatre of the stars. Time was birth, childhood, thirst and hunger, struggle, war, old age, death. Survival. On and on to another horizon while man survived, for ever changing, for ever the same.

The next morning we crossed the first dune chain of the Grand Erg of Bilma. The dunes were lumps of sand 60 feet high, placed at regular intervals and joined by sandy ridges. As we laboured up the windward slope, Marinetta took her camera and ran about taking shots. Mu'min and I engineered the caravan gingerly down the leeward side. Marinetta was nowhere in sight. We halted the camels and waited. Five minutes passed. I was itching to get moving, and the camels were fidgeting under their heavy loads. In another five minutes Marinetta appeared at the top of the dune. She had removed her thick jacket and her headcloth and tied them round her waist. I watched as she scuttered down the steep face, leaving a ladder of scallops where her feet had been. Her panther-slim muscles contracted and relaxed under her tight T-shirt as she ran, her dark hair swinging behind her in a weighty mass. Her eyes were alight with excitement and animation. She looked extraordinarily attractive, but that worried me. It seemed out of place in this harsh world. 'Marinetta,' I said, 'we can't keep stopping to wait while you take photos. Next time we won't stop.'

'You never give me a chance to take shots,' she panted. 'You never think about photography. Just to move on, that's all you want!'

'And cover yourself up.'

'Jesus, don't you realize what hard work it is, running about in this deep sand?'

'Perhaps you should have come in your bikini. You're no better than those Italians from Genoa in their swimming trunks.'

'You're just a British prude. No sex, please, we're British, ha, ha!'

'At least we don't wave our hands about as you Italians do. Look at you, giving off signals all over the place when you get excited!'

'I knew a Turkish woman once who was married to an Englishman. She told me, "Never marry an Englishman." '

'Pity you didn't take her advice,' I said. 'I don't know why the hell we got married.'

It was a lie, of course. I knew why we had got married. I had been in love with her. Her strict Sardinian upbringing had made her anything but promiscuous. She wasn't the kind of woman you could just live with. And my years among the nomads had made me as chauvinistic as they. It was only proper that a man should marry when he found the right woman. I had believed that she was the right woman. I had been determined to marry her.

My determination had taken me on a plane to Rome the previous January. I landed at Ciampino at night; the city was pulsing, electric in the winter heat. I booked into a pension in the Via Nazionale. It had doors a foot thick as if they had built them to withhold a siege. I met Marinetta there in the foyer next morning, looking tense and harassed. 'You're crazy!' she said, pushing me away as I tried to kiss her. She was afraid the manager would notice.

Warm rain was falling in the Via Nazionale. It was Epiphany, and most of the shops were closed. The city seemed deserted, and we spent most of the day wandering from street to cobbled square with our collars turned up. Marinetta told me about the bad dreams she had been having about the Sahara trek and how worried her parents were. We sat in the Café Greco among elegant paintings and antique mirrors, while the rain fuzzed the windows. I asked Marinetta to marry me. I was prepared for 'No', but it was the 'I don't know' that threw me. For two days we dawdled around the drizzly streets, rode in buses, stood in bars. She told me that she wasn't sure if she loved me. She didn't think she could ever be a wife. Marriage seemed to her like a betrayal of her parents. In all her twenty-nine years she had never taken a boyfriend home. In the end, though, my persistence won through. She looked at me gloomily and said, 'You'd better come home and tell my father. God knows what he'll say!'

The argument played itself out as we struggled up the next dune face. We inched the camels down again, while their legs trembled in the sliding sand. Suddenly there was a *Waaaaah! Waaaaaah! WAAAAAH!*, and we turned to see Abu Nakkas, the white camel, floundering in the sand and trying to wriggle out from under the heavy jerrycans that had fallen forward on to his neck. The other camels halted, watching the spectacle on unsteady legs. Mu'min and I rushed up to the thrashing animal, expecting the lead ropes to break at any moment. The white camel spat venomously at us like a cobra. We had to remove the saddle and carry the load down the slope to firmer ground. Then we replaced the saddle with a tail cord to prevent it from slipping forward again. Abu Nakkas hated the tail cord. He turned his head and snapped at me viciously as I slipped the rope around his tail, trying to lurch up and kick backwards with his rear leg. He was the most aggressive gelding I had ever seen. 'This camel,' Mu'min pronounced solemnly, 'is mad.'

On the next ascent the saddle slipped backwards. The big jerrycans thumped into the sand, and the tops came off. Water splashed across the dune. *Yaaaah! Yaaaaaah! YAAAAAH!* squealed the camel. Marinetta and I exploded with laughter. Mu'min scowled and hit the white camel with his open hand. *WAAAH! WAAAAAH!* the camel answered him. He ranted in incomprehensible Beriberi as we picked the saddle up.

On the next dune chain the hay bales fell forwards and pinned Abu Sanam's head to the ground. He wailed pitifully, and Marinetta and I laughed again. Mu'min raved at the camel as though the beast had done it on purpose to spite him. We fixed it, but the scratchy hay bothered the camel all morning, drawing dribbles of blood from his shoulders. It rocked backwards on the ascent and forwards again on the way down. Finally Mu'min hit on a way of hoisting it up above the camel's shoulders. I complimented him on the technique, and a flicker of satisfaction crossed his lips as he said, 'We know camels!' Ten minutes later the saddle rope broke, and the entire load of hay was deposited on the ground. With it went bits of firewood, dried waterskins, tent poles and the machete. Mu'min looked as if he would burst into tears.

Before we loaded again Marinetta suggested that we should eat. We sat down in the sand as she brought out the pot of cold macaroni and sardines. There were pieces of straw in the macaroni. Mu'min inspected each spoonful very carefully, removing the straw and flicking it into the sand with utter distaste. 'You should have removed the straw before you cooked it,' he declared. It was all we could do to prevent ourselves from laughing again. After the macaroni we ate a few dates. They were the dates we had brought from Agadez.

We reloaded the hay and marched on. There were more dune chains and everywhere the purple battlements of cliffs. Deep, rippling sand had been swept off the valley floor, revealing a network of patterns like mosaics. The sand made us pant with effort, and the afternoon sun brought slivers of sweat to our foreheads. Often we found the leeward slopes too sheer to descend and had to traverse far along narrow ridges to find a way down. There was no chance to ride. Dunes followed dunes, and bars of sand interlocked with each other. Sometimes we were lost in labyrinths of sand more frightening than anything I had seen. There were no comforting markers in the Grand Erg, and I prayed that Mu'min knew the way.

At sunset we stopped, tired out, and threw our baggage into the sand. The dunes were as sterile as ice, and a cold wind reared across them like a dragon. We laagered the camels in a circle, heads facing inwards, and fed them some chaff. Mu'min erected his shelter against the cold and I put up our open-sided tent. As we sat down to eat, he noticed more straw in the macaroni. He brought his flashlight and fixed it in the sand so that he could examine each mouthful before he ate it. To divert his attention, I said, 'There are *always* problems on the first day.'

The Beriberi looked at me morosely. He sucked his teeth and set his massive boxer's jaw. His eyes, each holding a speck of yellow light, were suspicious. He did not answer me. He kept on staring quietly out of the primitive soul of the Sahara, asking wordlessly, 'Who are you? Why have you come here?' I realized that he hadn't even asked our names.

In the morning the cold cut us like a knife blade. We looked out across a landscape of sand like polar ice. The camels were reluctant to get up. We picked at their hobbles with blue fingers and stood back as they heaved themselves to their feet, shivering. They showered us with warm urine and pellets of dung. Before we loaded, Mu'min drew on a pair of gloves with the air of a surgeon about to perform an operation. The gloves were of light-brown wool and had pictures of pink elephants embroidered on them. They matched the woollen bobble-hat that he wore beneath his headcloth.

The dunes got higher day by day. They towered above the ivory sands of the plain. Often I thought that the camels would never make it down the steep inclines, but they always did, with trembling legs and shaking loads. Always there were stoppages, though. The chaff had to be shifted higher; the jerrycans had to be rebalanced by pouring icy water from one to another; the firewood came unfastened, scattering twigs across the sand. Loads tilted forwards or back; headropes snapped; nose-rings were wrenched out as camel heaved against camel in the slithering sand. We tottered across scrolls of shimmering silicon, through bows of orange chiffon and draperies of pale cream. The Grand Erg was too big for the mind to take in, too featureless for the memory to gain hold. If it were not for the detailed notes in my diary, those days would have blurred with each other and become as featureless as the erg itself. In my dreams the action took place in a vast hall with austere stone floors and windows draped with sweeping curtains. It was as if my mind was desperately trying to define and limit the fearful dimensions of the sand-sea.

Mu'min never cheered up. He remained silent and aloof, asking us little and telling us nothing. His Arabic was poor. At first he stalked on ahead very fast, as if wanting to escape. Soon, though, his pace slowed. He became tired, and his left knee swelled up with the constant battle against the sand. After an hour of walking in the morning, he would start limping, a spindly, surreal figure in his flapping vampire cloak and his bobble-hat. When limping too got difficult, he would try to hop. Then he would couch his camel with a vicious expression and snarl at Marinetta threateningly, 'Madame! Why don't you ride?'

'Not yet,' she would answer. Mu'min would swing his lanky legs viciously into the saddle and urge on his camel at a terrible speed. It was a humiliation for him to ride before we did, and especially before a woman no higher than his chest. He drove the camels on fast, hoping that we wouldn't be able to keep up on foot and would be forced to ride when he did. We were determined not to give in to this pressure, and anyway we were very fit now. We had walked hundreds of miles. We refused to ride until three hours had passed, and only then would we couch our camels. Mu'min never paused to wait for us to mount. He just charged on madly across the erg, making us trot the camels in order to catch him up and tiring them out needlessly. If there were jinns in the Grand Erg, they had certainly got to Mu'min.

He never sang or hummed, as our other guides had done. He never told stories. Instead he smoked his Gauloises, one after the other, coughing and spluttering over them as he whipped on his camel. There was a hole in his pocket, and often the blue cigarette packet would slip through. Then I would be obliged to dismount and pick up the packet for him. He never thanked me and always replaced it in the same pocket. Once I pretended that I hadn't noticed the fallen packet, and he was very angry when he discovered it missing. He never dropped one again after that.

After a few days Marinetta developed a swollen ankle. She still refused to ride before the appointed time. One morning Mu'min drove the camels on so fast that she almost had to run to keep up. As she fell farther and farther behind, I saw the exasperation written on her face and the pain behind her eyes. I knew her well enough by now to realize that she wouldn't give in until she had to be carried. I lost my temper. 'For God's sake, slow those camels down!' I yelled at Mu'min. 'Let them go at their own pace. You're killing them!' He gave me a murderous look, but he slowed down.

When Marinetta caught up, she was fuming. 'Face of shit!' she said to the guide in Italian. Mu'min didn't understand Italian any more than we understood Beriberi. But it looked as though he'd got the message.

On 4 January we saw the oasis of Dibella beneath us. It was deserted and austere, lying in a deep depression in the sand. Ivory dunes and the dark machicolations of rocky crags loomed over it to the north. The trees were dim shadows, double-stemmed trunks of dom palms intertwined with the feathery headdresses of date trees. There were bushes of thorny *talha* standing in dusty squads among outcrops of rock. We made our way painfully down into the basin. It was a place that belonged to the wilderness, a haunting, spartan, dying place. The water, lying in a clear pool under the date palms, was brackish. It gave Marinetta stomach cramps within minutes. I noticed a tiny dead camel rotting by the pool and hoped it hadn't died from the water.

While we were hacking off bits of firewood from the acacias, Mu'min pointed out the ruins of Toubou palm shelters. 'There used to be plenty of Toubou here,' he said. 'They had to move on when the grazing failed. There are still some dates, but they aren't much good now.'

We hoisted on our full jerrycans and climbed out of the oasis. The ascent was exhausting. In the high sun we couldn't make out the sheer drops and angles of the dunes, and we ran the risk of plunging down them with our camels. At the top of the valley we emerged on to a groundswell of carmine-pink. There were occasional skerries of rock thrusting out of it, jet-black against the dazzling sand. We mounted our camels. The vastness of the landscape eased us into a familiar, compulsive, dreamy mood. It was sensual, languorous, a luxurious state between waking and sleep when the camels flowed on endlessly, rocking us back and forth like babies. My thoughts drifted back, as they often did, to those few frantic days in Rome almost exactly a year before.

Marinetta had taken me to her parents' home. It was a well-appointed apartment in the Viale dei Campioni, with automatic doors and polished marble stairs. Meeting her father was more frightening for me than crossing the Sahara. The fact that he had been captured by the Allies near Tobruk and had spent five years in a British prison camp only added to my apprehension. General Peru was a small man with a compensating powerful personality. His eyes were very bright. He wore tweeds and a waistcoat like an English country squire. Signora Peru was very slim and quite beautiful. She was dressed impeccably, and her English was as faultless as her dress.

The apartment was predictably plush. Prints from India and African carvings decorated the walls and shelves. Marinetta's brother, a small, dark-haired doctor, began showering me with questions almost before I had sat down. When his artillery barrage petered out, the General and his wife launched the infantry attack. They asked about education, religion and politics. I tried to drink the chocolate they offered me, but my hands were shaking. My mouth was too dry to eat the special Sardinian cake. After a while, during a lull in the battle, I said, 'One of the reasons I've come is that Mariantonietta and I were ... well, we were thinking of getting married, and I wondered if you might have any objections.' There was a moment's silence. Had I phrased it in the wrong way? I wondered. But the General's eyes were twinkling, as if he was remembering himself in the same situation. After this, I thought, the Sahara would be easy.

'No,' the General said. 'None whatsoever.' I let my bated breath out slowly. Nothing could ever be quite that hard again, I thought.

The camels shuffled on across the interminable erg. There was silence. My mind flexed back and forth across the terrible dimensions of the Sahara. It seemed that we had been here for ever. I could visualize no end to this journey. I could imagine nothing but a life of constant movement, searching for the next grazing, the next water. I reminded myself of my responsibility to this woman. She was my own small family now. The hundreds of miles I had travelled with her had made me far more like the nomads than I had ever been when I lived with them. They were family men, not lone travellers and explorers. The Sahara was not only a 'land of men' but also a 'land of women'. A man's first responsibility was always to his own. I remembered how Marinetta had showed me into her own room. It was the room in which she had grown from childhood to woman-hood, the room she dreamed about when she was homesick. There was her bed and a desk and a bookcase of photographic books. The shelves were inhabited by woolly toys – a turtle, a camel, a monkey – and various teddy-bears. We sat down on the edge of the bed, and she gave me a peck on the cheek and said, 'You are the first man I've ever brought into this room.' I felt almost that we were married already.

We rode on till sunset. A cold breeze chased away the last shreds of heat. The sun sank into a net of translucent clouds like angry scratches on the sky's belly. In a moment it appeared to balance uncertainly on the edge of the dunes. I thought suddenly of the tiny planet we were travelling on. An umbilicus bound us to it. It was not separate from us. We were as much manifestations of the earth as the rocks and the sand, the grass and the trees, the insects and the birds, the clouds and the rain. Our ancestry ran back into the unfathomable ages, through branches and junctions of the tree and down into the taproot of the mother plant. From this moment our kind would spread out into the future, through more billions of branches, plugging into eternity, colonizing the distant time to come. But the earth was the mother of all. Such feelings came to me often, together with a deep sense of the unity of everything around me. It was primitive, even pagan. Or perhaps I was only relearning what I and everyone else had always known. I can only say that these

intense feelings of the oneness of nature were the nearest to a genuine
religious experience that I have ever come.

The sun tilted and the streaks of cloud burned with purple fire.
Then the day was gone.

In the morning we were crossing the Modjigo erg when a sandstorm
began. Grey dust stirred along the clear horizon to the south. 'A
wind is very bad here,' Mu'min grumped. I could understand why.
We were heading for the oasis of Agadem, which was marked by a
long crag. In a sandstorm the crag couldn't be seen, and we ran the
risk of marching straight past it. When we halted for lunch the sand
filled the pot as soon as we opened it. Mu'min groaned and lifted
the wing of his cloak to protect the food. But after I had eaten I could
feel the grit lying on my stomach for the rest of the day.

As we rode on, I was attacked by a severe migraine. It was
probably the result of staring into the sun every morning for so long.
Jewelled snowflakes shimmered before my eyes, and when I closed
them pinpricks of light glimmered inside my head. I could no longer
focus properly. When I tried to talk the wrong words came out. The
sand-mist swirling about us mixed with the whorls behind my pupils.
My hands started to go numb, as if the circulation had been cut off.
I clung grimly to my camel. Within an hour the sensory effects had
passed and were replaced by a pain like a hot needle across my head.

The tempest grew more intense. The sand whipped against us and
piled up in miniature drifts in the folds of our clothes and on our
saddles. The grit penetrated everything. Worse than the stinging
sand was the maddening roar of the wind. Even the camels seemed
unnerved by it. I was startled by a shout and turned to see Marinetta's
camel disappearing into a nebula of dust. I had been towing the camel
behind me, but the headrope had broken. I shouted to Mu'min to
stop, and while he held my camel, I ran off to find her, my heart
thumping. Her camel was uncontrollable without a headrope, and in
a storm like this she could be lost in minutes. After that death would
be almost a certainty. It took me only a short time to find her; I retied the headrope and led her back to the caravan. As we moved on,
Mu'min peered constantly into the distance through the white strands
of mist. The cliffs of Agadem were nowhere in sight. At about five

the guide couched his camel and called me over. 'I think we should make camp,' he advised me. 'We'll never see the cliff tonight. In the morning the wind doesn't begin until after sunrise. Then we'll have a chance of seeing it.'

We unloaded the camels. They were tired and in poor condition now. The saddles had already left bald patches on their skin. Shaybani had the beginnings of a gall on the withers. Abu Sanam, the hay carrier, was bleeding from the feet. All of them were hungry. After we had fed them some chaff, Mu'min asked for medicine for his knee. I massaged it with analgesic balm, but by the time I had finished the wind had plastered the sticky ointment with sand and straw. At sunset the wind dropped. I felt sick from the migraine and all the sand I had swallowed. I worried about finding Agadem and about the possibility of being turned away from the Chadian frontier. Later Mu'min listened to his radio, and said, 'The French have bombed a radar station at Wadi Doum. Habri's men have dropped poison gas on Zouar. More than eighty Libyans have been killed.' In the darkness he seemed to be smiling.

Mu'min woke me the next morning to show me the cliff of Agadem cutting across the erg like a grey wall. It took us four hours to get there, but the camels perked up as if they could already smell the vegetation. We passed through a gap in the rock and saw below us a perfect saucer of green. Beyond the oasis the sand was bright red, tunnelled through by enormous worms of gypsum-white, which stood out like veins. There were drops of green *arak* on the valley floor, amid a purl of magenta and streaky blue. The dunes that swept down into the oasis looked dangerously steep. Mu'min dismounted, and at once his leg collapsed. I watched him as he desperately tried to hop down the steep slope on one leg. His black cloak flopped comically around him as he hopped. Abu Sanam pulled back from the slope, and we had to tie him by the jaw. The next time he pulled, the headrope broke. We had to unhitch all the camels and ferry them down the dunes one by one. Mu'min worked up and down, pogo-ing madly on his one leg like a dark flamingo and spluttering to himself. When all the camels were safely down, we rehitched them and led them into the oasis.

There was little sign of life other than the *arak* bushes. There was a brooding silence to the place. We moved through the bushes noiselessly, searching for the single well. In the distance stood the ruins of an old French fort, crumbling and full of sand. Two yellow-headed Egyptian vultures buzzed around it.

I heard the roar of a camel and looked up to see four men riding towards us. Their faces were veiled in white cloth but tied in a style quite different from that of the Tuareg. They halted around us in a semi-circle. They did not shake hands. The men carried arm daggers, and thick clubs hung from their saddles. I inched instinctively nearer to the handle of my machete, which protruded from a bale of hay. Their saddle gear was unfamiliar, and their camels wore strange headdresses of painted leather thongs. The men looked at us silently through the gaps in their headcloths. Mu'min began speaking to them in Toubou, very calmly. While he talked, they eyed us suspiciously and weighed up the state of our camels. Then one of them pointed to an *arak* grove not far off, and without another word they rode away.

There was a Toubou family living in the *arak* grove. The men were not wearing veils like the others we had seen, and without them they looked friendly and ordinary. Yet I marvelled that they could live permanently in this desolation. They were small, ragged men with black faces, narrow and finely boned. Their tents were made of dom-palm fibre, woven into sheets and stitched together to form an oval igloo with an opening at one end. By the tents stood a shelter of loose palm fronds, where some women in brilliantly coloured dresses were playing with tiny children. There was a rusty oil drum for storing water, and a rickety frame of Sodom's Apple stalks held old saddles, rolled up mats, water pots and stiff well buckets.

The Toubou owned some camels, which were grazing among the *arak* trees. Their herder was a girl of fifteen who swished about cheerily with a stick, her flowery dress billowing behind her. Her face was broad and pleasant, her tightly braided hair covered with a thin rag of cloth. I knew how tough these black nomad women could be. I had often seen women of the Gor'an, the eastern branch of the Toubou, when I was living in Gineina, in the Sudan. I remembered how they had ridden into Gineina market on their camels, carrying clubs and arm daggers and looking as dangerous as the men.

1. In Moorish dress at the door of our house in Chinguetti.

2. On the edge of the emptiness: Chinguetti oasis. The building on the left is a grain store.

3. High noon under the palms of Ganeb.

4. Mafoudh leading the caravan across the plains of Aoukar valley.

5. The real spirit of Ténéré: the face of the Tuareg herdswoman in Wadi Borghat.

10. Guide Adam climbs a great dune to look for Abu Tabara.

11. The edge of darkness: hitching up the caravan near Tegaru plateau.

12. A long-dreamed-of sight: the river Nile after 256 days.

13. The going gets tougher: Marinetta grabs a rest near Tegaru.

14. The wild man collects fodder for the camels on the banks of the Nile.

There was a bull-camel among the herd, strutting about, blowing out a pink air bladder, slobbering, lifting his head arrogantly and displaying his swollen neck. I had once seen an Arab boy whose arm had been almost ripped off by a bull-camel in this state. I told Marinetta to keep clear of him. The Toubou girl showed no fear of him, however, and shouted at the bull harshly when he came too near the females.

The Toubou brought us mugs of warm camel's milk and helped us to fill our containers from the well. They told Mu'min that there was just enough grazing here to keep their camels fat. The oasis had once been a French base, and many Toubou had camped here, grazing their animals and tending the palm trees. Now almost everything had gone but the *arak*. The ground between the bushes was a *sebkha* of scorched earth, scattered with the sherds of trees like bones. Of the original date palms only a few were left.

These Toubou were one branch of the black Saharan nomads whose homeland lay in the mountain massif of Tibesti, lying on the borders of Libya and Chad. It was this area that was now being fought over by the Chadian government of Hissein Habri and the Libyan army. The nomads of the mountains were called Teda, while the southern and eastern tribes were known as Gor'an. In Niger the black nomads were called Toubou, a name probably given to them by the French.

The black nomads were among the hardiest people of the Sahara. By nature quarrelsome, independent and prone to family feuds, they never managed to present a united front to resist the Turks and Arabs who had conquered them or, later, the French. Once they had been the most feared raiders in the eastern Sahara, riding thousands of miles across the open desert, striking as far east as the Nile. Now half of the Toubou were fighting on the side of the Libyans, and the other half were fighting for Habri. That evening Mu'min told us that Habri's soldiers had captured seventy-five Libyans in Tibesti. A third of them would be shot the following day.

As we moved nearer to Lake Chad, the temperature rose steadily and the signs of vegetation increased. The dunes of the Grand Erg were left behind us, and we moved instead through a graveyard of thornscrub. The trunks were smashed and bent and grotesquely twisted, as if hit by a tornado. Yellow gashes had been ripped across their dull, grey skin, and fantails of fragile fibres hung out where they had snapped and keeled over. The husks of acacias lay crushed and shattered, trampled into the lifeless, salt-grey earth. There was no speck of green among them. A monochrome confusion of deathly pale shapes and shadows stretched to every horizon. It was a landscape of hell in which the lifeless trees took on the forms of devil creatures from the edges of imagination. They were like the giant carcasses of insects, eaten from inside by unnameable parasites and left to stiffen in the scorching sun.

This kind of desolation was infinitely worse than the empty, featureless erg. It induced depression. Mu'min stared about him as if he were constantly lost. Marinetta said, 'It's the kind of place in which you imagine an assassin behind every bush and tree trunk. I keep thinking that Mu'min has led us this way to murder us.' I felt exactly as she did. In the clean, open desert you could see enemies approaching. The sudden closing in of the landscape after months in the open brought paranoia. It made you feel suddenly vulnerable. Once I sensed inside me a submerged pulse of unreasoning terror, the terror that makes you panic for no obvious reason, prompts you to yell out madly and run away. It was the first time I had felt such terror since Tijikja, five months before.

It was very hot now. The camels were hungry. There was no longer any hay to give them, and among this lifeless shell of a landscape there was nothing for them to eat. Abu Sanam left spats of blood in the sand as he walked. Abu Nakkas fought and whined constantly. My feet were blistered for the first time, and Marinetta's ankle was still swollen. Mu'min's knee was so inflamed that he could hardly walk at all. We lurched on silently through the desolation, our minds blank and empty. We were walking and riding more than twelve hours a day.

I could think of nothing but resting in N'Guigmi, but beyond it, I knew, lurked the deadly shadow of Chad. I wondered if they would turn us away at the border. I wondered if, once inside, we would be attacked by murderous political factions. The Royal Geographical Society had warned us against passing through this unstable region.

Quentin Crewe, writing in 1983, had declared Chad a 'closed country' and had said that the Chad–Sudan border was mined. It was a disappointment to have to enter the country so far south, in what was really the Sahel belt. If we were turned back now, our attempt to cross the Sahara from west to east would have been in vain. Marinetta and I were determined that we should try to get through Chad whatever the cost. But when I thought of the pitfalls that must surely await us, I felt bilious and sick.

One morning we met some nomads making camp. They were Shuwa Arabs with cheerful red faces. Their camels carried wooden litters like the ones I knew so well from my years in the Sudan. They greeted us in Arabic – not Hassaniyya, but the good, clear Arabic of the east. The familiar style, the familiar faces, the full, unclipped language at once lifted my melancholy. Chad lay ahead of us, but beyond it lay the Sudan, the country where Marinetta and I had met. Reaching the Sudan would be like coming home.

Two hours later we were walking through N'Guigmi towards the sweeping flag of the *gendarmerie*. The town looked like a French colonial base, with its villas and tin-roofed verandahs of mosquito-mesh. A group of small boys sat under a tree, chanting verses from the Quran in an ecstatic burble. They stopped chanting to watch us go past. Farther on a thick stream of reggae music poured from the window of a villa. It contrasted strangely with the Quranic chant that had resumed behind us. The reggae streamed on in the stillness of the morning, *cha-bunka-cha, cha-bunka-cha, cha-bunka-cha*.

Jibrin

A massive elephant skull stood at the entrance to the town *cercle* like a mute guardian. It was a souvenir of the time when N'Guigmi really had been on the shores of Lake Chad. That time of crocodiles and elephants was long gone now. Throughout history the lake had expanded and contracted like a concertina. It was now in a phase of contraction.

We were received sombrely by the *gendarmes*. The slim young officer in charge asked us, 'Doesn't it bother you that two people were killed last week entering Chad?' I told him that it bothered us but that we were still going. He shrugged as he stamped our passports, as if to say, 'Thank God, it's not *my* lookout!'

Then a drunken man escorted us to the town camp site. He kept trying to put his arm around Marinetta and crying, 'Madame!' in a loud voice. I sincerely wished he would go away.

The camp site, a rectangle of desert with a wall around it, was unoccupied except for a gang of small boys who perched on the wall like crows. They jeered at us while we erected our tent. Mu'min took his camel and went off to buy some hay. As soon as he had gone Marinetta said, 'Can't we go to Chad alone? I'm sick of guides.'

'And who's going to lead us into Chad?' I asked sarcastically. 'You?'

'Why not?' she replied. 'We can handle the camels ourselves. Why should we pay so much money to useless people like Mu'min?'

'The next guide will be better,' I promised.

'No,' she sulked, 'I don't like it. I hate having a third person watching all the time. I have to behave in a different way, and so do you. You treat me as if I'm a second-class citizen.'

'You have to respect the culture,' I told her.

'That's not respecting the culture,' she countered angrily. 'That's just being a chauvinist pig!'

Then Mu'min returned and left me to spread out the new hay while he threw himself into the shade, muttering, 'Thank God, I can rest! I've done what I promised to do.'

We sold Abu Sanam and Abu Nakkas in the camel market the following day with the help of a tout called Musa. He claimed to be a Targui but didn't bother to cover his rodent-like front teeth with the *tagelmoust*. He said that he had lived in N'Guigmi so long that he had forgotten Tamasheq. He spoke only Arabic now, he said. The market was held in groves of Sodom's Apples on the edge of the town. The camels were packed in like sardines. Caravans wormed out of the scrub in all directions escorted by tribesmen in nicotine-yellow shirts who rode on little ponies. The men had faces of charcoal-black, haloed with brilliant white headcloths. They belonged to the Toubou, the Gor'an, the Beriberi and the black Shuwa Arabs of Lake Chad. Their camels looked dumpy and lethargic beside our sleek Tuareg geldings. Merchants and butchers and touts marched about with white gandourahs flying. Women sat in snug lines, selling wedges of peanut cake and packets of chick-peas. One woman was churning out maggots of pasta from an imported machine. Coffee-sellers balanced trays of mugs and kettles on their knees, next to men selling blankets and belts and whips and saddles.

I met an asthmatic Moor wearing a burnous with a hood and spoke to him in Hassaniyya. He had been in Niger three weeks, visiting his brother. When I asked how he liked it here, his eyes narrowed. 'Everyone is a thief,' he said. 'You can't trust anyone here. This isn't Mauritania. Here the blacks are proud to steal from a white man.' I mentioned that I was English. He peered at me and said, 'There aren't any thieves in England, are there?'

'Plenty,' I said.

'But the thieves are all blacks, aren't they? I mean, white men wouldn't steal?' He introduced me to his brother, who had been a merchant in N'Guigmi for thirty years. He was leaving very soon, he said. He was as slight as the asthmatic Moor and with the same distorted face. He came from Atar and was anxious to know our opinion of it.

'Aren't you sorry to be leaving N'Guigmi?' I asked him.

'No, I'm looking forward to going home,' he told me. 'Everyone here is a thief.'

The tout Musa told us to wait while he took the camels into the selling area. It wouldn't do for the buyers to know that they belonged to a *nasrani*. We hung about, stamping our feet to dislodge the camel ticks that crawled up our legs from their burrows in the sand. The ticks were everywhere. They were small but particularly voracious. I noticed that everyone else in the market was stamping too. They were doing a sort of rhythmic shuffle, rocking to a silent beat. Even the camels were at it, slapping their flat pads in the sand. Men and animals were shuffling and stamping together around this little patch of desert. 'It looks like a dance!' Marinetta said.

The only people who weren't stamping were two Frenchmen of middle age. They were tanned and wore high jungle boots and the kind of peaked caps favoured by American oilmen. They worked for a French oil company prospecting in Niger. They were interested in our expedition and made a note of our names. Just then Musa appeared and spoke to me in Arabic. When I replied, the Frenchmen looked up in surprise. 'Of course,' one of them said, glancing at his scrap of paper, 'this isn't your real name, is it? I mean, you must have been born in the Middle East.' This reminded me that I was still wearing my gandourah and Moorish headcloth, unchanged since Agadez.

'You can't win,' Marinetta commented later. 'The Arabs think you're a *nasrani* and the *nasranis* think you're an Arab. What the hell are you?'

'I don't think I know any more,' I said.

We ran into the slim chief of the *gendarmes* who looked immaculate in his green uniform. He was wearing black shoes, highly polished, and was trying desperately not to stamp. He asked us if we had found a guide to Chad yet. 'Don't take a Chadian guide,' he advised us. 'Take a Nigérien. That way you're more likely to survive.' I thanked him for his advice. Suddenly he stamped violently and even bent down to scratch inside his shoes. 'Petrol!' he declared. 'That's the only thing that gets rid of them!' I looked down to see my own ankles covered in blood and alive with ticks. While talking to the chief, I had for some reason been standing at attention.

We left N'Guigmi for Chad on 15 January with three camels and a guide named Jibrin. He belonged to the Gor'an and had been born in the Kanem region of Chad. His family had moved to N'Guigmi when he was a child, and he now had Nigérien nationality. He styled himself 'Malam' Jibrin, in the manner of the Hausa. 'Malam' meant that he could read the Quran and write magical charms that would ward off the evil eye. He carried a copy of the Quran in a cardboard box slung from his saddle. I imagine that the Quran itself was intended as a charm because I never saw him reading it. I once asked Jibrin if he understood everything in the Holy Book. 'You don't have to understand it!' he told me, surprised. 'It's the words that are important, not the meanings!'

Of all our guides, Jibrin looked the least like a camel man. He came dressed in a thick, elegant gandourah and shiny black slip-on shoes. His hairless face was as shiny and black as the shoes, and his head was shaved as smooth as a cannon shell. When we made camp on the first night, a few miles outside the town, he took his food away and ate it alone. Then he went straight to sleep. When it was time to bring the camels in I woke him up to help me. 'I've got a bad leg,' was his reply. 'I've already put my ointment on. I'll help you tomorrow.' From then on I knew how it would be.

'So this is your better guide!' Marinetta jeered when she heard what had happened. ' "I've got a bad leg," indeed! He's the first guide who has ever refused to help with the camels. You must be mad or stupid to hire a man like him. We'd have been better off without a guide.'

'Steady on,' I said. 'We haven't made it into Chad yet, let alone through it. Jibrin is a Gor'an, and the Gor'an rule Chad.'

'Huh!' she scoffed. 'All I can see is that we're pouring money down the drain.'

In the morning, when Marinetta started to make her simple ablutions, Jibrin hovered near by, watching her. It made her very angry. All our other guides, even the uncouth Sidi Mohammed, had at least respected a moderate degree of privacy by turning their heads or busying themselves some distance away. Finally I told him, 'Give

her some space, Jibrin. You know, women don't like to be stared at.'
He moved away reluctantly. Instead of thanking me, Marinetta said,
'This is your better guide! Don't talk to me about guides again.' She
went into one of her sulky, silent moods and refused to talk for hours.

We set off over the clay-powder bed of the old lake. A herd of
ravaged camels fanned out among the brakes of salt bush. 'All this
used to be water as far as you could see,' Jibrin told me. 'There were
crocodiles and hippos and elephants. You saw the skull at the *cercle*
yesterday? Now there's not even enough grass for the herds here.
Look how thin those camels are. At first the water receded little by
little, then all at once it disappeared. Now it's miles away.' There had
been no Gor'an in this area once, he said. The Gor'an were nomads
from the north and east, and the lake was Beriberi country. The
Gor'an had come here only when the grazing in the desert had started
to die.

Jibrin was a government guide. He had taken travellers to Chad
dozens of times and knew the route backwards. Always, though, he
had taken them in motor vehicles. The year before he had guided a
couple of heavy trucks through the sandy country around the old
lake. 'Germans,' he said. 'I told them they'd never get the trucks
through. The country here is all deep sand. In trucks like those you
couldn't do more than 15 miles a day. It's all up and down. Very
hard on the axles. After three days the axle of one of them broke.
They just left the truck out in the desert. I wonder if it's still there.'

On the way back there had been an accident. Jibrin had been
travelling in the back of a Toyota pick-up when the steering had
gone. The pick-up had rolled over in the sand. Jibrin's leg had been
crushed and broken in several places, and he had not yet fully
recovered. 'I never got any compensation,' he said mournfully.

'Why didn't you tell me all this before?' I asked him, aware that in
N'Guigmi he had glossed over several important facts. 'You must be
mad to ride a camel after an accident like that.'

'Yes,' he admitted sorrowfully, 'you're right, *patron*. But I needed
the money. I've got seven children, and not even a wife to look after
them. My wife died last year.'

At mid-morning we were challenged by three Nigérien soldiers
hidden in the salt bush. They gawked at our camels, and they gawked

at our Western faces. 'Why don't you go by car?' one of them asked.
I thought of Jibrin's smashed leg. 'You know there's a war on in
Chad, don't you?' the soldier asked us. When we nodded wearily, he
said, 'Well, then, good luck!' and walked away. Two hours later we
crossed the Chad border.

For two years I had been a teacher in the Sudanese town of Gineina.
It stood on the Sudan–Chad border, on exactly the opposite side of
the country from where we now were. Often during those years I
had heard the thunder of artillery from across the border and had
seen thousands of refugees streaming over the frontier. They had
carried with them tales of massacre and rape, of torture, mutilation
and genocide. They had told of numerous political factions, armed
and desperate, roaming the ranges and killing at random. These
fearful tales had come back to me many times as we approached
Chad but never more vividly than now, when I was suddenly inside
the country with my wife and three camels. Chad had always reared
like a poisonous serpent in our plans to cross the Sahara. Recently
Marinetta had been kept awake by a recurrent nightmare about it.
She dreamed of a black man with ice-cold eyes looking at us down
the barrel of a machine-gun. I already knew that every step of the
way inside this war-torn country would be like walking in a minefield.
Always we would be expecting the worst.

    We arrived at the village of Dabua just after sunset. I wanted to
make camp outside and report to the border post at sunrise. I was
unwilling to approach the place at night, knowing how trigger-happy
Chadian soldiers were supposed to be. Jibrin advised us to report to
them immediately, however. He said that hanging back would make
it look as if we had something to hide. The village looked poorer
and more ramshackle than any I had seen in Niger.

    A young black soldier in combat dress came out to meet us,
clutching his rifle. After him came a security man dressed in a
gandourah like an ordinary tribesman. Both of them were Shuwa
Arabs. 'Christians with camels!' the soldier said. 'The world is truly
a strange place. You are the first Christians I have ever seen with
camels.' Another young man wearing a gandourah came puffing up.
The soldier introduced him as the 'chief'. 'You will leave your pass-

ports with me tonight,' he said, 'and tomorrow we will take steps to help you on your way.' After the months of worry this politeness made me feel like laughing.

The village looked almost derelict in full light. Outside the chief's office there were no flags or symbols of statehood. The office didn't even have a door, just a dirty blanket to keep out the cold wind. Inside there was a bench and a desk. The plaster was coming away from the mud walls. A picture of Hissein Habri hung tenaciously by a piece of tape. I had once seen Habri in Gineina while he was a fugitive. I was glad that he was back.

We had been expecting an interrogation or at least a search. Instead the chief inspected our visas and entered the details in a school exercise book. He shivered with cold as he wrote. 'You are the first Christians ever to come this way by camel,' he declared. He was wrong, but I was chary of correcting him. Two Christians had come this way by camel in 1899. They were Frenchmen, and one of them was called François Lamy. He had led a column of Algerian soldiers around Lake Chad and had attacked the stronghold of the previous ruler south of it. The opposition slaughtered, the French had added Chad to their list of colonies. They had founded a new town named, after their leader, Fort Lamy. It was now called N'Jamena.

The chief instructed us to report to the brigade HQ at Bol, where our passports would be stamped. Then he told us to send in Jibrin. The guide emerged with a face of misery, muttering, 'He took 1,000 francs off me. They say it's a "passage fee" but I call it a tobacco fee.'

We led our camels up the main street of mud-and-wattle buildings. It was like a film-set cowboy town. 'We passed the first obstacle so easily!' Marinetta said. 'Can you believe it?' Before we had walked 10 yards a voice shouted, 'Hey! Where do you think you're going?' We stopped dead and saw a lean and hungry-looking soldier in soiled combats looking at us over the barrel of a sub-machine-gun. His eyes were icy. 'We're going to Bol,' Jibrin told him diffidently. 'We've just passed the chief.' The soldier took Jibrin aside, and there was some furtive whispering. Then Jibrin handed over a further 500 francs. He looked dejected when he rejoined us. 'Tobacco fee again,' he said. 'It's always the same. By the time you've finished, it's not worth your coming.'

A few minutes later we were back in the desert. The day was very hot. The ground alternated between spits of soft sand that had once been the lakeside and the hard, empty bed of the old lake. You could see where the lake bed had been moulded by the water into troughs and shallows. I tried to imagine this place as it had been then, with the steel-grey, licking waters underfoot. Change had come quickly and completely. Earth's great machinery trundled on incomprehensibly. Our lives were no more than a breath of wind that spun the sand across the desert's surface.

At prayer time Jibrin would select a shady tree and couch his camel under it. He would clear a space around him fastidiously with a twig, then remove his shoes and socks and make his ritual ablutions with water. He took far longer over his prayers than any other guide we had had. Before mounting he always asked me to hold his camel. He was understandably afraid of falling and breaking his leg again. His injury made him too static to be a good rider. His camel went its own way at its own pace. 'This camel won't go straight,' he grumbled. 'It's afraid of the bushes.' Often he would place a hand gingerly on his side and say, 'Riding this camel gives me a pain in the liver. It's killing me, by God!' If we descended a hill, he would lean so far back in the saddle that he was almost horizontal, holding his side with his free hand and groaning. It looked so comical that we couldn't help mimicking him. We must have looked a mind-boggling sight to an observer: three camel riders descending a hill, one after the other, all leaning back with their hands on their sides and groaning miserably.

Jibrin found it difficult to walk for more than ten minutes in the morning, especially in the deep sand. He complained loudly that we never rested in the afternoon. 'This isn't the way the Gor'an travel,' he said.

'This is the way the British travel,' I told him.

'The British don't breed camels.'

'The Gor'an don't make cars, but they still drive them.'

I never criticized Jibrin for his infirmity, but I felt cheated. He hadn't mentioned his injury before I hired him, and a journey like this could cause him harm, I thought. Our guides had been steadily less effective as the journey continued, and for the first time I seriously considered crossing Chad alone. I had hired Jibrin only to take us as far as N'Jamena, where we had to obtain visas for the Sudan. After N'Jamena, we decided, we would not hire another guide unless it became essential.

Jibrin tried to compensate for his weakness by giving orders. 'Make rice with sardines tonight,' he told Marinetta. 'Keep those camels away from the *arak* trees,' he said to me. Another time he instructed me to hang an empty waterskin high in a thorn tree. 'So the jackals don't get it,' he said. Such remarks made me doubt his full sanity. And we were not the only victims of Jibrin's instructions. He was inclined to give them to anyone we passed. Once, for instance, we met some Arabs with a herd of camels feeding across the track. One of the animals was a bull-camel, blubbering and blowing out his mouth bladder. I noticed that the bull was hobbled by the knee. 'Keep that beast out of the way, you Arabs!' Jibrin ordered. 'Don't let it come near human beings!' The Arabs ignored him.

Another time a woman with a little boy begged us for water. She said that her husband had stormed off in a temper after an argument and left them to walk home. 'Don't ever argue with your husband,' Jibrin ordered her. As we passed some villagers later, he called out to them, 'There is a woman coming along this track who has had a row with her husband. Look after her and take her to your village.' Like the Arabs, the villagers showed no signs of having heard. Perhaps one of them was her husband.

Jibrin used a piece of twig as a camel stick. He never struck his camel with it but constantly flailed around with it in the air, extending his arm forwards and back and twirling it around his head. As he did so, he hummed to himself. 'Either he's doing arm exercises or he's practising to be a conductor,' Marinetta said. Whenever he saw a dog, he would point at it with his stick and recite something in a loud voice. The dog would watch us go past in bemused silence.

We made camp in a bald patch among some *heskanit* grass. After we had unloaded Jibrin said, 'I feel tired and a bit sick.' He uncovered his paunch of belly and asked me to feel it. It was fat and flabby. It was not the belly of a desert man. I thought of the rope-muscled Mafoudh and Moukhtar and of the powerful Sidi Mohammed. 'I've got a bad stomach,' he said. 'The doctor told me not to drink coffee or tea or eat kola nuts.' He lay down while I made a fire. Then I went off to watch the camels a little way from the camp. From where I stood the fire was the only bright spot in the pitch darkness, and my eye was automatically drawn to it. I saw Jibrin get up and approach the fire slowly. He looked round furtively, and I guessed Marinetta must have left the camp. He began to remove his shoes and socks. He dangled one bare foot over the flames, then the other. Then he lifted his gandourah and let the flames warm his bulging belly. Finally he squatted over the fire, pulled down his *sirwel* and warmed his backside. Then he retired into the shadows. When I returned to the camp he was already asleep.

The moon came up later, and I brought the camels in and hobbled them near by. At an early hour of the morning I was woken up suddenly by a terrifying scream. I jumped out of my sleeping-bag, startled. My first thought was that Marinetta had gone out and was in trouble. Then I realized that she was lying next to me. 'What is it?' she gasped as she woke up. We peered into the moonlight. Just beyond the place where the camels were hobbled I caught the sinister glimmer of yellow eyes. The camels had stopped chewing and were shifting nervously. I took the machete and went to investigate. Suddenly there was another ear-piercing scream and a great blunt animal shambled away into the shadows. It was a hyena with an ungainly head and a fat, bloated body. It was the first time I had ever seen a spotted hyena close-up. In the morning I asked Jibrin about the animal. He said that he hadn't even heard it.

That morning we came across a set of gnarled footprints in the sand. They were no more than hours old, and they were gigantic. It needed no skill as a tracker to see that they could belong only to an elephant. Jibrin began to gaze about him anxiously. 'You get herds of ten or twenty elephants here sometimes,' he said, whispering. 'They're all right – but an elephant on its own is dangerous.'

'Why are you whispering?'

'Because they can hear your voice a long way off.'

Now it was my turn to look around me. The landscape was still very arid. I was amazed that elephants could survive here. The previous night I had taken my machete to chase off the hyena. I asked myself what you could do against an elephant.

We reported to the *gendarmes* at Liwa, where dozens of screaming schoolchildren left off their games to pursue us into the brush. Jibrin paid out another 1,000 francs as tobacco fee. Outside the village we found ourselves in a tropical landscape. There were deep dells full of fluted dom palms, tangled in thick undergrowth, dank and humid. Great *siyal* trees towered above the brush, with canopies like massive parachutes and boughs dripping with lianas. Arabs and Gor'an watered animals in clearings. There were places where elephant herds had moved, rooting up trees from the soil and splitting them like straws. Their enormous droppings lay everywhere. A pack of red baboons skittered across the track and dived into the foliage. We emerged from the forest into rolling prairies scattered with tiny villages. They were set above fields of golden stubble, where the millet had recently been harvested. The houses were domes of twisted cane, built on high ground above the floodwaters of the lake, small fortresses against wild animals, drought and war.

Some time during the afternoon I was startled by a shout. I turned to see two soldiers charging towards us on camels. A third soldier, running across a field of stubble, was trying to head us off on foot. The soldiers surrounded us and regarded us with predatory faces. Two of them were young and the other old, but all of them were black, lean and aquiline. They reminded me of weasels. The soldier on foot was pointing his rifle at us, saying, 'You can't be tourists. Tourists come by car. They don't come by camel.' We replied only in French, afraid to use Arabic. Libyans spoke Arabic.

The other two troopers dropped from their camels. The younger one was wearing a pistol in a holster, which dangled heavily from his hip as he inspected our camels. 'We'll go through every-thing they've got,' the older man said. 'I bet we'll find some nasties!'

'Open all your baggage,' the pistoleer said. 'We're looking for firearms or drugs. You'd better not have anything illegal.'

'You can search us in Bol,' I protested. 'It's not right to search us out in the bush.'

The young soldier stood very close to me. I could see the red veins in his eyes. 'We'll say what's right,' he snapped. 'Open your baggage!'

'Better do as he says,' said Jibrin.

'So you speak Arabic,' the older man cut in, noticing my nod of understanding.

'Only a little,' I said in French. Resentfully I began to lay out our things on the ground. I realized that these men could steal anything they wanted from us. What worried me most was our emergency flare pencil. I thought that they might take it for a firearm. We were beyond the bounds of any protection, I knew. We had only ourselves. I was instinctively fearful that they might touch Marinetta. If they did, I found myself thinking, I hoped I would have the courage to fight.

The young soldier was going through Marinetta's personal effects. The bag containing the flare was in front of him. I watched as he held up some sticky pieces of soap, a dirty hairbrush and the two pairs of socks, very soiled and unwashed for months. I watched the look of disgust on his face with something like satisfaction. He rubbed his hands on his sleeve. 'Come on,' he told the others. 'There's nothing here.' Marinetta and I exchanged a look.

The older man said, 'Go straight to Bol. Don't leave the main track.' They watched us as we reloaded and set off.

'I wish we'd never brought that flare,' I said to Marinetta.

'Yes,' she agreed, 'but can you imagine what would have happened if we'd brought a satellite navigation unit?' We discussed whether we should throw the flare away, or bury it, but it occurred to me that if we should be seen, even by Jibrin, we would look very guilty.

We reached Bol before sunset the following afternoon. It was built on a peninsula surrounded by the glinting blue waters of the lake. We had only just entered the town when a narrow-faced youth shouted out that we were Libyans. Other youths and children crowded around us, looking ugly and firing questions. One of them, a barefoot adolescent with a skeletal face, stared at Marinetta and rubbed himself on the groin. We managed to get away from them and marched on through the sandy streets. Children pointed at us out of barred windows, and people scurried past, whispering.

The brigade HQ was set on a bank above the lake in some trees. A line of men in uniforms, all different, were sitting on a bench outside. They carried clubs and pistols. Their faces were unpleasant mahogany masks, and I saw mockery in their eyes as they looked at our camels. A big, pot-bellied man with yellow teeth told us to come back in the morning.

We were leading our camels back out of the town when someone bawled at us to stop from the open door of what was obviously a bar. He was of the young, thin-hipped, weasel-faced type that had already become familiar to us. His civilian clothes were unkempt, and he lurched over to us on unsteady legs. The odour of beer followed him. 'Where do you think you're going?' he demanded. I told him that we were heading out of town to find a place where the camels could eat. 'No, you aren't,' he said. 'Not unless you hand over your passports.'

'And who are you?' I asked.

He fixed me with an evil stare, as if the question were unthinkable. Then he showed me a pistol stuffed into his belt. 'I am in charge of passports, that's who I am,' he said. 'Police. You don't leave this town till I get your passports.'

'Where's your ID card?' asked Marinetta.

'I don't need an ID card. I have this.' He gestured at the pistol. 'Now, you give me those passports or you'll be in trouble.'

Jibrin volunteered nothing. I looked at the pistol and at Marinetta. Reluctantly I handed over our precious documents. I dared not think about what might happen to us in a country like Chad if our passports were stolen. They were our only way of proving that we were not Libyan spies.

We made camp in a field of stubble. It was infested with mosquitoes from the lake. Jibrin had a personal mosquito net but was too tired or lazy to cut wooden supports for it. Marinetta and I had only our tent. To cap it all, Jibrin told me, 'This place is well known for camel thieves. You'd better watch the camels well tonight.'

'How about you watching them for a change?'

'I wish I could, *patron*,' he said, 'but my leg, you know ...

At that moment there was an ear-shattering explosion. All three of us jumped. A Jaguar aircraft flew over us, so low that I could see the pilot in his cockpit. The noise of the machine shook our raw nerves, but it reminded me that this was a country at war. Our journey was a war too. Now we had to gather every ounce of courage and endurance to keep going.

I thought of Ibn Battuta, the Moroccan traveller. He had covered 75,000 miles in his lifetime, all without benefit of the internal combustion engine. He had visited every Muslim state then in existence. I remembered how he had been captured by Negroes, who had forced him to sit down and placed a rope in front of him. 'That is the rope they will tie me with when they kill me,' he had said to himself. Things had never been easy in the Sahara. Not even in his day.

We were amazed to find other tourists at the brigade HQ when we arrived there the following morning. Two Land-Rovers and a Toyota were parked outside. One of the Rovers belonged to some students from Edinburgh University. They had been heading down into Central Africa but had found the Nigerian border closed.

The four male students all wore olive-drab safari suits, like uniforms. The fifth member of the group was a woman, rather attractive, with a full figure and black hair. She sat in a folding chair, looking sick. The men had fresh, earnest faces. 'I pairsonally didnae want to come this way,' one of them told me. He was a short Scotsman, a little shy, with an angular face and a fluff of golden beard. 'I knew this soft sand would ruin the vehicle.' He showed me the sadly cracked chassis of the Land-Rover, saying with affection, 'She's thairteen years old. Now we'll have to leave her here.'

The gendarme chief was the same yellow-toothed man we had seen the previous night. With him was the ragged youth who had confiscated our passports. He was sober this morning and smiled at us nicely when we entered the office. We smiled back in relief. The chief asked to see our bills of sale for the camels, to which he applied his rubber stamp. Then he charged us 250 francs for each camel and 1,000 francs for our guide. I presumed it was a tobacco fee.

An hour later we were searched by the gendarmes. Three troopers went through our baggage with a mixture of curiosity and greed. Marinetta and I held our breath as they came to our emergency flare. 'This is a pistol,' one of them said. My heart missed a beat.

'No,' Marinetta said, smiling sweetly, 'it is a flare in case we get lost in the desert.'

'It looks like a pistol,' the trooper repeated, but already he was laying it down again disconsolately. Our sighs of relief must have been audible.

Another soldier was fingering one of our water bottles. 'This is military equipment,' he declared. 'It's illegal in Chad.'

'It's just a water bottle,' I said. 'And it's not in very good condition.'

The third soldier was already gazing towards the Land-Rovers, where the pickings looked more tempting. 'Ah, what do people with camels have?' he said. Later they confiscated two pairs of 'military' boots from the students.

Outside the commissar's office was a fat man in a long blue gandourah who addressed me in Arabic. He said that he was a Sudanese and came from Darfur, in the western Sudan, a region I knew intimately. He worked in Bol as an Arabic teacher, he said. He didn't look like a Sudanese. I had never heard of the village he claimed to come from. I must have looked puzzled because he said quickly, 'I was brought up in Khartoum.' I told him that I had lived in Khartoum and knew the city well. He changed the subject very rapidly.

The occupants of the second Land-Rover were a cheerful French couple with two small children. The children were both suffering from conjunctivitis. The couple were addicted to travel and were driving to India; they expected the journey to take two years. When they came to wait outside the commissar's office the fat 'Arabic teacher' asked me, 'Don't you think this French woman has some Arab blood?'

'I wouldn't know,' I told him.

The commissar was a youngish, handsome man. He was very silent. After a few moments he pointed to the picture of Hissein Habri on the wall. 'Do you know who that man is?' he asked. He told us that he had been a refugee with Habri in the Sudan. 'That's all history now,' he said. 'We were on the run then. Now we're back.' He tried to get us to talk about the relative conditions of Chad and the other countries we had passed through. Sensing danger, we both went silent. He went quiet too, and I guess he was wondering what profit could be made out of a pair of camel riders. Then a man came in and told him, 'Orders have just come through, sir. No one is allowed in or out until tomorrow.'

The commissar tried to look upset, but his 'Merde!' didn't sound convincing. It looked as though he was enjoying himself. 'I don't know if we can allow you to continue,' he said before we left. 'This is a country at war, you know.' He told us to return the next day.

We marched out, feeling confused. In Niger we had been held for six days but had never doubted that everything was official. Here, though, you had the feeling of being the victim of a cat-and-mouse game the object of which was exploitation. I had the uneasy sense that these people were capable of stripping me of everything, camels, money, even my wife. That night we resolved that we would refuse to be separated, whatever happened. We would refuse to give an inch. We would not abandon our plans. We would not relinquish our camels. We would not pay a penny in bribes. The only way forward was to fight.

The following morning, the commissar called for me alone. I made sure Marinetta was sitting with the French couple before I entered his office. I had noticed the fat 'Arabic teacher' hanging around like a vulture.

The commissar had one of the British students in his office. The man was sitting nervously on a stool, lean and aesthetic-looking with bright blue eyes. On the desk between them was an ordinary cassette deck with a separate amplifier, which had obviously been removed from the students' Land-Rover. The commissar asked me to translate his Arabic into English for the sake of the student. I sat down next to him, feeling equally nervous.

The commissar began to explain the situation. At sunset the previous day, he said, someone (could it have been the 'Arabic teacher'?) had seen the British students listening to a radio with an antenna. Then one of them had been seen speaking back into the radio. When the 'someone' had approached them, the students had quickly hidden the apparatus. The gendarmes had searched them later but had not found it. He wanted to know where the transmitter was. I listened incredulously. The story was an obvious fabrication. Still, I was obliged to translate.

The student, whose name was Graham, listened to me with increasing discomfort. 'It's not possible!' he exclaimed.

'I know,' I said, 'but I'm only translating what he said.'

'There's no radio,' Graham said shakily.

I translated, feeling just as shaky. Another man with an aggressive, bull-like face came in and stood next to the commissar, regarding us both threateningly.

'If that radio isn't found, you will be in big trouble!' the commissar said.

Graham went red. 'All we have apart from this,' he said, gesturing at the cassette deck, 'is a Sony Walkman.'

The commissar ordered him to go and get it. 'I really don't think they've got a radio,' I ventured, after he had gone out.

'What about these two?' the bull-faced man said. 'Shouldn't we confiscate one of their camels?'

Graham returned with the small Walkman. 'This isn't what we mean,' said the commissar. 'I've already got one like that.'

'There's nothing else,' said Graham. 'Only this car stereo.'

'Ah, yes!' said the commissar, as if noticing the stereo on the table for the first time. 'I think this is too powerful to be an ordinary stereo. It could be used for other purposes.'

'It's powerful because a Land-Rover engine is loud,' said Graham. 'It has to be louder than the engine.'

'Listen,' the commissar said, 'four hundred tourist vehicles came through here last year, and not one of them had a stereo as powerful as this. What's this "graphic equalizer", for instance? That's no ordinary stereo! It could be used for Morse Code – tele*graph*, you see!'

I watched the game that he was playing with tight insides. I watched Graham struggling, dying to tell him not to give in. I felt a natural sympathy for him, a member of my own people. A man must look after his own. But my immediate responsibility was to myself and my wife, and I was afraid that our own journey would grind to a halt here in this gloomy room on the banks of Lake Chad. I was reminded of my resistance to interrogation training in the SAS regiment. The bullying, the pressure, the disorientation all seemed very familiar. These people were using cold-blooded threats to steal this piece of equipment. I knew it, and Graham knew it. The commissar knew it, but he didn't care.

'I'll tell you what!' the commissar said suddenly. 'We'll let you keep the little Walkman. That's the important one for you. But we'll keep this big one. Either it stays here, or you stay here.'

Graham thought for a moment. 'All right,' he said, summoning as much dignity as he could. 'I didn't realize that the rules were so strict.'

'Now, don't you go telling bad stories about us when you get home,' the commissar said, crowing in triumph.

'I'll tell only the truth,' Graham answered bravely.

And so will I, I thought as we went out.

Marinetta was waiting for me in the sunshine outside. She said that the fat 'Arabic teacher' had tried to get her alone and had asked where she had slept the previous night. Just then Jibrin called us over and introduced us to an elderly man dressed in a smart gandourah. Much to my surprise, the man turned out to be the *préfet* of Bol. He asked us interested questions about our journey, then inquired, 'What's the delay with your passports? You shouldn't have been here for two days.' A few moments later the commissar emerged from his office, and the *préfet* called to him. The commissar saw us standing with the *préfet* and perhaps thought that I had reported the story of the car stereo. He looked a guilty man as he sidled up. 'What's all this business about the passports?' the *préfet* asked him. Before answering, the commissar sent us to wait outside his office. Half an hour later we were given our passports back.

Just before we left, I saw the chief of *gendarmes* remonstrating with the French couple, who had tipped the entire contents of their rubbish bags in a pile outside the commissar's office. Normally I detested litter. But on this occasion I thought it a fitting comment.

For another five days we prowled around the edge of Lake Chad. We travelled through cultivated country where the bulrush millet stood as tall and stately as a Guards battalion. The crops were full of people, rattling tin cans and shouting hoarsely at the attacking flotillas of birds. Between the fields were neat hamlets, four or five mud houses angled around a square. Huge old trees covered the smooth ground with black shade. In other places tangled jungles of dom palms and acacias stretched to the horizon, like equatorial rainforest. There were *merikh* and *tundub* trees, with fat juicy shoots, red berries hanging like grapes among the branches. Golden *heskanit* grass sprouted along the crevices of fractured clay that gradually replaced the sand.

Once we met a caravan of camels carrying millet sewn up in leather sacks. The Arabs with the caravan told us that the town of Messaguet lay only a day's journey away. That night we made camp in a dense forest. Within moments the camels were out of sight among the trees. Jibrin was already snoring. I had to track the animals down in the undergrowth and watch them while they fed. The ground was alive with the scampering of thousands of mice, which crawled over my feet. The sound of a drum came throbbing through the trees. Above the speartips of the branches the stars were clearer than I had seen them for days.

The next morning we entered Messaguet. The village was depressed and dilapidated, stewing in the heat. Children with swollen bellies looked at us with wide eyes as we passed through the labyrinth of houses. We traversed the rollicking lines of market stalls, where tins of Food and Agriculture Organization pilchards seemed to be the only food available. Everywhere was the brooding sense of defeat.

The sergeant of *gendarmes* was the smartest soldier I had yet seen in Chad. His face was broad and black, and his mouth dropped open slightly as we trooped into his room in our filthy clothes. There were two unused cannon shells standing on his desk as ornaments. You could see that he was trying hard to keep his cool. His scrutiny of our passports seemed very professional at first, until he snapped at Marinetta, 'Your height is only 157 centimetres [5 feet 2 inches]?' His mouth tightened and his eyebrows went up, as if this fact was of a most suspicious nature.

'I am very small, yes,' she giggled. 'It's not my fault.' I realized suddenly that the figure was probably the only thing in the passports which he'd understood. Her answer was too much for him, and he stood up and called a soldier to watch us, then strode out of the room.

The soldier was small and cylindrical and had only one eye. His face had a robotic blankness. His cap was pulled low over his single good eye, and he wore a combat suit that was evidently meant for someone slighter. He stood next to us awkwardly, then pointed to a poster that I had noticed on the wall. It showed a group of bearded

Libyan soldiers, presumably the ones recently captured in Tibesti, being led around a town in chains. 'The enemies of Chad!' the soldier said fiercely. One of the Libyans looked uncomfortably like me, I thought.

The sergeant reappeared, looking relieved. He instructed the soldier to take us to the office of the state security police. We couched and unloaded our camels outside some rambling brick buildings staggering around a courtyard. An old man in a black gandourah interviewed the three of us together. He had a seamy brown face and a silver stub of beard. Mostly he spoke to Jibrin in Gor'an, but once he asked me in Arabic, 'Is this woman your wife or your daughter?' After we had explained everything, he said to us, 'This is what you will do. You will leave your camels here with us. You will go to N'Jamena with a guard, and you will see the chief of state security. You can explain everything to him. Get ready. There is transport to the capital today.'

After we had moved our baggage into their store room Jibrin lay down in the shade of a straw shelter and groaned, saying that he had a fever. I gave him a dose of chloroquin and some aspirin. There was a wc in the corner of the yard, a hole in the ground guarded by a matting screen. We went behind the screen to change into our Western clothes. We had not changed our clothes at all since leaving Agadez forty-three days earlier. My hands were pitted with rough callouses; my fingers were covered in deep ruts, burned by fire ash, nicked and scarred by stones and plants. My face was deeply roasted by the sun except for a pink line across my head where the headcloth had sat. I watched Marinetta changing into her salopette. Her muscles were hard as an athlete's now. Her skin was dark bronze where it had been exposed. Gone was the look of touching innocence that I had first seen in that office in Khartoum. In her eyes was the ferocious fire of a strong woman.

Just as we finished changing someone shouted that the transport had arrived. We gathered our few possessions and went outside. The transport was an articulated lorry with about 500 people perched shoulder to shoulder on its spine. Jibrin groaned again. 'We can't ride on that!' he said. A young and chubby-faced Arab soldier with a Kalashnikov appeared and cleared tiny spaces for us after we had climbed up. We sat down with our legs hanging dangerously over the side. Jibrin's cup of misery was full. He was still feverish, and his leg hurt him in this crushed position. He was probably also white with fear that the vehicle would roll over, which seemed a distinct possibility given the hundreds of passengers. Behind us people pushed and shoved and elbowed each other, jabbering in Arabic and Gor'an and complaining about lost seats. As the vehicle lurched forward an old woman began to prod Marinetta in the back with a bony black finger. The woman had a horrific face. I told her to desist, but she ignored me and started making obscene remarks in Arabic. The men laughed but looked sheepish.

N'Jamena was only about 40 miles from Messaguet. Sunset came, and then the lights of the city showed ominously through the darkness. The lorry shuddered to a halt by a checkpoint, and the passengers scrambled down and began opening their baggage for inspection. We were ordered to transfer to a waiting Land-Rover. Things began to look more serious. I was surprised when the Land-Rover dropped us in the street and our guard said that we must get a taxi to the state security HQ – at my expense, of course. It was then that I put my foot down. 'Why should my wife and I spend the night in a police station?' I demanded. 'It's not possible. We are not spies or criminals, and we have visas for this country. All we have done is to enter the country riding camels, and that is not a crime.' I insisted that we go to a hotel and sleep properly. Then we could visit the state security HQ the following morning. Our guard was very young and obviously unused to making decisions. He wavered, and in the end I persuaded him. After all, I said, where were we going to run to when he had our passports?

The hotel was called Hôtel du Lac and it was run by a nervous Bornu. At first he wanted nothing to do with us. Then he obliged our guard to call his HQ by phone to make sure it was official. He showed us into a room with no furniture and a mattress on the floor. He smiled apologetically. 'The war,' he sighed. 'There used to be tourists here before the war. Ah, well, that's life. God is generous.' Before we slept our guard searched our belongings and removed our knives. I wondered what he imagined we intended to do with them. He sat down outside the room with his Kalashnikov across his knees and prepared for a long vigil. Jibrin sprawled out next to him. Inside we lay down on our mattress, shattered. A Jaguar flew low over the city, rocking the buildings with the boom of its engine. Just before sleep took me I heard the metal bolt being shot across our door.

Wild-beast Land

The state security H Q was a dark citadel from a nightmare. You could imagine rat-infested dungeons, racks and manacles hidden away behind its crumbling façade. A man in ragged clothes and unlaced boots sat by the gate. He nursed a sub-machine-gun lovingly on his knees.

The building was set behind high stone walls that were eaten away by bullet holes. It was heavy and broken, full of narrow corridors where nameless men stalked past us silently. Rows of plyboard doors were smeared with the grease of many hands. After an hour of sitting on the floor in a corridor, Jibrin was called into an office. The door snapped shut behind him. Someone told us roughly to wait outside in the yard.

There was a school bench to sit on. Six or seven red-bereted soldiers clattered back and forth around us. They were teenagers with all the arrogance of youth in uniform, They played cards and shouted at each other stridently in Gor'an. After that they wrestled and threw clods of earth. One of them seized his rifle and pointed it at another. Both of them seemed drunk.

We sat on the bench for eight hours. No one spoke to us or called us inside. The soldiers slurped tea and attacked a bowl of lentils but never offered us any. Jibrin never reappeared. Once a tall, stout man in a very clean gandourah emerged from the building, followed by a soldier who was evidently his bodyguard. Our soldiers left off horseplaying and saluted, while the man climbed into a Peugeot saloon. Then they went back to their horseplay.

'What do you think Jibrin's saying about us?' Marinetta asked. The soldiers glared at her, silently forcing her to shut up. But she had voiced my own fears. I remembered with great clarity the disparaging remarks I had made to Jibrin about the commissar in Bol. Jibrin was Nigérien, but, like the ruling elite in Chad, he was a Gor'an. He was one of them. As the hours passed, my mind explored the possible result of this captivity. Nothing I had seen here inspired my confidence. If things went against us, I thought, we could expect at best to be put on the next plane to Europe. At worst we might be suspected of spying, separated and thrown into prison. The idea of separation was too hard to bear after the hardship we had endured together. I was utterly horrified by the thought of being forced to leave Marinetta to the tender mercies of soldiers like these. Better, I thought, for us both to be taken out and shot.

Once I got up to fetch my pipe from the rucksack. 'Sit down!' one of the soldiers scowled. 'Don't move until you're told!' He looked about sixteen. When I sat down, he began describing to the others, in French, how he had once shot a man.

The sun grilled us. The soldiers retired into the shade of a broken-down shelter. The stout man returned in the Peugeot, and the soldiers scuffled out of the shelter to salute. Marinetta and I sank further into despondency as we were ignored. Our backs ached constantly from the now unaccustomed effort of sitting on a bench. We were hungry and thirsty. We had almost reached the stage of wishing that someone would start asking questions, no matter how brutally, to remind us that we were human beings.

At about two o'clock a man in a thick blue safari suit came to the door holding a flimsy paper. He beckoned to us. 'Go!' the soldiers said.

The man handed me the paper solemnly and said, 'Here it is.' I looked at the single sheet. It was an authorization to cross the whole of Chad by the land route as far as the Sudanese border. It had been signed by the Minister of the Interior himself.

When we looked up in shock, the man said, 'Stick to the main track. Do not go right or left. Report to any police posts you meet on the way. *Bon voyage!*' As we trooped out of the yard, with Jibrin and our guard from Messaguet trailing behind, I felt strongly inclined to make a very rude gesture at the red-bereted soldiers. But I refrained.

Jibrin parted from us hurriedly outside the gate, hobbling off with his few belongings and his Quran in the cardboard box. The young

Arab from Messaguet was less easy to dispose of. He had been instructed to stick to us like glue. We knew our next step. We would make a bee-line for the UNICEF HQ. It happened to be farther down the same street, and we had noticed it on the way in. As soon as the blue UN flag came into view, Marinetta ploughed towards it like a bulldozer. The guard had to stride out to keep up.

We arrived at the office just before closing time. The yard was full of cars with gunning engines, ready to go. A stream of employees poured out of the glass doors. We were searching desperately for a friendly face when someone said, 'Good God! Hallo!' It was Pamela Clifton, a slim, elegant Englishwoman whom we had met in London the previous year. She had then been a pillar of UNICEF's London press office. Now she was their information officer here in Chad. Within minutes she had taken charge of us and sent the soldier away with perfect diplomacy. When she invited us home it was the most welcome offer I had heard in nine months.

The walls of Pamela's house, like those of all the houses in N'Jamena, were scarred with bullet holes. Behind them, and behind her Chadian doorman, we sank into the downy opulence of a sofa and gulped down glass after glass of fresh mango juice. An air-conditioner purred behind us. The room was cheerfully decorated, and a bookcase crammed with English volumes stood in one corner.

Pamela's voice had a soothing quality. She was petite and very trim, with corn-coloured hair cut short and stylishly. Her mouth formed easily and quickly into a smile, and her blue eyes were constantly alive with excitement. 'You can't really blame them for being so sensitive,' she said. 'The country is at war, and don't forget that it's one of the poorest countries in the world.' The average income in Chad was only $90 a year, she told us. Huge gifts of dollars from the United States were almost all that kept the country on its feet. Yet still they were fighting the war against the far richer Libyans with courage and tenacity. The recent push that Habri's men had made in the north had been initiated by a change of allegiance among many Toubou. Once a fighter with the Libyans, their leader, Gikoni Wadai, was now discredited. This had given Habri his chance to expel the Libyan army from the north. French units had been brought in but were playing only a defensive role. We thanked our lucky stars for this change in the fortunes of war. Without it we should never have been allowed to cross Chad by camel.

N'Jamena's scars were the result of the battle that had raged between the Habri and Gikoni factions in 1985. You scarcely saw a building undamaged by artillery or peppered with bullet holes. The rival armies had expended ton upon ton of lead. When Habri had finally taken the city, however, the United Nations had moved in to help pick up the pieces. One of the first Westerners into the capital after that battle had been the UNICEF representative, Ulf Kristoffersson. He was a charming Swede, built like an Olympic weightlifter, whom both Marinetta and I had met in the Sudan.

Ulf picked us up by chance the following day in a sleek Mercedes limousine, chauffeur-driven, with the UN pennant flickering on the bonnet. Even Ulf's muscular bulk seemed dwarfed by the massive seat of blue velvet as he beckoned us inside. The car smelled of new leather. The door closed almost soundlessly. 'I don't like using this car,' Ulf explained, 'but I'm on my way to see the President. You have to put on a show, or they think it's weakness. Then you lose your bargaining power.' I have never liked motorcars, but those few moments in that limousine, easing along the taut streets of N'Jamena, seemed almost dreamlike after nearly 2,500 miles by camel.

Ulf surprised us by saying that he was interested in camels too. He intended to buy a herd of them. The camels would be used by UNICEF's health workers to reach remote places in the Chadian deserts. He had even ordered a miniature fridge, which would be carried on a camel's back and would preserve valuable vaccines during long journeys. 'It's still got some teething problems,' he said, 'especially the solar battery.' We saw a photo of one of Ulf's camels later. It wore the tasselled leather headpiece of the Toubou and had the word 'UNICEF' branded all the way along its neck.

Ulf dropped us at the Sudanese Embassy, where we met the Minister Plenipotentiary, Nureddin. He came from Wadi Halfa in the north of the Sudan but was as near to being British as any African could get. His evident good nature warmed your heart. 'It's too dangerous to travel through the northern Sudan just now,' he said. 'There have been new developments.' The new developments were the Libyans. 'You could take a truck to the Nile,' he suggested diffidently. I showed him the letter that I had received from the Sudanese Embassy in London. He sighed and agreed to issue entry visas as long as we signed a letter accepting all responsibility. 'You ought to take a gun with you,' he said. 'There are some bad people in the Sudan just now.' When the visas arrived they had the words 'By camel' written neatly over them in pen.

The man responsible for orchestrating the redevelopment of Chad was François Tissot. He was Swiss and lived with his wife Susan in a palace on the outskirts of the city. Tissot was the director of the UN's Development Programme, which was the paymaster of the other UN branches. He invited us to dine with them the day before we left.

He was a tall, sardonic man with a dry humour and a composure produced by thirty years of elations and depressions and reversals. He and his attractive wife had been almost everywhere in Africa. Susan Tissot kept us spellbound by a description of Uganda under the regime of Idi Amin. I asked François how UN aid worked, and he told me that every country had a certain amount of credit, depending basically on how poor it was. 'But there is an ethical factor,' he said. 'In the case of Chad, we support Hissein Habri because Libya has clearly invaded a foreign country.'

At dinner we sat down to a magnificent banqueting table of heavy oak, designed to seat twenty. Marinetta seemed so far from me across those acres of polished wood that we could scarcely hear each other talk. 'We brought this table from Tanzania,' Tissot said. 'Not an easy thing to carry about, I can tell you!' It seemed a superb feat to have got such a thing into this landlocked country at all. As we ate pizza and ice-cream I was once again filled with a dream-like sensation. It hardly seemed possible that only four days before we had been eating in the sand out of a fire-blackened pot.

Jibrin, wearing a new white gandourah, was waiting for us outside the UN building. 'Pay me my money, *patron*,' he instructed me. 'I've had enough of this place.' I handed over the money rather grudgingly, aware of how little work Jibrin had done by comparison with our other guides. I was tempted to say, 'Never was so much paid by people so poor for so little,' but then I thought of Jibrin's crushed leg and seven motherless children in N'Guigmi. The ten days he had been with us must have been a torture for him. I didn't even blame him for cheating us now: he had done the right thing from his point of view. A man must look after his own. And, actually, we had much to thank him for. He had done so little work that Marinetta and I had become experts in every aspect of handling our camels. As a guide, Jibrin had been excellent practice in not having one.

The door of the store room in Messaguet creaked open, and a beam of light stove in the darkness. Three figures were sitting hunched up among our saddlery and equipment. The light left yellow smears across their ragged shirts and greyish faces, and they blinked, screwing up their eyes in the unfamiliar brightness. The old security chief told me that they were three felons who had been caught stealing clothes from the market. They were to be locked up here until their case was decided. The grey, defeated faces looked at us blankly as we shifted our things. I was suddenly very glad to be setting off that night.

Our camels had been grazing in the fields around Messaguet, and while we were waiting for the herdsman to bring them in, we bought provisions in the market. A young state security officer insisted on accompanying us. Like most of the others, he must have been no more than twenty. I guessed that almost everyone older was away fighting the Libyans.

Hassan was a stringy, nervous man, impetuous, impulsive and obviously bright. He had been a refugee in Nigeria and spoke English and Hausa as well as French and Arabic. He said that the state security was 'like the CIA', but before long the romantic façade crumbled and he admitted to being worried about the future. He was a Bornu, he said, not one of the Gor'an who were the ruling elite. 'You can't get anywhere without having friends in high places,' he said. 'When the war finishes, that will be the big problem.' As we walked back towards the office Hassan revealed the true reason for his interest in us: could we, he asked, get him a job with the UN? 'You can never get near it unless you know someone,' he said. 'To see a white man you first have to get past a black man.' I wondered if that was a saying from colonial times.

The camels looked refreshed after their rest. As we loaded them hastily, the chief repeated, 'You should take a guide. There are plenty of bandits in Chad. There are subversives and rebels who all have guns.' We resisted adamantly. Our authorization did not specify that we must take a guide. After Jibrin we felt that we'd be better off alone.

A great conga of people followed our camels to the town gate, where a beer-reeking soldier examined our passports again. It was sunset. Beyond the wooden barrier low acacias lay in brooding darkness. The soldier lifted the barrier, leaning clumsily on the weighted end. Hassan looked at us with hooded, trustless eyes. 'Watch out for wild beasts and wild men!' he shouted. Then the plexus of light fell away behind us.

The town, its weapons and its police were a dim sheen of memory on the hugeness of the desert sky. Cicadas vibrated in the thornscrub. There was the rattle of rats and scampering lizards. The night, the whispering brush, the shadows of the stars and the last white rind of day formed a pattern that seemed suddenly dangerous. 'It's a bit scary,' Marinetta said. The Sudanese border lay 600 miles to the east. In all that vast expanse of desert it seemed we were alone.

Work was harder now that there were only two of us, but we were rewarded by a new sense of freedom born of the fact that no third person was watching us constantly. After the frightening experience of our arrest and brief captivity in N'Jamena we felt closer. I knew that we could make it to the Nile without a guide, but I doubted if we could do it without each other. There was no question of one of us going on alone: we would do it together or not at all. Sometimes I thought that, in its raw, harsh, desert form, this feeling must be love.

Over the next days Marinetta worked with a determination that I had only glimpsed previously. She struggled with jerrycans that were heavy even for a strong man, and strained on her side of the weighty provision sacks. When the camels were loaded she would take her turn at leading them, always walking as long as I did. When it was my turn to lead she would drive them on from the rear, swinging her little stick and making clucking sounds of encourage-

ment. We moved fast now, faster than we had done with almost any
guide. It was a rare day when we did not march for twelve hours
and cover 30 miles.

At midday we halted in the shelter of a tree and ate the remains
of the previous night's meal. It was hot again. The winter's span had
been abruptly cut short as we moved south. Again we drank copious
quantities of *zrig*. As soon as the light began to fade we would search
for a place as far off the track as possible. I knew that Hassan had
not been joking about 'wild men'. We would unload the camels,
making a tiny island in the desert, then hobble them and send them
off towards the grazing. We set up our equipment like a three-sided
fortress against the prevailing wind. Our saddles formed the cross-
wall, and each saddle bag and container had its place along the
battlements. Inside this tiny *querencia* we laid out our groundsheet
and, on top of that, our blankets. Then, as the darkness thickened
around us and the camels shuffled among the stunted trees, we would
sit on our blankets and Marinetta would make tea. We each drank a
whole mug of it, scalding hot and very sweet, with dried milk added.
It was the most welcome experience of the day.

After tea, which we made on our gas cooker, I would collect
firewood for the main meal. Making fire was a dicey business in this
uncertain country. A campfire was like a beacon; it attracted enemies
and unwanted guests. On the second night out of Messaguet I left
the camp to watch the camels while Marinetta was cooking our meal.
Suddenly I heard her shout, 'Maik! Come quick!' In the long, flickering
shadows, three men were standing, watching her. Their squat forms
threw ugly dark shapes on the uneven sand, and their faces were
demonic in the firelight. Each of them carried a spear with a leaf-
shaped blade and a haft taller than the tallest man. The wide speartips
glittered in the flames. The men stood motionless, staring at
Marinetta, as I emerged from the darkness. I was unarmed except for
the knife that I now wore constantly. I shook hands with each of
them, but as they made as if to sit down, I suggested firmly that
there was a better place to camp farther on. Close up, the men had
simple, farmers' faces. Most likely they were ordinary tribesmen. But
I had seen and heard enough of Chad to know that it was not worth
taking chances.

After this incident we used our gas cooker as much as possible. It gave out little light and could be concealed behind our baggage. Before and after our evening meal I would be coming and going with the camels. Watching them was a constant problem, especially when there was no moon. I tried to keep them always in view, which meant following them and driving them back to the camp if they wandered too far. They would be awkward, meandering this way and that or dipping their heads under the branches of very thorny trees. Often one of them got his nose-ring caught in the thorns and would stand their wailing until I released him. In bright moonlight, though, I was afforded a little rest. I could watch the camels from our camp with a pair of binoculars, a generous present from a friend in N'Jamena.

When our meal was ready Marinetta would call me over to eat. We always ate rice or macaroni, with the same old sardines or dried meat. We ate with Tuareg spoons, which we had acquired in Niger, scooping the food from our pot, which had been with us since we had left Chinguetti. It had been used as a drinking bowl, a washtub, a well bucket and a watering trough for the camels as well as a cooking utensil. The original shining silver had long since matured into a smooth patina of fire-black, yet after the thousands of miles it still maintained its shape. That pot was more than just an old friend to us: it was home.

After the meal we would spend half an hour writing up our diaries by torchlight. When that was done we would both drive the camels into the camp and knee-hobble them for the night, near enough for us to touch them. They made the fourth wall of our little redoubt in the wilderness. We would crawl exhausted into our sleeping-bags, and only then, as the last act of the day, would I light my pipe. Those few puffs of tobacco, as I sat in the sepulchral silence listening to the belching of the camels as they chewed the cud, seemed to make the whole day worth while.

We had been instructed never to leave the track, but when villages appeared on the horizon we often made a detour around them. Most small villages had a *gendarme* or two, some of them illiterate, whose fear of us could be a greater obstacle than our fear of them. There were few vehicles on the road, but once a military convoy rumbled past us, ten or a dozen heavy trucks, each with a compliment of guards riding shotgun on top. The guards looked ferocious with their headcloths across their faces and their combats bleached with dust. The convoy halted somewhere ahead, and we left the road at once, making a semicircle and rejoining the track farther on. The last thing we needed was to be mixed up with the military. Another time we heard gunfire, and saw some jeeps parked along the track. A squad of soldiers were firing across the road and into the bush on the other side. I had no wish to find out what they were shooting at, though the middle of the road seemed an odd place for target practice.

Occasionally we were forced into the villages to find water. On 3 February we sighted the settlement of Ngoura. It lay among some languid thorn trees, squatting under a nugget of flinty grey shale. A wooden barrier blocked the track with a sign reading 'Stop' in squinting letters. Near by stood a blockhouse, where a Chadian tricolour flapped drowsily. A teenage boy with a rifle and wearing the uniform of a *gendarme* came out to meet us. He wore broken sandals and a wiry undergrowth of hair instead of a cap. His eyes were wide and shiny with fear as he moved towards us. I produced our passports, and the boy clicked his fingers for them, keeping us at arm's length. Then he disappeared again into the blockhouse. At once a mob of tribesmen came stampeding out as if someone had lobbed a grenade among them. They circled us like vultures, a sea of grey faces and dirty gandourahs, gabbling, 'Are they Arabs or Christians?' Eventually a more responsible-looking *gendarme* pushed his way through, carrying our documents. He spoke to us in French. 'You are going to the Sudan?' he asked.

'Yes, but we need water for our camels.'

'The camel is a very sturdy animal,' the man said. 'It can go without water for a very, very long time.'

Marinetta caught my eye for a fraction of a second. I looked away. 'Are there any wells around here?' I asked.

Water was pumped up from a deep-bore well and fed into some concrete basins near by. The water was too bitter for us, but the camels swallowed it thirstily. There were some Arabs there, watering a brace of plump ponies. The men had brooding brown faces and carried giant spears and arm daggers.

'Where have you come from?' one of them asked.

'From Mauritania,' I said.

'Isn't that the country of Moukhtar Ould Dadda?' he asked. 'The people there are Arabs, aren't they?'

'Yes, but my own country is Britain,' I said, fearing confusion.

The Arab wrinkled his face. 'Where's that?' he inquired.

In the village women with slim, black bodies sat at the doors of one-roomed huts of mud. Along the main street a line of little girls were selling drinking water in earthenware jars. A man was frying a very flat chicken on a charcoal grill. We bought the chicken and the water, and while we squatted down to eat, the little girls formed a procession to fill our jerrycans.

Such villages punctuated the monotony of the arid landscape through which we plodded hour after hour, day after day. It was bushland of red sand, sparse yellow grass, clumps of greying gorse and brambly trees and the curious double trunks of dom palms like enormous fluted flowers. Once we ran into a herd of *kudu* cattle driven by Arabs on horses. The cattle flowed across the track like a many-coloured oil slick, brown and tawny, black and white. The men were small and dark, wearing knotted turbans, and sheaves of assegais swung from their saddles. We saw men riding camels, schools of five or six of them sweeping along in a bolus of dust, their faces intent and dark under their cowls of cloth.

There were whole families on the move: strings of camels carrying worm-eaten old saddles and crude cowskin saddle bags. There were children riding on bullocks with strings through their snouts and women sprawling on cohorts of grey donkeys – handsome, muscular women, naked from the waist up, displaying sleek breasts and lean shoulders of copper bronze.

These people were mostly nomads of the Baggara cattle Arabs, who were spread across Africa from Lake Chad to the Nile. Their tents, made of woven palm fibre like those of the Toubou, dotted the landscape like igloos and could be identified by the helixes of smoke from their campfires.

As the days passed the constant corrosive fear of both authorities and bandits whittled us down to the level of pure survival. We were like commandos behind enemy lines to whom every move is potentially hostile. After a twelve-hour march each day we would hug each other tightly in silent celebration of having survived. But the evening brought little relief. There were the camels to be watched against thieves and the cooking to be done in secret. There were a thousand and one jobs to be completed: restitching torn sacks, repadding saddles, tightening ropes and repairing hobbles. Always our ears would be scanning the night for the slightest sound, the softest footfall, a momentary halt in the camels' chomping. Our senses became as sharp as those of hunted beasts. We smelled woodsmoke long before we saw the flash of fire. We picked out the tiny shapes of camels in the landscape long before they came near. When selecting a camping place at sunset we would search the surrounds for the tracks of men and animals and would even examine the environment methodically with binoculars to make sure that no one was lurking near by. If we heard voices as we were drinking tea or eating, as we did several times, we would stop and try to pick out the figures in the darkness. We would not relax until they had gone by.

At night we slept on a hair-trigger with our poor weapons by our sides. The slightest sound would wake us instantly. Often the camels got hungry and crawled off as far as a hundred yards away. I would be forced to get up and bring them back to the camp by torchlight. We rarely enjoyed a full night's sleep, yet we would be on our feet before dawn, loading the camels for another day's march. Marinetta endured it all without complaint now. Her red-raw face set itself into a new mould of weary determination. We both knew that we had to make it to the Sudan.

When we stopped for our midday meal we were plagued by ticks. Marinetta had a special loathing for the leathery little mites. They were very cunning. If you inspected the area around the base of a tree, you would see nothing of them. Then, just as you sat down to your food, the earth's crust would crumble and out would troop a detachment of blood-suckers. Nothing seemed to deter their kamikaze raids. They would crawl up our legs and dive into the joins of our sandals. They would scale the sheer wall of the cooking pot and abseil down into the food. They were always a mystery to me. I knew that they could live for years between meals. But why were they found under some trees and not others? How did they sense a warm-blooded presence? I reasoned that it could only be by vibration of a certain magnitude, but in that case why the delay before they appeared? Very often they drove us out of the shade into the hot sunlight, and some persistent individuals even followed us there.

At nights we were so shattered that we could hardly move. Since leaving Agadez in December, we had 'rested' for a total of eight days. Almost every other day we had marched for between ten and twelve hours. The constant work, even on 'rest' days, had drained the strength out of my muscles. My skin glowed charcoal-hot from exposure to the sun. Often I suffered crippling migraines accompanied by nausea and palpitations, as if the working parts of my head had slipped out of gear. A mesh of glittering lights would form before my eyes, inducing disorientation. At those times I couldn't do anything but ride or walk, and Marinetta would take over leading the caravan. When I came to write my diary, the events of the day had already become a pot-pourri of dislocated images. One village blurred into another, lost in a landscape that was bleak, hot and comfortless, spreading over everything and dwarfing any feature that man had made on its surface. The one act of significance each day was when I marked our position on the map and worked out the distance that still remained between us and the Sudan.

The Sudan became our promised land, and Chad dissolved into an endurance test. As the exhaustion ate at us like poison, we grew paranoid. Any figure or group travelling behind us was following us. A shepherd with a spear asked us for water; while I filled the bowl from our waterbag, I told Marinetta to watch him, imagining that leaf-headed lance being plunged between my shoulder blades at any moment. When we moved on, the man followed us, his spear balanced over his shoulder like a rifle. When we moved faster, so did he. When we shifted to another track, he shifted with us. When we stopped, he stopped. In our paranoia he was an enemy to be thrown off at any cost. We mounted our camels and drove them on relentlessly. Still the persistent figure remained behind us, striding doggedly with his spear. The camels were panting as we whipped them forward. Trails of dust like muslin layered the air behind us. Each time I turned my head, Marinetta gasped, 'He's still coming!' I heard the urgency in her voice. I felt the same near panic inside. The man had been tried and condemned as a bandit in our own minds, and nothing seemed so important as getting rid of him. An hour before sunset we found ourselves in a forest of dom palms. We ploughed along beneath fluted foliage. It reminded me of Malaya rather than the Sahara desert. The man finally dropped out of sight. We continued until the sun was sinking through the trees in the background. We turned far off the track and made camp in a hidden place behind some low palm shrubs.

Just as we sat down to drink tea, I heard voices. They seemed very near. 'Ssh!' I whispered to Marinetta as I put my tea down. There were the voices of two men, and I could hear the creak of a camel saddle in the darkness. I took the binoculars and leopard-crawled out of the camp. Marinetta lay silently in our concealed baggage. Our camels were grazing in the bushes a hundred yards away. I scanned the forest. Two camel riders were moving stealthily through the groves of palms, apparently looking for something. I could see the pale moonlight gleaming on their gnarled faces and the hafts of the spears slung across their saddles. I wondered why they weren't on the track. Suddenly one of the riders couched his camel and slipped off. I thought they might have sighted our animals. Then, as I watched, the man squatted down and urinated. Afterwards he led his camel by the bridle and they passed within a few yards of our camp. I watched them disappear into the palm fronds with relief.

Our camels were thirsty and in poor condition. Their feet had cracked from the hard ground, and old Shaybani had a bad gall on the withers, which had become infected and smelled revolting. There was little for them to eat among the dom palms, but I dared not let them wander far. In those trees they would have been lost in minutes. I had to tighten their hobbles and watch them constantly. After a short time I would have to unhobble them, attach their headropes and move them to another place, then hobble them again. It was a painstaking process, which seemed to last hours. All the time I was longing to lie down on my blanket. Once I stopped to watch Marinettta working at the fire. She was making bread, pummelling the dough into flat loaves and cooking them on our steel plate. The delicious smell of baking bread filled the night. The flickering firelight played over her face, absorbed with the job, set with incredible patience and determination. No one, I thought, could be tougher than this small, ordinary, extraordinary woman. I was suddenly, irrevocably, glad she was my wife.

We arrived in the town of Ati in the early morning. It was the regional capital, from where we needed yet another stamp if we were to proceed east into the province of Wadai. The town was wreathed in new mesquite trees. The troopers at the barriers smiled at us and shook hands as we arrived. We moved through a wide boulevard, shaded with giant canopies of trees, until we came to the state security office. The security men checked our authorization and passed us on to the commissar of police.

He was a shy man, dark enough to be a southerner, who spoke French and pretended not to know Arabic. He was sympathetic and talked with affection of the three UNICEF nurses who worked in the town. He stamped our passports almost at once and was about to hand them back when his face clouded over. The hand with the passports in it halted in mid-flight across his desk. 'You'd better have a word with the *préfet*,' he said. 'It's only a formality, but he likes to know what's going on.'

As soon as we entered the *préfet*'s office I realized that we were in trouble. He had a broad, dark face and was fastidiously dressed in a safari suit and a stiff collar and tie. A severe pince-nez decorated the end of a slightly aquiline nose. He winced at the effort of shaking hands with us. As we sat down the hooded eyes raked us from head to foot. He unfolded our authorization carefully. He seemed unimpressed. When I showed him a letter of recommendation given to us by Ulf Kristoffersson, who had helped us in N'Jamena, he scoffed visibly. 'We cannot allow you to go farther by camel,' he said. 'There is the problem of *sûreté*. This is a country at war.' A cold flush of fear fizzled down my spine. The man looked as though he meant it. The Sudanese border lay only twelve days' march away. Was it possible that, after all we had endured, we would be stopped now?

'No,' he went on. 'What if you were captured by the enemy and held hostage? Then there is the problem of robbers on the way. No, it's impossible!'

'We've had no such problems up to now,' I said.

'You weren't in Chad,' he answered, then he peered at our filthy clothes more closely. 'I think you are a couple of *intellectuals*. You think all this is a game.'

'Look,' I said, 'we've got permission from the Minister of the Interior himself to travel as far as the Sudan.'

He scrutinized the authorization again, holding up the pince-nez with an effete hand. 'This authorization,' he said triumphantly, 'does not mention the word "camel".'

The commissar blinked at us apologetically in his office. He must have been guiltily aware that we had already seen our passports stamped. 'I'm sorry,' he said, 'but my hands are tied.' Then he dropped the bombshell. 'You'll have to go back to N'Jamena,' he said.

I flushed. I tried hard to control my anger. I just couldn't believe it. My instinct was to fight. 'What if we refuse to go?' I asked him.

'That would be unfortunate,' he said, 'but there won't be any question of that, will there? You'll be going with a guard.'

So this was it, I thought, after such a distance, after seven months of travel. This was the end of the road.

There were no passengers on the truck except ourselves, a soldier called Musa and three goats tied to the chassis by string. Each time the truck lurched over a rut, which was every few minutes, the goats fell sprawling over one another, almost strangling themselves. 'At least they're worse off than we are,' Marinella declared, bouncing a foot off the roll of matting that was our only seat. The only difference I could see was the string.

The three days of that journey back to N'Jamena convinced me, if I had any last doubts, that motor vehicles are not the ideal means of travel in Africa. We were jolted and shaken like rattles until our bones ached; we were blasted by the sun and strangled all day by the exhaust fumes. Our guard, Musa, was a disarmingly friendly Arab with very large ears and prominent teeth, which gave him a humorous appearance. Marinetta quickly named him Topogigio after the Italian equivalent of Mickey Mouse. There was little that was comical about the sub-machine-gun he carried though, except perhaps that it was badly pitted with rust.

Each time we halted in a village that we had passed through people would gather round us asking, 'Where are your camels?' Then they looked at Topogigio and his sub-machine-gun and were confirmed in the belief that we had been, after all, dangerous foreign spies.

At the state security HQ the man in ragged clothes and unlaced boots was sitting by the gate. He leered at our small cortège.

We waited two hours, sitting in a corridor, then we were called into the presence of the Director of National Security. He was a young, handsome, expansive type. He wore a red-and-black shirt or *batikh*. He smiled at us over the desk. 'There's been a message about you from Ati,' he said. I showed him our authorization indignantly. His dark, handsome mouth split into a wide grin, and he threw his head back and laughed. '*Il n'a pas bien compris!*' he chuckled. 'He didn't understand! There has been a mistake. When would you like to go back to Ati? At once! Why don't you stay here the weekend? Don't you like dancing?' He must have read the answer in our grim faces, for he called in a shaven-headed police superintendent and instructed him to write a letter to the commissar in Ati.

Two hours later we were still waiting for the superintendent to finish his breakfast. Then he called us into his office and said, 'You will go from here to Ati by truck. Then you will sell your camels and go to the Sudan by lorry.'

My head reeled. I shut my eyes for a second. Marinetta was looking at him with her mouth open. I gripped the superintendent's desk and tried to master my emotions. 'We will *not* go by truck,' I told him, as calmly as I could. 'We have been given permission to go by camel. We will go only by camel.'

The superintendent looked at me in genuine surprise. Then he stood up and rushed out of the office. We sat there waiting, too confused and miserable even to speak. I cannot recall how long we waited, only that it was the most tense and agonizing wait of the entire journey.

Then the superintendent came bustling back. We waited with bated breath as he sat down. 'I'm sorry,' he said. 'There has been a mistake. You will proceed to Ati by truck. From there you will proceed to the Sudanese border *by camel*.' Half an hour later he pressed a brown envelope into my hand. Marinetta and I looked at each other. Then we both clenched our fists in a spontaneous victory sign. That letter was our passport to the Sudan.

In the UNICEF building François Tissot regarded us with a dreamy half smile, and invited us into his office. We sank into his leather armchairs and drank coffee from a thermos. Tissot called in a man named Schiller. He was another Swiss with a lifetime of work in troubled places behind him. He had long, grey hair and giant sideburns: perhaps it was the sideburns or the name that reminded me of Albert Schweitzer.

'I'm sure Mr Schiller can do something for you,' Tissot said, 'can't you, Mr Schiller? Unofficially, of course.' Schiller nodded in agreement. Within ten minutes he had arranged for us to return to Ati in a UN car with a local driver.

'And don't put *that* in your bloody book!' Tissot said.

We watered at Umm Hajar in a slick of pea-green liquid left over from the rains. Naked children were splashing about in the murky water, and others were trawling for fish with square nets. An Arab called Yasin escorted us through the village. He was an educated man from the Baggara and was helping to run an OXFAM nomad project in Umm Hajar, which was a watering centre for the cattle Arabs.

Yasin said that there were three grades among the Baggara: those who had both cattle and camels, those who had cattle and cultivation and those who had just cattle. All the cattle were the shorthorn *kudu* type, which, he told us, were more resistant to drought than the longhorn cows we had seen in Niger. But many nomads were changing to camels as the Sahara marched inexorably closer each year. 'The rains haven't been bad this year,' Yasin said, 'but half of the millet crop has been lost to plagues of mice and locusts.' The locust plague had been the worst for decades, and the grasshoppers had blackened the streets with their presence.

A Belgian aid worker called Pierre told us that he'd seen a locust swarm so thick that he'd had to use his windscreen wipers. 'They breed near Lake Chad,' he said. 'The eggs can lie fertile in the sand for three years. The drought killed the locusts' natural enemies, like rats and birds. When the rains came the hoppers emerged from the eggs with plenty of food and no predators. Then you've got a plague!'

Pierre was half Flemish, and looked like a nineteenth-century French cavalry officer with his short hair and neat moustache. Ironically, he had come to Africa to avoid military service. 'It's all above-board,' he said. 'If you find yourself a job and keep it for twenty-two months, you're no longer liable for the military.' After he had finished his spell in Chad, he intended to settle down with his Camerounian wife in Yaoundé. His wife was a master brewer who worked for Brasseries Cameroun.

We left Umm Hajar in blistering heat and made camp before sunset among some fields of yellow stubble. In the grass we noticed two large burrows where the sand had been cast out and piled up by some powerful animals. 'What are those?' Marinetta asked.

'Ah, probably ant-eaters,' I replied.

Just after we had set up our camp, in the last grey shadows before total night, we were frozen by the terrifying screeching and chuckling of three or four hyenas. The animals sounded very near, their cackling and crowing almost like the gloating of some very evil human beings. Then the sound faded, and there was silence. The camels, a few yards away, had stopped grazing and were looking around nervously. 'Oh, Jesus!' Marinetta exclaimed. 'We've camped right on top of a hyena's nest!'

She began telling me about a film she had once seen. There had been an exclusive gambling club in which rich clients played roulette for huge stakes. Those who were unable to pay their debts disappeared mysteriously. There was a certain debtor who tried to escape after welshing on a debt. You heard the hollow sound of his footsteps on the deserted street at night. Then a big black limousine pulled up and a gang of thugs seized him. The next thing you saw was a dark cellar and the yellow, glowing eyes of starving hyenas. The man was dropped, screaming, through a trapdoor, and the hyenas pounced on him. The last thing you heard was his cries of agony as the animals crunched his bones.

'Don't worry,' I told Marinetta. 'Hyenas don't attack people. They're scavengers.'

I didn't feel as confident as I tried to sound. The belief that hyenas were purely scavengers was a myth. Since they were afraid of the light and hunted only at night, few people ever saw them making a kill until infra-red photography was developed. Then a woman zoologist had made a chilling film showing hyenas attacking and killing wildebeest in Tanzania. It was a film that I had never forgotten. Then there was the instance of the British biologist who had been travelling by Land-Rover in the Serengeti park at night. The vehicle had run out of petrol, and the man had decided to walk back to his camp. He knew that there would be hyenas about, but they were said never to attack humans. As he walked, a pack of hyenas began following him. The biologist had begun to feel uneasy and had walked faster. The hyenas had come closer and closer, and finally one of them had sprung at him. Terrified, the man had made a super-human leap into a tree, and the hyena had grasped only the seat of his shorts. The beasts had pawed around the tree until sunrise, then disappeared. When the length of his leap was measured the following day, it was a new Olympic high-jump record.

At exactly one in the morning we were woken up by a blood-curdling screech. A dark shape lurked in a thorn tree not 5 yards away. Behind us, in the middle distance, my torch caught the glow of golden-yellow eyes. I grasped the machete, and Marinetta grabbed her stick. Our camels had stopped chewing; one of them, Pepper, had crawled away from the camp in search of more grazing. We shouted and banged on plates and pots. The dark shadow disappeared from the thorn tree. While Marinetta fixed the torch on the pairs of gleaming eyes, I built up a fire quickly. The eyes withdrew into the darkness. When the fire was blazing, I went out to fetch Pepper nearer to the camp. The eyes did not reappear, but we kept the fire going until dawn.

All the next day we were troubled by thoughts of hyenas. 'I haven't come all this way to be eaten by a hyena,' Marinetta said.

'Don't worry,' I told her. 'The old explorers thought nothing of hyenas.'

'The old explorers had armies of servants and guns that would have knocked down an elephant,' she said. 'Here it's just you and me and a machete.'

'And our emergency flares,' I answered.

'Bah!' she said.

At noon we halted in the shade of some thornscrub as usual. A few minutes after we had stopped a Hilux pick-up came along the track, loaded with soldiers in combat gear. As soon as they saw us, the driver pulled up and the soldiers leapt out. They ran towards us with their rifles. Their faces were grim and unfriendly, their combats soiled and ragged. I hoped that they were government men and not rebels. Marinetta and I took up a defensive position in front of our camels. The men circled us threateningly.

I felt nervous but also annoyed that they should find it necessary to threaten people who were obviously helpless. 'Do you want to see our passports or what?' I asked, a shade too abruptly.

A youth with the face of a street-corner delinquent examined our papers. 'What is your nationality?' he inquired.

'British and Italian.'

'The British and the Italians are our friends,' he said and handed the documents back.

'With friends like you, who needs enemies?' I said, but not until the truck had safely pulled away.

There were no sounds of crying hyenas when we made camp at sunset. 'Thank God!' Marinetta commented.

After we had eaten I went to collect the camels and returned to find her clutching the machete in one hand and her torch in the other.

'What is it?' I asked.

'There!' she gasped. 'There's something in that bush, moving!'

'Rubbish!' I said, and just then there was an ominous grunting sound, ugh! ugh! ugh!, and a heavy creature shifted out of the bush ten yards away. At once there was a shout, and the curtain of darkness was sliced open by a piercing beam of light. A dog yapped and belted past our camp into the trees. The powerful beam came straight towards us, blinding us. I took the machete from Marinetta. 'Who is it?' I yelled.

Behind the flashlight were two Arab boys. One held the torch and a club and the other a huge spear. 'Did you see the hyena?' one of them asked. 'We were looking for the hyena.' The boy told me that they had come from a Baggara camp near by and that every night they were plagued by hyenas, which took lambs, kids or even calves.

'Don't you hear the barking?' he asked. 'That's the herdsmen and their dogs. They never sleep in this place. It's well known for hyenas, big ones. They are the worst hyenas in Wadai.'

'Do they attack humans?'

'Yes. It has happened several times. They aren't afraid of anything but light and fire. But you shouldn't stay out in the open like this. Stay in a camp or a village. The hyenas attack camels too.'

That night, for the second time, the fire was burning until morning.

The next day we crossed a sandy plain almost devoid of trees. Humpbacks of rock appeared on the horizon. Quite suddenly military vehicles began to pass us. First there were two jeeps with high radio antennas, then 3-ton lorries, then heavy trucks. The drivers were Frenchmen, bare-chested and insect-eyed behind their black sand goggles. Some of them stared at us in surprise. Others drove past without looking. There were military cranes and excavators and jeeps equipped with mounted machine-guns for desert fighting. I guessed that it was a French column bound for the Abéché region, where they had recently installed an early-warning device. The column was passing us for ninety minutes.

Their effluence was scattered all over the plain. There were book matches, empty tins and scores of plastic mineral-water bottles. I stopped to examine them. The mineral water was 'Made in France': how incredible, I thought, that they should bring their own water with them all that way. Just then Marinetta pounced on something and giggled in glee. It was an economy-size roll of military toilet paper, still sealed in its wrapping. 'That will last me till the Nile!' she said.

The hills came nearer in the afternoon. They were gnarled carbuncles of granite, pink and grey with smears of white, rising in terraces over a plain of stunted grass, red sand and a few trees. We made camp early, tired from stoking the fire all night. Later I brought the camels in close. The fire was dying, and I was about to light my pipe when Marinetta hissed, 'The camels have stopped chewing!' She was right. They were still and were staring upwind at something that neither of us could see. 'What's that sound?' Marinetta gasped, catching her breath. There was a distinct rhythmic wail coming towards us, a mournful sound.

'It sounds like a goat being slaughtered,' I said.

'Goat, my foot!' yelled Marinetta, getting up. 'That's a hyena, and it's coming straight here!'

I flashed my torch into the night and immediately caught the glow of almond-shaped eyes, smouldering gold, a stone's throw beyond the camels. *Ugh! uuugh! uugh!* came the chilling call out of the shadows. 'It's coming!' Marinetta whispered. I seized the machete. She followed the animal with the beam of her torch as it passed around us warily, close enough for us to see its bulk and to hear its heavy footfalls. It had a bloated belly and an enormous black head. 'My God!' Marinetta wheezed. It was the biggest hyena either of us had seen.

The hyena turned to face us downwind, sniffing the air appraisingly. I looked straight into the hellish eyes, and for a second I was certain it would attack. I was looking down a tunnel into the remote cave-man past, grasped by the same instinctive fear felt by my distant ancestors: dark night, open bush, wild animal. 'Get the flares!' I yelled.

Marinetta rummaged feverishly in the saddle bag. 'They're not here!' she wailed.

'They damn' well are!' I swore, holding up my machete behind our barricade of luggage. At last she handed me the flare pencil and I fitted a cartridge. I pulled the trigger and released it. There was a sickening dry click. Nothing happened.

'He's coming, Maik!' Marinetta wailed again. I pulled the trigger a second time. Again there was a click. 'Quick!' Marinetta was urging me. The third time there was a gratifying *bang!*, and the night was drawn back by a brilliant corona of crimson fire. The dark bulk of the hyena dissolved into the shadows.

For minutes we surveyed the battle area for any signs of movement. Then Marinetta hugged me tightly. I could feel her body trembling. 'What if it comes back?' she asked. 'There might be more of them!'

'We'll build a fence,' I said, 'a defensive position. You get that fire going!'

For two hours I sallied forth into the darkness with the machete and hacked at any bushes within range. Marinetta built up the fire and raked the surroundings with her torch. I cut wood until my hands were blistered and bleeding, hurrying back to the camp with thick

branches for the fire and long, thorny boughs, which we twisted into
a stockade around our tiny position. There were few trees, and each
time I had to venture farther afield. Once I saw a tempting piece of
wood lying in front of a gaping hole in the sand. I backed away,
expecting a bloated creature to appear at any moment. At last we
had enough wood to keep the fire going. We sat down, dog-tired,
inside our barrier.

Marinetta asked, 'You're not going to sleep, are you?'

'No, no!' I answered. 'We'll take turns to stay awake. Two-hour
stags. Sentry duty, just like the army. My stag first.'

Ten minutes later I was slumped across the luggage, probably
snoring. Marinetta woke me. 'So much for your sentry duty!' she
said. 'You'd have been shot by now.'

We passed through Abéché in the late afternoon and received another
stamp from the commissar there. We led the caravan out of the town
into pitch-darkness. Jeeps passed us with blaring headlights, forcing
the camels off the track. Twice we had to stop to adjust loads.
Suddenly a sharp voice shouted, 'Alt!', and there was the awful
metallic ring of a rifle being cocked.

'Oh, God!' Marinetta choked. 'Now they're going to shoot us!'

I shouted out that we were tourists, and a minute later we almost
barged into two young Chadian soldiers, nervously pointing their
rifles. They advised us to remain near the guard post that night.
There were bandits on the road, they said, and hyenas. At the guard
post there was nothing for the camels to eat, but at least there were
no hyenas.

On 27 February we arrived at the rainwater pool at Adré, where
some tribesmen were watering their camels. The tribesmen had
familiar faces, and I was certain I had seen one of them before. Then
I remembered: I had seen him often in the market of Gineina when I
was a teacher there years ago. He obviously didn't recognize me. He
examined our strange saddlery and the nose-rings of our camels.
'These camels are very tired,' he observed. I said nothing. Agadez
would have meant nothing to him, I knew. That was how far these
camels had come, I reminded myself: we had left Agadez almost two
and a half months before. Tombouctou and Chinguetti were lost in

the mists of time somewhere beyond.

We crossed a wadi full of low *arak* trees. On the far side we met a bent old woman collecting firewood. She had a friendly face. 'Is this Chad or Sudan?' I asked her.

'Eh! This is Sudan!' She beamed at us.

When she had gone we dropped the headropes and embraced, squeezing each other's emaciated bodies. 'Thank God!' Marinetta whispered.

'We made it!' I gasped, kissing her.

Three thousand miles of desert lay behind us. We were in the Sudan. The nightmare was over.

Bandit Country

When I first went to live in Gineina I was given a colonial-style house at the border post. It was one of a long rectangle of buildings, mostly concerned with immigration, that stood 2 miles outside the town. On the Chadian side the rectangle was closed by a thick acacia hedge, in the centre of which was a gate and a sentry box. The gate had a barrier, which was always left open. On the far side was a track of loose sand that led across the plain towards Chad. Over the two years I lived there, making my first clumsy experiments with camels and writing my first book, that gateway took on an almost mystical significance. For me it· was no less than the gateway to the Sahara. One day, I dreamed, I should emerge through that gate from the Chadian side, having crossed the entire distance from the Atlantic by camel.

The gateway was symbolic in other ways too. It was the place where Francophone North Africa ended and Anglophone Africa began. Gone were the lands of C F A francs, *préféts* and *gendarmes*. Here there were pounds, district commissioners and good old-fashioned constabulary. I had always found it irritating that the French, in their arrogance, had considered that the Sahara ended at their borders, whereas the British, in their arrogance, had called the parts of it within their sphere by a different name. It was all the Sahara, from the Atlantic to the Nile, and the gateway to Gineina now reflected no more than colonial history.

Still it was with some excitement that we approached the border post with our small retinue of exhausted camels on the morning of 28 February, coming up the sandy track along which my imagination had wandered so many years ago. The first shock was that the thorny hedge had gone, leaving only the stumps of trees. The gate was still there, its masonry cracked and crumbled, and the old barrier was still stiffly erect, rusted in the upright position. But the track no longer passed through it. Instead a new track curved away to the left, to some gleaming new warehouses for aid supplies that had been built there. The 'Gateway to the Sahara' was left stranded like a monument in the middle of land scorched and withered by drought. I led the caravan off the new track and passed through the gate anyway.

The captain at the passport control was very apologetic. 'I'm afraid you'll have to come back tomorrow for your stamp,' he said, 'because the stamp is locked in the safe, and I've lost the key.' We moved on, chuckling, towards the town, past the house where I had lived and nearly died of malaria, past the school where I had taught for two years and grown to love the Sudanese. Some students were leaning on the wall near the school entrance, waiting for classes to begin. For the first time in 3,000 miles I was treading on ground my feet had already trod. I thought of Mafoudh saying, 'You will come to the place where the earth ends,' and of another man, an Englishman, who wrote:

> We shall not cease from exploration,
> And the end of all our exploring
> Will be to arrive where we started
> And know the place for the first time.

T. S. ELIOT, from 'Little Gidding', Four Quartets

The district commissioner, with typical Sudanese hospitality, let us stay in the town rest-house. The only other guests were three Quaker volunteers who had arrived that day from Khartoum. Their journey had been rough. One of the women was violently ill, and the others, a couple called Wright, looked pale and tired. Annie Wright told us that they had come to begin a forestry project in the nearby village of Assirni, where thousands of Chadian refugees had gathered. 'We don't know anything about forestry,' she said, 'but we'll learn.' They intended to build their own house and to learn Arabic. They were here to stay. Annie showed me a snap of the picturesque cottage in Yorkshire that she had shared with her other half, Howard. He was a big, gristly man with cropped hair who had worked in Halifax with Pakistani immigrants. Annie was soft and black-haired and might have been a nurse. She had taught at nursery school and had run a course for adult women. They had burned their boats by selling up their lovely cottage. They were here to devote their lives to Chadian refugees and trees, for which they were being paid next to nothing. I admired their grit and felt humbled by it.

Projects like theirs were much needed in the western Sudan, where years of drought had destroyed trees, withered the millet crop and devastated grazing land. Old friends told me that the drought had been terrible here in Gineina. Thousands of displaced people had wandered the streets like ghosts, begging for crusts and scouring the garbage dumps for edible morsels. Many had just curled up in doorways and died. It was only the emergency EEC airlift, which had brought in ton upon ton of grain by Hercules transport, that had saved the situation. The rains had been better this year, but a great deal of money was needed to reconstruct the province.

We restocked with food and exchanged old Shaybani for a nervous Sudanese bull-camel. I would have preferred a gelding, having seen how patient and enduring they could be, but the Sudanese rode only on full-blown bulls. The security police shook their heads over our proposed journey to El Fasher. It lay 200 miles east, over some of the wildest country in the Sudan. There had always been trouble from bandits in this region, but since the drought and the war in Chad banditry had reached epidemic proportions. Only a few days before, we heard, a group of bandits had attacked a herd grazing in the Kawra mountains and had shot the owner dead. They could not guarantee our safety, the police said.

For days we moved across rolling sand waves, avoiding settlements and hiding at night in wadis and sandy depressions concealed by trees. Each day began at first light and ended with the setting sun. The camels gave us little rest, and Abu Wirim was a constant source of worry. A gall, which had begun in Chad as a hardly noticeable nick on the withers, had expanded into a badly infected wound. He was thin and tired, the skin of his feet worn painfully frail. We never rode him now, but despite his light load he found it difficult to get to his feet in the mornings. I doubted that he would live long enough to reach El Fasher. Unfairly I blamed Marinetta for not agreeing to sell him in Gineina and for wanting to take him to El Fasher, where he would fetch a better price. 'He won't fetch anything if he's dead,' I told her sullenly.

We watered in a wadi near Tojuk, where there was a shallow pit lined with creepers. The water was muddy and slightly brackish. There was no one at the well when we arrived, but as we hoisted up the water in our cooking pot, some Arabs encircled us. One of them, an old man with a tufty beard, asked us, 'Are you pilgrims going to Mecca?' I replied that we were going to Egypt. 'No God but God!' he exclaimed. 'But haven't you got too much water?'

'Perhaps they want to take a bath?' sniggered a younger Arab mounted on a camel.

'No, no!' a third Arab said. 'He who has water has the blessing of God. Always take water when you can.'

That evening we made camp near Wadi Barei, a great swath of giant *heraz* trees that divided the northern and southern parts of the province of Darfur. Abu Wirim had moved shakily all day, and near sunset he collapsed so heavily that the nose-ring ripped through the flesh of his nostril, leaving flaps of bloody, useless skin. I had been fearing this for some time. It meant that the ring couldn't be refixed without making a new hole in the nostril. After trying several methods, we eventually tied him by the jaw. Even then, though, he refused to get up. The light had gone out of his eyes, leaving the opaque sheen that told of approaching death. We frantically tugged on the rope and kicked from behind. I knew that if we failed to get him up and into some grazing, he would certainly die a lonely death here. Nomads, I knew, will do almost anything to budge an exhausted camel, even lighting a fire under him. We cursed and shouted at the poor animal until, at last, he dragged himself trembling to his feet. He staggered another half mile, where we found a camping place with some sparse grazing. He did not move after we unloaded his saddle. I wondered if he would still be alive at first light.

He seemed a little better the following day, and we moved into the village of Birka Sayra, where a friendly police corporal bought him for a ridiculously low price. 'It's a risk,' the corporal said. 'He's only the shell of a camel. I will feed him grain and salt, little by little. But only God knows if he'll live or die.'

*

We skirted the edge of Barei, where dozens of nomad families were camping with their herds and flocks. Many of them were moving back from their winter grazing lands in the north, making for the well fields where they would spend the summer. Once we had the luck to see an entire Arab clan migrating. First we saw a sea of camels undulating through the dead scrub. They were being driven by little boys wearing only torn grey shirts and sliding along the backs of huge bull-camels without saddles. Then we saw the goat flocks and, half an hour behind them, the procession of camels and horses that carried the families. We saw strings of seven or eight camels carrying litters like tiny cabins on their backs. We saw the dark faces of women peering out, some of them young, smooth and beautiful, others ravaged, haggard and brutal. We saw the bobbing brown heads of small children clinging to their mothers. We saw camels laden with rolled-up beds of palm fibre and hide, blackened cooking pots, urns of water in wooden cages, threadbare blankets neatly layered, drinking gourds and wickerwork hampers, cauldrons and skillets, knee-high mortars carved from tree trunks, bashed-in tin coffers locked with padlocks, cowhide satchels grown shiny with age, string sacks of charcoal, curved ridges for tents, camp beds and rope beds and spiked stakes of wood. Finally, when these rattling Christmas trees of camels had creaked by, we saw men on sprightly ponies carrying javelins and rifles and nests of spears. Then, perhaps an hour later, some dark commas on the horizon materialized into yet another branch of the clan, creaking past on an eternal trajectory: pasture to water, water to pasture, year after year, generation after generation.

Kobkabiyya was a small town sitting on the edge of the Kawra mountains. It happened to be market day when we arrived, and there were some camels for sale. We bought another nervous bull-camel, with an angled-down snout that gave him a curiously unintelligent look. There were hordes of Arabs in the market, small, tight men in knotted headcloths. Everywhere there were whispers about bandits in the Kawra hills, and one tribesman went so far as to tell us, 'If you go into Kawra, you will never come out again.'

At dawn we marched out of the town and saw the great peaks of the mountains rearing up out of the nebula of dust. There were many camel herds scattered across the lower slopes. As the day grew hotter, the mist evaporated and the rocks came into focus, a symphony of shape and size. There were ponderous blocks and gentle, swelling curves, fluted volcanic cones and needle-sharp pinnacles. With every step the mountains closed in on us, claustrophobic after the endless vista of the plains. The track wound on higher, cutting through wadis shrouded in the foliage of lime and mango trees. The hillsides were edged with bushes and strange cactus-like plants with red flowers. We saw a tribe of baboons playing among the trees. On the steep cliffs above us were the abandoned villages of the Fur hill-people, after whom this region, Darfur, was named. We descended into a valley where a waterless river stood, decorated with blue-and-white boulders. Suddenly Marinetta said, 'Look there!' Her sharp eyes had caught the figures of three men standing under a thorn tree some distance away. I brought up my binoculars. There was no doubt that the men were observing us with great interest.

Suddenly, aware of my momentary lack of attention, the new camel bolted. I leaned back on the headrope for all I was worth and, unexpectedly, the camel began to butt me with the back of his head, growling and spitting. I had never known a camel to do this before, and for a second I was stunned. Then I jumped out of the saddle and got the animal under control. 'Maik!' Marinetta shouted urgently. 'Those men are coming!' With a furious effort I slapped the headrope through the camel's teeth and pulled it tight around the jaw. I set off, almost at a run, trying frantically to distance the caravan from those steadily moving figures. Marinetta rocked behind me, gasping, 'Jesus!' every few seconds.

We plunged down a rocky slope, crossed another wadi and climbed the twisting track on the opposite side. It was midday. The heat thumped down, magnified by the rocks, lacing my body with dribbles of sweat. Soon, I knew, I would have to stop and drink. The track opened out through some low bush, and a few minutes later our way was blocked by a herd of twenty camels. There were females among them, and as soon as he scented them the bull from Gineina started rumbling and arching his neck, the prelude to mating behaviour. A moment later a gigantic, full-muscled male answered his challenge, stepping out menacingly from behind a bush. He was completely unfettered and stood directly in our path like a fire-breathing dragon, lifting his head and fixing us with malevolent black eyes. He blew out his disgusting mouthbladder like a warning flag and slobbered, dropping spats of foam on the rocks. Our bull, not yet fully mature, whimpered ineffectually, and on his back Marinetta was shaking. We knew that mature males would attack mounted camels ferociously.

I halted for a moment and drew out of the baggage our new secret weapon. It was an 8-foot-long spear that we had bought in Gineina. I held my headrope gingerly in my left hand, keeping the spear pointed at the enemy bull. I edged out into the bush, making a careful semicircle around him, my eyes never leaving him for a second. The bull watched us suspiciously. Then, just as I thought we had escaped, two young females lurched jauntily in front of us. Our bull burbled again. 'Oh, God! Let me down!' Marinetta wailed, afraid, like me, that the great male would come to the rescue of his females. I whacked one of the cow-camels hard across the rump with the haft of the spear. She and her sister exploded into action, leaping away in fright, and we raced off down the track. When I looked back I saw that the bull had lost interest and had gone back to his grazing.

An hour passed, and we stopped to drink. Marinetta climbed down to join me on foot. We were walking on silently when she suddenly cried, 'Maik! Those men have got Pepper!' I looked back incredulously and saw that the red camel was no longer with us. He was standing more than a hundred yards back along the track and was being held by an Arab in a red headcloth. I recognized the headcloth at once. It belonged to one of the men we had seen under the thorn tree.

My blood went cold. I told Marinetta to hold the other camels and to follow me. I was painfully aware that we were in the midst of one of the most notorious bandit regions in the Sudan. I walked hesitatingly towards the man and the camel, glad of the spear in my hand. As I walked, two more Arabs appeared from behind the rocks, driving a small herd. Steeling myself, I went right up to them. I was about to say, 'What are you doing with my camel?' when Red Headcloth spoke. 'You should learn to tie your camels better,' he said. 'It's lucky we were behind you. You might never have caught this one.' The Arab had an ugly, humorous face. He wore a short, white gandourah and a sleeveless waistcoat. He grinned at me. I realized at once that Pepper's headrope must have come loose and that he had fallen behind without our noticing. 'Thanks!' I heard myself saying.

We retied the camel and travelled along together for a while. The two men with the small herd drove their animals down the track in front of us. 'What are you doing here?' the Arab asked. 'You shouldn't travel on your own in this wild country. There are people here who would say you had camels and plenty of money. They wouldn't let you live.'

'If anyone touches us, the government wouldn't let them rest,' I blustered, thinking that it was as well to sow a few seeds of fear.

'The government!' The Arab spat. 'They never leave the towns. They're afraid of the bandits. The bandits have better guns than the police and move more quickly. They won't help you, by God!' He said that he and his brothers were camel traders and had bought their camels in Kobkabiyya. They were taking them to El Fasher, where they would fetch a good price. 'Almost every time we come this way we have trouble with bandits,' he said. 'They live rough, sleeping in the wadis. Most of them are Chadians, by God!' When I mentioned that we were heading for Egypt, he said, 'Don't go to Egypt. Take a plane to Khartoum. That's the best way for people like you.'

He caught up with his brothers, and just before sunset they turned off the track towards some secret hiding place of their own. We carried on down into a sandy creek bed shadowed by thick foliage. Steep cliffs rose out of the wadi, stubbled with bush. We heard the sound of axes and saw half a dozen Fur women hacking among the bush, some of them carrying babies in sashes on their backs. The track took us up into their village of wood and grass. As we approached it, a shimmer of goats came bristling down from the high pastures. We led the caravan through the stockaded streets of beehive huts and couched them in the square. Later we asked the headman if we could stay the night. He gave us a place on a wide rocky shelf beneath the walls of the mountains. Some small boys brought us sheaves of yellow straw for the camels. The boys told us that the village was called Om.

When we set off in the morning the headman told us, 'If you meet bandits, it's just bad luck! There aren't as many as people say. God protect you!' We paced along the rocky track below a great fluted cone of ebony black. By midday we were passing the salty spring, also known as Om, where the nomads of Kawra watered their herds. The water spilled out silver in a shallow pool in the rocks, and hundreds of goats and camels gathered around it. We crunched through wadis where blue stones glistened and passed through gorges where the green shoots pressed themselves out like pimples. Gradually the hills got smaller. The track descended. By late afternoon we had come to another village of beehive huts, where we were greeted by a villager in a woolly hat. 'There are no bandits here,' he assured us. 'Not like Om. There's plenty of grazing from here to El Fasher. Just take your time and enjoy it.'

Two days later we saw the belt of green tobacco fields that surrounded El Fasher. The dunes above the tobacco fields were full of huts and people. A woman sold us hay for the camels and asked where we had come from. I told her, 'Mauritania,' but as we started loading the hay, I heard a man comment, 'Liars! They couldn't have come from Mauritania. It's too far!'

The sharp scent of tobacco filled the air. The way through the fields was a maze of narrow lanes. We heard the churning engines of lorries from somewhere across them. Night caught us in the maze, and it was moonless. I was terrified that a truck would trap us with blazing headlights in one of these narrow lanes and make our two nervous camels break ranks and run off. Only Pepper was placid: he had been with us all the way from Agadez and was still going strong. I remembered with nostalgia how we had nearly lost him on that first day with Udungu and how the old Targui had fallen off his back. As for the other camels, it was like walking with a box of sweating gelignite. Any noise or unexpected light would make them bolt. We went on for hours, Marinetta leading with a torch in her hand. I brought up the rear, ready to stop any truck that threatened to approach. We were lucky: none did. That night we made camp in a tiny, clear space in a tobacco field. We had been walking for fifteen hours. I wrote in my diary: 'El Fasher. This is where I began my first journey with desert nomads. That was 1980, seven years ago. Coming here, with the Sahara behind me, is a kind of pilgrimage. Now I am too dog-tired to see it as any more than just another camping place. Marinetta, you're wonderful.'

He was sitting in the same restaurant, at the same table, as when I had last seen him here, three years before. He wore a pure-white *jellabiyya*, white leather shoes and a pure-white, perfectly layered headcloth. He was an Englishman but as near to being Sudanese as any Englishman was likely to get. His name was Rabi', but I called him by the one I had first known him by, Rob Hydon.

Rob came from Reading. He was an educated man, trained as a lawyer, who had worked in a bank and as the manager of a petrol-retailing company. He had never been happy in Britain. A broken home had led to a broken marriage. He had come to the Sudan as a volunteer teacher, as I had, intent on starting a new life. He had been in the Sudan almost seven years and had been a Muslim for five.

The Sudanese sun had not bronzed Rob. Instead it had left him stony-grey. There were new lines of strain on his face since I had last seen him. Rob invited us to his house. He would have taken the camels too if we had not already sold them in the market. He was about to leave for Khartoum, he said. The Ministry of Education had perpetrated the ultimate treachery of terminating all contracts with English teachers in Darfur province. The teachers were volunteers and were paid a pittance anyway, but for Rob the change could not have come at a more inconvenient time. He had just proposed marriage to a young Sudanese girl, one of his students, and had every reason to suppose that his offer would be favourably received.

'I had to ask her in the office, between classes,' he told me. 'That's the only way I could talk to her alone. I told her, "Look, I won't give you all the chat, because everyone else will be here in a minute. I want to marry you!" You know what she said? "It's no problem with me, professor!" Imagine that! I went to see her father with a Sudanese friend, and the father told me she was engaged to a cousin. They always say that. She told me she's not interested in the cousin, so I still have a good chance. In the end they listen to what the girl wants, you see.'

Marinetta was not impressed with the Muslim way. 'It's like choosing a wife from a catalogue!' she said.

*

The police chief wore a green bush shirt decorated on the collar with silver secretary birds, the national emblem of the Sudan. His mouth was small and tightly closed as if he normally wore dentures, which were for some reason missing. 'It's out of the question,' he said. 'You can't travel by camel in Darfur. It's a security matter.'

I explained that I had a letter from the Sudanese Ambassador in London granting us permission to cross the Sudan by camel. Surely a police officer couldn't overrule an Ambassador?

'This letter is a year old,' the officer said.

'Eleven months,' I corrected him. 'That's how long we have been in the Sahara.'

'There have been new developments since then,' he said. I already knew what they were. Colonel Gaddafi's shadow was everywhere.

Marinetta suggested the UN. They had helped us in the past, and we hoped that they would be able to do something for us now. The UN Development Programme boss in El Fasher was a Texan called Bob Siddell. He looked trim and cunning with his spectacles and neatly brushed, silvering hair. 'I yewsta be an oilman,' he said, 'but the company went bust. I kinda miss the oil business, though.' Bob's war had been Korea, where he had been an intelligence officer for General Westmoreland. He spoke fluent Japanese, and his Arabic was coming along. Bob's task in El Fasher was to supervise the spending of $76 million donated by the Italian government to the province of Darfur. I asked him to repeat the figure. 'Seventy-six million dollars,' he said. The money was being used to build a new road joining El Fasher to Gineina, to sink a hundred new wells and to rebuild or refurbish ten hospitals. There were also projects to build warehouses containing stockpiles of seed in case of future drought and to establish projects for cultivators. I told Bob the nature of our problem. 'I'll do what I can,' he promised.

When we called at his office the next day Bob told us that he had spoken to the man in question. 'I said that you were British and Italian and that the Sudan is currently in receipt of a lot of aid from both your countries. He said that even if he wanted to give you permission to go north, he couldn't. Only Khartoum can do that.' My heart sank. Khartoum lay 400 miles away, and the hot season would soon be upon us. Our money was short now, and we had to reach the Nile before high summer or we would be in trouble. I explained this to Bob, who smiled knowingly, like a Cheshire cat. 'He did say, however, that if you were to leave *without* permission, there wouldn't be much the police could do about it once you were outside the city. The only areas barred are Kutum and Mellit.' Marinetta and I looked at each other. We had been given the green light.

That evening we held a conference of two at Rob Hydon's house. Rob had left for Khartoum and had generously allowed us to remain there. We had been barred from Kutum and Mellit, both of which lay to the north of El Fasher. Mellit had been on our proposed route, which would take us across the south Libyan desert to Egypt. Now we realized that this way would be fraught with problems. We decided to head north-east from El Fasher into the neighbouring province of Kordofan. There, just across the provincial border, lay the camps of the Kababish, a confederation of Arab tribes among whom I had lived and had many friends. In Kababish country we would be out of reach.

The first, most dangerous, task was to get out of the town without being seen or stopped. If the police caught us within its perimeter, they would be obliged to arrest us to save face. We had bought three fine new bull-camels in El Fasher market, ferrying them back to Rob's house one by one under the cover of darkness. We had tested them carefully before buying them to make sure they were placid and unexcitable. We restocked with food and bought a new set of waterskins and a new saddle.

We were up well before dawn on 23 March. It took two hours to get the new loads right. When the three new camels were loaded, I told Marinetta to open the street door of the yard. She took a deep breath, and the zinc door creaked open. She peered out into the sandy avenue that tilted down towards the market. She looked both ways, then beckoned to me. 'Come on! There's no one!' she said. I led the camels out into the street. Then it was 'Eyes front! Left-right-left-right!' down into the marketplace where women in many-coloured robes were setting up piles of limes and oranges among the stalls. There was the warm smell of animal dung. Men on donkeys were

trotting across the sandy square. Some goats mooched about, nuzzling at yesterday's peelings. We marched straight across the square,
expecting to be stopped at any moment. No one took the slightest
notice of us. We coiled through the wooden stalls and plunged into
a steep alleyway that, I knew, led directly out into the desert.

No sooner had we entered the alley than Marinetta hissed, 'Maik!
There's a lorry full of policemen coming!' Thinking that she was
joking, I looked behind. A battered Commer truck was following us,
carrying half a dozen green-jacketed policemen. The driver hooted,
and the camels snorted nervously. As bold as brass, Marinetta held
up her hand, shouting, 'Stop! Stop!' to the driver. The man grinned
back at her and slowed the truck to an idle. I quickly manhandled the
camels into an intersecting alley. As the truck swayed past, the
policemen waved to us cheerily.

Moments later we emerged from the town into a vast, rolling
plain of amber laced with green. At the plain's edge we saw the
carved black husks of the Wima hills, darkly silhouetted against the
carmine sky of sunrise. Beyond those hills, seven days across the
desert, lay the borders of Kordofan. Beyond that lay the homely
camps of the Kababish Arabs, where I had spent three of the best
years of my life.

Edge of Darkness

We crossed the Kordofan border near Umm Gozayn and turned north towards Umm Sunta, where the chief of the Kababish Arabs, At Tom Wad Hassan, always pitched his tents. Marinetta was excited at the prospect of meeting an Arab chief. 'I knew an Arab prince once,' she told me. 'It was in Somalia. He was a Saudi – I'd read about him in the newspapers.' She had met him at a conference, and he had liked her because she spoke Arabic. A few days later she found herself with an invitation to his quarters in the palace and a chauffeur-driven car to take her there. 'Can you imagine it?' she said. 'It was like a dream. Here was a man who had everything, even his own private plane, inviting *me!*'

'What was he like?'

'He was fine at first – quite romantic. He recited a poem for me. Then he started talking about sex. He said it was unnatural for a woman like me not to have a boyfriend.'

'What did you say?'

'That I was quite happy as I was. I wasn't interested in sex. It was the romantic idea of meeting a prince that I liked. You know what he told me before I left? He said that even though he had enough money to do anything he wanted, he wasn't happy. He said that money was a lot nicer when you hadn't got it. "When you've got it, it means nothing," he said. "It's getting it that matters."'

That just about said it all, I thought.

Sheikh At Tom wasn't that kind of prince. He was the hereditary sheikh or *nazir* of the Kababish confederation, the largest nomadic tribe in the Sudan. His tents were arranged in family groups, standing out like slices of fresh cream from the dull, metallic cages of the acacias in Wadi Umm Sunta. As soon as we arrived in the camp, old friends surrounded us. Other hands than ours unloaded our baggage and hobbled our camels, setting them out to graze in the scrub.

The *nazir* was about my own age, a big, husky man with a broad face, capable of both charm and fury. He was a diplomat, generally liked and respected by his people, an able leader and a just mediator. He had inherited the nazirate from his father Hassan only two years before and was the great grandson of Sir Ali Wad At Tom, KVCO, one of only three Sudanese ever to have been knighted under British colonial rule. At Tom welcomed us with dignity and genuine warmth. As we sat in his presence, almost everyone in the camp came to greet us. Many of them were old acquaintances and travelling companions of mine, who were curious to see 'Omar's wife'. One of my closest friends, Juma' Wad Sinniin, told me, 'Now you are a complete man, Omar!' He had often told me a man was not complete without a woman.

The sheikh too had married since I had last seen him, as had several of the younger men I had known. Marriage seemed to be in fashion here after the deaths of scores of children and old people in the drought. The Arabs pulled my leg about the duties of marriage and asked me if my wife was pregnant yet. When I answered, 'No,' they shook their heads and laughed, saying, 'It's not possible the way you've been travelling! You haven't had time for it, by God!'

'Either that or they were too tired!' someone else joked.

None of them was surprised by our extraordinary journey. A certain section of the tribe was of Moorish origin; all of them had come from Mauritania on foot or by camel. The Moors were known here as Shenagta, a corruption of the word Chinguetti. Most of them had passed through the Sudan on their way to the holy cities of Mecca and Medina in Saudi Arabia, making the pilgrimage that is a duty of Muslims. All of them had taken wives from among the Kababish and had settled down contentedly in a village north of the *nazir's* camp.

Sheikh At Tom ordered a sheep to be slaughtered in our honour. We were famished, and it seemed hours before the meat was ready. We sat on rope beds in the *nazir's* great guest tent. The Arabs sat cross-legged around us or crouched by the walls on their haunches, tilting their heads to one side in the familiar, half diffident manner.

Their faces were both black and brown, exhibiting their mixed African—Arab ancestry, many of them as wizened as parchment with sprouts of whisker and headcloths the colour of dust. A pair of muscular salukis were stretched out by the door gap. From beyond it came the twittering voices of women and the mixed smells of woodsmoke, roasting meat, urine and animal dung, a comforting, homely matrix of odours. Some servants brought us glasses of red tea. There was a feeling of peace that was almost tangible, a sense that everything was in its rightful place, hallowed by timeless tradition. I was comforted to see that little had changed since the Great Drought. Yet I learned that this serenity was an illusion.

The Kababish were gloomy about the future. Their main complaint was that supplies of American grain, which they had received until recently, had been stopped. The rains had been poor again this year. 'The British said when they left that this area would become uninhabitable within a few years,' the *nazir* said, 'and they were right. It's already almost impossible to live here.'

Another friend, Salim Wad Musa, told me, 'If the rains aren't good this year, there will be another famine and no doubt.' I asked him what had become of the OXFAM restocking programme that had been started in the region. Its aim was to supply goats and sheep for poor nomad families that had lost their livestock in the drought. 'They give six sheep and four goats to each family,' Salim said. 'Then after a year they take the stock back and the family keeps the offspring. That's supposed to encourage them to look after the animals. But it won't, of course. They'll end up by eating them.'

'How can you be sure?'

'Because you can't look after animals without grazing, and OXFAM can't provide that. Only God can provide grazing. Then you need to buy salt for your stock and a donkey or two to fetch water.' Ninety per cent of Kababish donkeys had died in the drought. 'They will end up by eating them,' Salim repeated. 'What the Arabs need is rain.'

We were distracted by the arrival of the meat. I had already warned Marinetta that the first offering would be the raw heart, lungs, kidneys and liver, which the Arabs considered a great delicacy. But when the tray of diced red flesh was placed in front of us I noticed a momentary look of disgust cross her features. I hoped none of the Arabs had seen it. 'Come on,' I told her in rapid English, as the expectant faces turned towards us, 'they're waiting for us to eat.'

She gulped and took a large, slimy cube of liver from the tray. Her hand paused for a fraction, then she popped it firmly in her mouth and chewed with every sign of enjoyment. 'Delicious!' she commented.

Later the servants brought in trays of roasted meat and steaming millet polenta, and we ate until we could eat no more.

We left Umm Sunta under a frail sickle moon and walked north for two hours towards the village of the Shenagta, the Moors who had settled among the Kababish. Our camels glided behind us in the darkness. They were heavily laden now, lugging sacks of sorghum for their feed in the empty desert ahead. The three camels were adolescent males and had been bred by the Gor'an nomads from the Chad border. The largest and strongest was called Wad An Nejma or 'Son of the Star', and Marinetta had chosen a trim camel called Wad As Suf, 'Son of the Fur'. The third camel was called Galil Al 'Agl, which meant that he had the brains of a simpleton. A chorus of barking dogs announced the proximity of the Shenagta village. We spent the night in the wadi near by and watered at the well there at sunrise.

The village was dominated by a white stucco dome that marked the grave of a marabout called Feki Ibrahim. He had walked here from Mauritania in 1940. The Moors at the well were lighter-skinned than the Kababish but wore the same nicotine-yellow shirts and headcloths. We shocked them by speaking Hassaniyya. 'Where did you learn that?' they asked.

A Moor called Talib invited us into his store for tea. 'Red tea, not green tea like we have in the old country,' he said apologetically. He must have been sixty, I thought; his eyes were edged in crow's feet, and his hair was silvery-white. He belonged to the Laghlal tribe, which made him a distant relative of Mafoudh. 'I came here by camel in 1948,' he told us. 'It took us fourteen months to get to El Obeid. From there we went to Mecca.'

I asked him why so many Moors had settled there rather than returning to Mauritania. The environment was very similar – indeed, this place could have been anywhere in the southern Sahara. 'It was because most of us are marabouts,' Talib said. 'There were few marabouts in the Sudan, so we could make a good living.' At first they had sold charms and performed religious services; later they had branched out into trade and commerce. I wondered why they had made such a long pilgrimage from the western Sahara when the journey was not compulsory for those Muslims who hadn't the means to make it. 'The Lord rewards those who make sacrifices in His name,' Talib said. 'There is hardship in such a journey: but in hardship there is *baraka!*' It was the word Muslims used for the magical power of God.

As we loaded our *girbas* and jerrycans, Talib advised us, 'Don't tell anyone you're going to Egypt. Life is dust here!' And on that note we led our camels across the scrubland towards the curving crust of Jebel Hattan, the great plateau that marked the horizon to the north.

The sunlight glazed the dust-bowl surface, and the heat dripped down like hot fat, cooking our brains under the thick headcloths. The way was punctuated by wells where teams of Arabs drew water for their hustling, stamping camels. Jebel Hattan stayed on our right, dwarfing the desolate scrub. To the north-west was the rampart shadow of another plateau, Jebel Meidob. It was the home of some black nomads who had been bitter enemies of the Kababish for generations. The two mountain blocks faced each other like grim frontier citadels, contesting the no-man's-land in the valley between.

The heat was sudden, and it made us dizzy and depressed. That morning we lost not only one of my sandals but also one of our priceless new *girbas* from El Fasher. Even our camels were sweating. The Nile still lay 600 miles away, the Egyptian border at least 1,000. We were already beyond the normal limits of human endurance. If the heat remained like this, we should be lucky to survive.

In the afternoon we met three Arab boys who were herding sheep. They begged us for water, and as I poured it, one of them asked, 'Is your land far?'

'Yes, it's far,' I answered him.

'Will you get there by tomorrow?' he inquired.

'Only if I went in an aeroplane,' I said.

'Can't you take your camels in an aeroplane?' he asked disarmingly.

We arrived at the bore well at Greywit not long after first light. There was a graveyard of saddles and camel litters like a funeral pyre; they had been abandoned there by nomad families that had fled to the cities during the drought. I supposed that many of those who went had never returned. The well head was crowded with beautiful girls carrying waterskins and dunking them in the steel troughs. The girls were coffee-brown with buttered hair, braided and quartered by leather thongs and cowries. The young men were wolf-lean with vortices of wild hair. The older men wore headcloths and thick leather belts. I asked around for a guide who could take me across Jebel Hattan as far as the next well, Khitimai. An Arab called Ahmed volunteered. He had a round, cheerful face and was very honest-looking. He took us to his camp, riding on a lame little donkey and leading his small son on a camel laden with five or six shiny waterskins.

His tent was white cotton with a camel's-wool roof. We unloaded at some distance from it and greeted Ahmed's wife and daughter. The wife, with her slim body and jet-black tresses, was still very attractive, though among these Arabs it is difficult to pinpoint age. The Arabs evidently had the same problem with us. Ahmed's pretty daughter, a little girl of perhaps ten, was much taken with Marinetta. The girl had an almond-shaped face and short velvety braids of hair. Her limbs looked strong under her swinging, flowery dress. Later Ahmed asked me if my wife had reached womanhood yet. He looked shocked at my weathered, sun-baked face when I explained that she was exactly three years younger than me. 'My little girl wanted her as a playmate!' he said.

Inside the tent we all huddled together on the bed, a mat of palm fibre joined by skin and resting on pegs driven into the ground. Balls of carded goat's wool hung from the ceiling like baubles, and beneath them was a wooden frame supporting three large sacks of grain. The grain was all that the family had to live on until the next rains.

Ahmed said that he owned some goats and a few sheep, two donkeys and a camel for bringing water. 'It hasn't rained here at all this year,' he said. 'Any grazing left here is two years old.' I asked about the American grain. 'It should never have stopped,' he said. 'Many people haven't got on their feet again yet.'

A woman called Amni came to ask if she could travel with us as far as Khitimai. She was not old, but she was cadaverously thin, her skin drawn tight around her mouth, her black hair rotted to grey. She looked hungrily at Marinetta's earrings, and said, 'That woman is loaded with gold!' A boy of sixteen arrived. He had recently married, and Amni asked him to enumerate the animals he had received as presents on his wedding day. She kept count on her fingers as he described them, one by one.

Another youth appeared and asked Ahmed for a sack of grain. 'It's not for sale,' Ahmed told him. 'Take one, and give me one back when your family can afford it. One for one, that's all I want.'

Ahmed's wife had cooked a goat's head as a parting feast. Ahmed stripped the succulent flesh off the skull, ears, eyes, nasal membranes and tongue. The tastiest part was the brains, but you had to smash the skull open to get at them. I asked Ahmed if there were any bandits in this area. He told me that during the Great Drought people had stolen animals to feed their starving families. Now things were better, and the main threat was from the Meidob. They would come out of the mountains at night in raiding parties with nothing but their rifles and waterskins. Many people had been shot and wounded. A few days earlier some Kababish had gone off into Jebel Meidob following a party of raiders. They hadn't yet returned. 'We never light a fire when we're travelling,' Ahmed said, 'not while we're in sight of the Meidob hills. The Meidob would come to you like vultures.' I could hear the fear in his voice as he spoke.

We left at sunset, Marinetta and I with our three camels, Ahmed astride his slow watering animal and Amni on a thin camel with a twisted rear foot. Amni looked very poor and begged from Marinetta constantly as we rode. 'If you don't give me something, I'll cause you problems,' she insisted.

Ahmed looked embarrassed. Later he told me that she had been driven half crazy by the drought. 'The women had to sell all their gold, the stuff they had inherited,' he said. 'Now they have nothing, and it drives them to distraction!'

We rode until midnight and made camp under the wall of Hattan. Camping here by the mountain was dangerous, but Ahmed said that it was too dark to climb the pass. He strictly forbade the lighting of a fire; this was nothing new to Marinetta and me.

At daybreak we climbed the pass and found at the top a mob of camels with a herdsman. He belonged to Ahmed's clan and greeted us warmly, insisting on giving us a bowl of camel's milk. On his camel was a Kalashnikov rifle. In return for the milk he asked for news of the pursuit party that had gone into the Meidob hills.

The skin of the plateau was stony and veined with wadis and the dry beds of pools. A family of Arabs was holed up on one of the pool beds. They had no tents. Their rifles, *girbas* and cooking utensils hung from trees. We halted with them, and they made us tea. The Arabs were hungry and had nothing to eat: they filled their bellies only with the milk from their camels. They were watering their herd at Khitimai wells every nine days and, in between, lived here in Hattan.

We mounted and rode down into Khitimai valley. The plain stretched as far as the eye could see, parched and dead. At noon we rested under a thorn tree and let the camels graze. Neither Amni nor Ahmed had seen powdered milk before; they sipped our customary *zrig* suspiciously. 'It's just like cow's milk,' was Amni's verdict. We ate rice and dried meat, since neither of the Arabs had heard of sardines.

As we were fetching the camels later, a rider approached. He was a watchful Arab with a rifle and a waterskin. After he had greeted us he took a look around our camp and rode away. 'My stomach feels bad about that man,' Ahmed declared. 'That's how a bandit travels: with a rifle and a *girba*. The Meidob aren't the only robbers here.'

In the afternoon we ran into a herd of camels being driven from the wells by a young Arab boy. Ahmed rode up to him for the news. 'He says not to enter the well at night,' he told me afterwards. 'There are bad people about. Better to rest with the Arabs tonight and go to the well tomorrow.' I was not to be put off so easily after 3,500 miles, and I insisted on reaching the wells. It was late when we spotted camp fires and heard the thud of the donkey engine across the sand. Amni rode off to stay with her relations, taking two of our spare sacks with her. A sack was nothing, I knew, but Ahmed noticed and looked embarrassed again. We made camp by the well and were joined by some Arabs. Marinetta was exhausted and went to sleep at once.

Later I made the mistake of waking her up to eat and drink tea. She jumped up as if bitten, with a terrified look on her face. She stared at me with wide eyes as though I was a stranger, stupefied by Ahmed and the faces of the other Arabs illuminated by the firelight. Her hands were trembling, I noticed. She tried to help make the tea, but her co-ordination was unsteady. She kept looking at me as if I was a monster. After we had sat down in our small den she said, 'I feel as if I've lost touch with reality. I forgot who Ahmed was. I even forgot who *you* were for a minute. It was as if everyone was a stranger.' The conversation made me afraid too. Deep within us was something more fearful than bandits or hyenas. It was the fear of the disintegration of the self.

Our depression increased in the morning when we filled one of our jerrycans and discovered a leak. We unrolled the three remaining new waterskins and were shocked to find them unusable. Two of them had been punctured in brushes with thorn trees, and the third cracked like paper when we tried to open it out. We patched up the jerrycan with melted plastic and bought a new waterskin from the Arabs at the wells. We filled all our water vessels. Then we bade farewell to Ahmed, and an Arab from the well led us out into the sand and showed us the direction of Wadi Howar where, five days away, we would find the next well. The man told us, 'From here to Wadi Howar you won't see anyone. No one at all. No one will know if you live or die out there.'

Those words stayed with me all day as we moved across the featureless sand hills, following the compass. No one would know if we lived or died. No one. There was no one here but Marinetta and me, and we hardly counted as separate people any more. The vast emptiness weighed down on us like a stone. Deep exhaustion had changed our feeling for the void. The freedom that we had sensed in Ténéré had become terrible. There were no restrictions on us. We could have done anything, performed any perversion, stripped naked and copulated on the sand without any observers, slit each other's throats, mutilated and murdered each other. It was not the desert itself that frightened us but the raw, unreasoning power inside us that might become unharnessed and run wild, a crazy cave-animal force, across these sands of nothing. Only my responsibility to Marinetta kept me going. She kept me alive with her strength and her weakness, her unquestioning faith in my ability to lead her to safety.

The following morning we crossed the Wadi Mafarit, a wide wedge of trees in a deep chasm. The wadi was inhabited by two black crows, which hovered around us, croaking. I had slept off the terror of the previous day, and my spirits lifted. Soon we saw the cliff of Galb Al Ba'ir, the southern tip of the Tegaru massif, which we would follow for three days. By late afternoon we were already in the shadow of the plateau. After the empty sands the rocks felt like live, friendly spirits. We scrambled over screes of gravel and larger boulders and found a sandy place among them where we made camp.

We had begun on the cooking when I suddenly spotted two lights. They were as yellow as hyena's eyes, hanging in the darkness and seeming to move towards us over the rocks. But there were no hyenas in Tegaru — unless they might be human ones. 'It's two men with torches,' Marinetta said. 'They're searching for us!' I considered the possibility of bandits grimly. Here, in the open desert, there were no people and no villages from whom to seek help. We were totally alone. No one would know if we lived or died. Even the authorities wouldn't bother to inquire. We weren't supposed to be here.

I quickly doused the fire and picked up my spear. Just having a weapon in my hands gave me a primitive confidence. I examined the lights with my binoculars, which told me nothing. They came no nearer. The camels shifted slightly in their narrow pits of sand. The desert was as silent as the sea. 'They can't be men with torches,' I told Marinetta. 'They would have been here by now.' As we watched, the lights seemed to undergo a strange fission. Each one split into two separate cells. Now at last they moved faster, and in an instant the entire perspective changed. Instead of seeing something small, very near, I was seeing something large, far away. 'Good God!' I said, 'They're lorries!' We had been watching the headlights of two vehicles, miles and miles away — so far away, in fact, that their engines couldn't be heard, and their two headlights appeared as one. Yet our minds had already produced an intricately detailed scenario of bandits with menacing intentions.

'I was even wondering what I would do if they murdered you and tried to rape me,' Marinetta said.

I watched the lights disappearing into the darkness, knowing that our enemy was no longer the desert. Our enemy was ourselves.

Tegaru was our only friend in the wilderness. Its blue-and-orange buttresses stayed with us comfortingly from dawn till sunset. We rode over rocky ground littered with the remains of prehistoric settlements. We saw billions of sherds of bone and shattered red pottery and picked up many diorite stone axes. I wondered who these stone-tool makers had been. Were they hunters, or nomads, or farmers? Marinetta held up a different type of relic that she had found: it was the brass cartridge case of a modern bullet. 'It's like reading a book about history,' she said. 'Stone tools transformed into bullets. Humans always find new ways of doing things, but underneath they don't change, do they?'

In the doldrums of the day we fantasized about the future. Marinetta told me that she dreamed of being clean and perfumed, dressed in her most expensive outfit. 'We will both dress smartly,' she said, 'and we will drink a bottle of Champagne. Then you will take me out to a nightclub. We will dance very close together in a dark corner, and you will kiss me on the neck.'

'And then?'

'Then you will take me home, and we'll drink more Champagne. We will sit down by a log fire.'

'And then?'

'Then you will slowly begin to undo the buttons of my dress ... You can imagine the rest.'

I looked at her, at her face grained with sand, her long shirt and *sirwel* tattered and yellowed by unnameable stains, and laughed. The world she had talked about didn't seem to belong to either of us.

We followed grooves in the rock etched by camel caravans over centuries. Here and there were shreds of motor tyres and discarded chunks of engine, oil filters and broken suspension units. We crossed a sheet of rippled sand, with the occasional umbrella of trees. A cold wind blew from the north. The sky filled with uneasy clouds, and suddenly a miracle happened. Silver rain fell across the sand, touching the dryness with a billion tiny blades. To the east a perfect rainbow formed over the plateau. Marinetta stared at it, entranced, with tears in her eyes.

At sunset we made camp in the sand-sheet. The shower had lasted only minutes, and the soft sand was still dry. After we had eaten we sat back in the moonlight. 'The hugeness of this place really scares me,' Marinetta said. 'But it's beautiful, too. It's like an enchanted world – the colours, the rainbow, the stillness. It's like a place that is sleeping under a spell. You can't believe there's really no one. I keep looking at the horizon for a person or a camel, but I never see one.'

'We're alone,' I said, smiling, 'just as two people should be on their honeymoon.'

'This must be the strangest honeymoon in history,' she answered. 'Plenty of moon but no honey.' She laughed. It was the same lovely, fresh laugh that I had heard in that office in Khartoum. It made me fall in love with her all over again.

'Perhaps we can do something about that,' I said, cradling her. Her body felt hard in places and soft in others, like the desert's crust. I began to kiss her very slowly on the neck and to move my hand under her shirt.

'What comes next in the fantasy?' I asked her.

'You have to imagine the rest,' she said.

A few minutes later our clothes were scattered around us in the desert. The camels gurgled quietly in the great silence, seeing all, hearing all.

We were savages now. There was no shame, nothing hidden from one another. Our bodies and minds, bent on one unflinching purpose, fitted like hand and glove. There was no barrier between us, no possibility of pretence. We were no longer Michael and Mariantonietta but two fantasy characters of our own making, who sang bawdy songs across the barren sands and made up stories about their adventures. Our faithful followers were our camels, which padded on silently, carrying our tiny, half-crazy world across the emptiness to our next source of water.

The sun splattered colours across the rippling sands. The plateau cracked and crumbled into piles of black boulders, perching atop each other like hats. The erg gave way to a gravel plain. There were hummocks of grass in places and basins filled to brimming with soft pink sand. There were more arteries of sand along the skirts of the mountain, glittering, undersea colours of turquoise and starfish-orange. Behind them the black jacket of the plateau seasoned into mauve as the sun moved higher. There were trees with red flesh that crumbled at the touch. This forest had become extinct long ago. Near sunset we climbed over a ridge on foot. The camels' feet left neat ladders of tracks in the velvet sand. Over the hill we found ourselves shut inside an amphitheatre of rock, where the only movement was that of our grotesque, elastic shadows, thrown before us on the earth.

There seemed to be no way out of the box. We moved one way, then another. Rocks that seemed only a few feet away retreated into the distance as we moved towards them. We turned back towards the way we had come, but the hill behind us was unrecognizable. Our tracks did not show on the hard ground. I felt panic welling up inside me, and I fought to keep it under control. The compass was in my hand, and my mind clicked with detached precision. To drift away from the red needle was to lose oneself in this labyrinth. We moved back towards a ridge that my eyes told me bore no relation to the one we had already crossed – how many hours before? On we stumped, dog-tired after the day's march. Nothing looked familiar, and the sun would soon be gone, leaving us stranded in the night. We climbed over the ridge and looked down on a plain quite different from the one we had traversed so jauntily that morning. Nothing matched. The sun balanced on the edge of the desert and hovered there. Without the compass, I would have sworn I hadn't seen this part of the desert before. The shapes and forms that I held in my memory had changed. A different light, a different angle, a different mood, had brought us into a new dimension, another world. We were travelling not through rock and sand but through an illusion, an ever-changing mirage.

Then, in the last glow of golden light, I came upon a skein of camel prints punched neatly into the sand. My first impulse was to look about, wondering to whom they belonged. Then a disjointed voice inside told me, 'They're yours, you stupid fool!' We had come back to where we had started.

We were too disorientated and tired to try to make up the hours
we had lost. Marinetta sat over the cooking pot miserably. The extra
effort of getting lost in the maze of rock had taken us beyond fatigue.
We were treading dangerously near to the edge of darkness from
which there would be no return. Marinetta started crying. 'I don't
know what's happening to me,' she sobbed. 'I keep having strange
feelings. I hear sounds behind me like walking people, but when I
turn around there's no one. Then I see monsters hiding in the rocks.
The worst thing is that I feel there's a monster inside me waiting to
come out. I'm afraid I might turn into a werewolf and cut your throat
and not be able to control myself.'

I shivered involuntarily and looked down into the flickering flames.
The day had been a sobering lesson in the relationship between the
real and the unreal. Now I had begun to doubt that there was any
dividing line between the two. As I watched the flames holding
back the night, even they seemed alive with a malevolent, sentient
force.

The day dawned into a horror of sun and sand. We left the last
tatters of the plateau and moved out into the dreadful, yawning
emptiness of the sands. Strange silver lights were blinking like eyes
across the erg. From the moment we started a demon of terror had
me in its grip. It was fear without rhyme or reason. It came from
somewhere deep in the hidden ravines of my mind. Some dragon of
fear had been lurking down there all my life, and now it was rising
to the surface. Some fifth-column subversive was in open revolt
against my will to go on. My voice seemed to come from somewhere
else, far away. It was not me speaking. My heart was palpitating, and
there were sudden surges of adrenalin through my body, urging me
to flee maniacally across the desert. The world seemed unreal and
sinister. It was as if Udungu's jinns were squabbling like vultures over
my mind, its psychic defences worn down by utter exhaustion.

I couldn't communicate my feelings to Marinetta, but I guessed
that they were the same as those she had felt the previous night,
signifying the presence of something alien inside. I remembered
reading about the mysterious psychic ailment that the French call the
cafard. It was supposed to affect expatriates who worked for too long
in the Sahara, a disorientating, maddening illness. I wondered if I was

experiencing the *cafard* and whether, indeed, it was just another way of saying 'jinns'.

Wadi Howar lay a day's march ahead. The hours unrolled with horrific emptiness. The sand seemed to be turning to flame and smoke. There were outcrops of rock, weird, bloated pillars of carmine and ochre. Scintillating diamonds of moisture appeared temptingly on the horizon. By afternoon another fear had gripped me: we were marching too far east. I was afraid we might miss the wadi completely. I stopped and took out my map and compass. I had marked the well of Ghobeishi carefully, knowing that of several wells on the south side of the wadi it would be the easiest to find. 'If we don't get this right, we'll die,' I told Marinetta. I was not exaggerating. Literally hundreds of men had died of thirst in this wilderness over the years, even recently. Only two years before, forty men had lost their way on a journey to Libya and had died in this desert.

Marinetta looked at me calmly. There was no trace of the sobbing fear of the previous day. It was as if she had found some new strength in the night. 'God will look after us,' she said. It was the first time I had heard her assert her faith. I understood then where her new strength came from.

Her calmness gave me new courage. With an effort I scoured the map and identified the rocky outcrops near by. I took a grid bearing from there to Ghobeishi. It was a gamble, I knew: there were scores of outcrops, and not all of them were marked on the map. If I had identified this one incorrectly, then the bearing would be wrong. I checked it twice. Then I oriented the compass, and we turned to face the empty desert.

We never strayed from the bearing all afternoon, even when the fresh tracks of two camels intersected our path. They were the first tracks we had seen in five days, and we were both tempted to follow them, yet we knew this might be a fatal error. Hour after hour went by, and I felt the same hot terror smouldering on the edge of my consciousness. The camels paced on determinedly, and we fell silent. There were no jokes or bawdy songs today, just two very small beings praying that they would not die.

Just before sunset Marinetta said, 'Can't you smell something?' I sniffed deeply. There was a slight but unmistakable scent of acacias in bloom. Then I noticed that the camels were covered in flies, the small black flies that bred in the wadi. A little later we climbed a ridge and saw a line of trees below us and the rocky hump of a hill. It was Ghobeishi. It seemed that no less than an act of God had brought us straight to it, using a bearing from a landmark chosen almost haphazardly from the map.

Adam

The Nile lay only ten days' march away, but when we awoke the next morning it might as well have been a hundred. We lay in our sleeping-bags, staring at the sky and not caring if the drifting desert sand should bury us under its skirts and build a sandy tomb over us for ever. My body felt hollow and aching. My nerves were as raw as gristle. Finally we dragged ourselves out into the morning of another day, made our fire, drank our coffee and loaded our camels.

Beyond the strip of ravaged greenery called Wadi Howar stretched the most desolate rocky plains in the southern Sahara. There was but one well in that desolation, Abu Tabara. I had visited the well from the east side two years before and had come nearer to dying of thirst then than on any of my other journeys. The well was concealed in a vast area of wind-sculptured rock and was impossible to see from a long way off. To find it from the west side I knew I would need a guide.

We moved only half a mile from the camp site. On the crest of a dune, among green *araks*, we saw the figures of people, with camels and goats and a tiny shelter. An Arab came slithering down the dune to greet us. Glad to see another soul, I ran up to meet him, and we clasped hands like two lost strangers in the solitude. 'Who is that other man?' he asked, pointing at Marinetta.

'That's no man,' I told him, with a touch of pride. 'That's my wife.'

We settled in some *arak* trees, and the Arab's wife brought us a bowl of fresh camel's milk. The Arab, whose name was Ja'adallah, suggested that we should take his father-in-law, Adam, as a guide. 'Does he know Abu Tabara?' I asked.

'He certainly does!' replied Ja'adallah.

Adam was a reedy man with opaque eyes and many missing teeth.

His face might once have been stern and aristocratic, but the desert forces had now riveted it with a network of lines. He had lived almost all of his life in this desolate wadi. He had never even been as far as Umm Sunta, nor met the family of the *nazir*. The only towns he had seen were those along the Nile, many years before. The only other Westerners he had seen were some archaeologists who had undertaken excavations near by. 'God knows what they were looking for,' he said. 'They were digging up the sand and putting it into sacks as if it was valuable. "If that sand is valuable," I said, "then we'll all be rich, by God!"' His body was almost skeletal, but his years in this harsh world had given him tensile strength. The seasoned grey eyes looked as if they had been misted over by decades of wind-blown sand. He wore a shirt that was crisp with dust and human sweat and torn in many places. He owned a woollen hat and two plastic sandals that did not match: one was red and the other blue.

He was pleased that I was English. 'When the English ruled this country, everything was cheap and plentiful,' he said. 'You could buy a pound of tea for 50 piastres. After the English went, it rose to £1.50. Then it became £3.00. I said to the trader, "How can it go up in one day from £1.50 to £3?" He said, "You Arabs with your thick skulls! One day it will go up to £9 and your camel will cost £1,000!"'

Adam had come to Wadi Howar as a child, in the days of Sir Ali Wad At Tom. His family moved here from the south-east. 'There were no Arabs living in Wadi Howar then,' he told us. 'There was too much trouble from Gor'an raiders. Then the English sent some cars and soldiers to deal with them, and they fled. Those cars were the first I'd ever heard of. Now there are cars everywhere.' I asked him, as I had asked all our guides, whether he preferred cars or camels. 'Eh,' he said, 'camels are for men. Cars are for children.' Camels were the *raison d'être* for Arabs like Adam. Without camels they would have been unable to live in this remote place. 'When we first came here there was only one well in the entire wadi,' Adam went on, 'but the Arabs got to work and dug two or three more, and the camels learned to eat *arak* leaves. God is generous. The *arak* stays alive when the other trees die. In the year of the Great Drought everyone left the desert but us. Our camels stayed alive by eating the *arak*. They're still in good condition, by God!'

The camels we saw grazing among the *arak* groves were fat and healthy. A large white bull steamed up to challenge our troop of three as soon as we hobbled them. Wad An Nejma bubbled a little in challenge, but the bigger animal spat and slavered with all his might, ballooning out his air bladder until our animals retreated into another *arak* grove. The bull swaggered back to his females. One of them had just produced a fluffy white foal, which stood a yard high on spindly, unbalanced legs. When Marinetta tried to photograph it, the mother rushed up and stood over the baby protectively.

We watered at a near-by well that afternoon. Camels waited for their drink in nervous squadrons. A ring of tousle-haired youths took turns, two by two, to hoist up the sandy water. I took my turn with them. Water splashed into the rusty halves of oil drums. The camels pressed shoulder to shoulder, slurping up the water, lifting their heads and shaking their floppy wet lips. There was the warm, sweet smell of dust and dung, the savoury scent of uncured leather. The Arabs chattered and laughed; one of them dropped a leather bucket into the well by accident. The others jeered mockingly. The boy looked embarrassed and went off to find another bucket. The camels roared and howled, and the mature bulls fought and had to be separated with whips. A haze of dust rose over this small well, a small island of activity in the vastness. Wells, above all things, were the symbol of life in the Sahara. I knew that we would not be seeing many more.

The next morning Adam led us across the dunes and towards the fantasy-like mountains of Rahib, at the easternmost end of the wadi. The black frames of the hills and the amber glaze that covered them gave them the look of drawings on a backcloth. The camels paced well after their day in the *arak* groves. The heady perfume of *sallam* trees drifted about us in clouds. The camels pulled out of our line of march to investigate the sweet smell. Adam said that it was eighteen years since there had been a good rain in Wadi Howar. 'When it rains once properly, there is grazing to be found as far east as the Nile,' he said. 'The whole desert blooms!'

At Rahib there was a beautiful girl called Fatna, with butter-smeared hair and wreaths of cowries around her neck. She smiled at us with ivory-white teeth and helped us to fill our *girbas*. They were in bad condition now, but Adam said they would be sufficient as long as we refilled them at Abu Tabara. When they were filled we rode out into open desert.

We camped near a rocky hill called Dabbat An Nahas, or 'Kettle-drum Hill'. Adam told us that sometimes you could hear a great drum booming from inside. 'It happens before somebody dies,' he said. 'You can hear it from miles away. Even the ground trembles.' I asked him what he thought it was.

'It's the Drummer of Death!' He shivered.

That night the Drummer of Death remained silent.

Another hill blazed on the horizon the next day. We climbed into its heart, where we found a hidden spinney of very dead thorn trees. There would be little firewood to be found farther on, and Adam advised us to collect as much as we could. After we had eaten Adam presented Marinetta with a leather bag made of gazelle skin. She accepted it eagerly, saying, 'This is really special! You can't buy things like that in my country.' That afternoon, Adam asked Marinetta for her blanket. He didn't own a blanket, he said. Anyway, you couldn't buy blankets like that in *his* country.

We scaled a huge dune that was laid against a gorge of rock and cut through a split in the hills down to a basin of glittering mineral salts. Patterns made by camel grooves intersected it in all directions. An occasional knoll of granite peeked above the plain, stretching on east until it dissolved into the aquamarine sky. We trawled across the plain like skiffs drifting on a tranquil ocean of dreams. We rode on until the sun roared and the shadows telescoped and shrank beneath the bellies of our camels.

Adam sat uncomfortably on the firewood and chewed tobacco like a ruminant. He chewed all day and made clicking noises to encourage his camel. He said that he had taken tobacco first to get rid of a headache. 'That's how I got into the habit,' he said, 'but now, any time I *stop* taking it, I get a headache.'

'Doesn't it make you thirsty?' I asked him.

'No,' he answered. 'It helps your thirst. Once I rode from Wadi Howar to Dongola with some of my family. We had no water: only camel's milk and tobacco. After a few days the camel's milk went sour. Then it doesn't quench your thirst. It was only the tobacco that kept us going.' He said that it had been ten days before they reached an oasis. 'There were some Arabs there,' he told me, 'and they offered us camel's milk. "Keep your camel's milk!" we told them. "Just give us water!"'

'Thank God you were alive!'

'Yes. But the Arabs can endure thirst more than any other people,' he went on. 'I've seen so many townspeople going to Libya by camel who don't even know what thirst is. They take too little and drink too much.' He told me the story of some camel riders who had come to Ghobeishi the previous year on exhausted camels. They had been sent back from the border post on the Libyan frontier. The men had left their camels in Wadi Howar and had hitched a ride on a truck going to the Nile; it had broken down near Abu Tabara. 'Eighteen people died of thirst,' Adam said, 'and one of the few who didn't was an Arab, one of our family. He couldn't speak when they found him, and his mouth wouldn't take water. They put liquid into his veins with a tube, I heard. He stayed alive, by God! He was a true son of the Arabs.'

Once we came to a pair of oryx horns that had been stuck firmly in the earth. They were more than the record of an unknown hunter's skill. They were a requiem for a bygone age. 'The oryx are all gone now,' Adam said, 'but there used to be plenty when I was a lad, in the time of the English. The English brought us luck, you see.' On another occasion he pointed out a ridge called Zalat Az Zabit, 'The Officer's Ridge'. 'It was named after an English officer,' Adam said. 'He's buried there.' The story ran that a young British subaltern had moved a detachment of camel corps from a local oasis to the Nile. A fearful sandstorm had blown up, and the guide had panicked and refused to go on, even though the column was short of water. In the end the officer had shot the guide dead. Then the sergeant had shot the officer dead, declaring that he was mad. They had buried the officer near the ridge.

'Do you think the officer was mad?' I asked him.

'The desert can do strange things,' Adam said. 'Only the Arabs can live in the desert.'

On 12 April we spotted a double-headed rock in the distance. 'That's it!' Adam cried. 'That's Abu Tabara!' An hour passed and the guide's elation waned. He fell silent. I kept on checking my compass. The double-headed rock looked way off the bearing. Suddenly Adam broke the silence. 'I don't think that's it after all,' he said.

Marinetta and I stared at him in alarm. 'You don't *think*!' I exclaimed. 'You mean you're not sure where it is?'

'Not again!' Marinetta gasped. 'Oh, God, not again!'

As the sun dropped lower we found ourselves in a landscape of moulded rock, which broke the sunlight into a pattern of long shadows. The rocks grew larger until they blocked the view on every side. They were like dream creatures of the night, closing in on us, moving beyond the corners of our eyes as we turned our heads away.

At last light we camped in a nest of sand and boulders beneath a granite stump. Adam sat down heavily in the sand. 'I've forgotten it, Omar,' he said. 'It's twenty years since I've been here, you understand.'

I grinned and choked back the anger I felt. 'Everyone makes mistakes,' I said, 'even the sons of the Arabs.' But I was savagely aware that I had listened to stories of the Arabs' remarkable powers with incredulous naïveté for the last time. 'If we don't find it tomorrow, we'll have to head back to Rahib,' I told him.

'No,' he protested. 'We can still reach the Nile.'

I knew that he would lose face if we returned to his home and that he was worried about his money. But I also knew that reaching the Nile was out of the question: our water would never last us that long. 'Adam,' I said, 'the Nile is six days away, maybe seven. We have water for two. You may be an Arab, but you aren't a gazelle. You still have to drink. Everyone does.'

Later I climbed the stump of rock and surveyed the desert with my binoculars, hoping to catch sight of a camp fire. I even set off a flare, praying that it might flush somebody out. The night was dark, starlit and endless. In the whole whispering canopy of the desert nothing moved.

Back in the camp, I found Adam reading the sands. He was making patterns with his palm and thumb and looking at the results intently. It was the favourite form of fortune telling among the Arabs.

'What do you find?' I asked him.

'We'll see people tomorrow,' he said. 'The sands say we'll see people.'

'Will we find the well?'

'I don't know if we'll find the well, but we'll see people.'

As soon as it was light Adam went off on foot to search for camel spoor or tracks that might give us a clue to the whereabouts of the well. I watched his long, bony feet making a swirl of footprints through the gentle ripples of the sand. 'Oh, God!' sighed Marinetta. 'So near to the Nile and this had to happen.'

I put my arms around her. 'You don't regret doing this journey, do you?' I asked.

'Not for anything, Maik,' she said. 'And there's no one else I'd rather have done it with.'

'Do you realize you have never told me that you love me?' I said.

She looked at me with her great, soft, brown eyes as if she were about to burst into tears. Then I saw Adam coming back across the dunes and released her.

'It's all right,' Adam said. 'I've found camel tracks in the sand.' But the camel tracks he had found led us nowhere. They were old and wove in and out of the boulders, not even showing us a direction. After an hour of moving south we climbed another great tower of rock and sand. Adam's gaze swept across the desert. 'Nothing!' he said. I scanned the east, west and south with the binos. Suddenly I stopped and back-tracked. I had picked out the tiny shape of a grazing camel. Then I picked out another, and another. There were five camels grazing together in tufts of grass, several miles away. Adam screwed up his old eyes but couldn't pick them out. There was no trace of any human beings with them. 'Camels are watering every nine days at this time of year,' Adam said. 'That means that these camels could be up to five days' journey from the well.'

Now we were all confused. Should we move towards the camels? Should we continue on the previous day's bearing? Adam was at a loss and said he would try anything. We retraced our steps and then moved east for a further hour. It was mid-morning, and the sun was already burning, raising a gas haze from the sand and steaming out of the rocks. We came to the edge of the rocky maze and saw a smoother plain spreading east with a three-peaked orange hill rising out of it. I was certain I had seen that hill on my previous visit, coming from the east. That indicated that Abu Tabara lay somewhere behind us.

We turned the caravan around and, with little real hope of finding the well, marched south-west. We traversed ridge after ridge, each time thinking, 'Now we might see it!', only to be met with the same blank rocks and lifeless shapes. We saw camel dung. Once I was sure that I smelled woodsmoke, but Adam shook his head. We saw sprigs of ferny tamarix among the crevices and fissures. I strode ahead with the binoculars. Marinetta pattered behind, holding her big zoom lens like a weapon. The towering, wind-moulded boulders looked down on us mockingly like giants and demons. Then the rocks disappeared, and we were on the edge of a grey plain stretching south. Abu Tabara could not lie in that direction.

It was almost midday now. We had been on foot since dawn, without a break and without drinking. My mouth was sore and as rough as gravel. 'That's enough!' I said. 'We'll have to go back to Rahib.' Adam turned the camels west reluctantly. I felt equally glum. This was only the second time in our journey that we had turned back. That Abu Tabara was our last well made it doubly infuriating. We moved over the sand haltingly.

Then, without warning, Marinetta shouted, 'Maik! Over there!' I turned and saw, directly behind us, the faraway shape of a camel and the distant silhouette of a man drawing water from an invisible well. 'It must be Abu Tabara!' I said. 'We've found it!' Then I kissed Marinetta. It was the first time I had ever kissed her in front of the guide.

The man drawing water stopped as he saw us coming, and as soon as we had shaken hands he held up the leather well bucket and poured the water so that we could drink. It was cool, cool, cool. It was the most delicious water I had ever tasted. The water spilled out of the bucket and ran in icy streams under my shirt. The sunlight caught it, dividing the liquid into priceless gems, dancing over it like a spirit. The Arab said that he had seen us passing and thought we were making directly for Rahib. That was why he hadn't shouted to us. We had been going in the opposite direction, I realized suddenly. That chance look backwards by Marinetta had probably saved our lives. On such small chances do life and death turn.

The Arab was black with a knobbly face. His shirt, *sirwel* and headcloth were so close to the colour of the sand that he would easily have been camouflaged but for his black features. There were three other Arabs in a small tent near by and an attractive woman with two small children. The tent was an oblong of camel's hair just large enough for all five adults and two children to sit in, very upright, all together. There wasn't a single tree on the horizon. The only other shade was to be found under some giant tilted boulders that trapped black ovals of shade around their bases. The woman's camel litter stood outside the tent, with a few moth-eaten blankets and some ropes and waterskins. Other saddles and saddle bags had been crammed into fissures in the rocks. The Arabs were small and unkempt, with tangles of hair and stubbly beards. They carried rifles and daggers and wore wooden rosary beads around their necks.

Two of them sat down with us in the shade of the granite chunk. I asked them why they lived in such a place, without even a tree for company. 'This is the real place for the Arabs!' one of them answered. 'There are no people. It's quiet. There's no coming and going, and you don't have to worry about thieves.' The coarse grasses that grew here were good fodder, he said, and the Arabs didn't even have to herd the camels. They merely let them wander. Every nine days, without fail, they would turn up at the well.

Not long afterwards the point was illustrated for us. There was a shout of 'Herds! Herds!' and the two men jumped up and rushed towards the well. We followed them, wondering why the sudden frenzy, and saw a picket of camels careening out of the desert and converging on the clay watering trough near the well head. The Arabs fought them back with sticks, afraid that they would break the fragile trough. Only two or three animals were allowed to water at once, and the Arabs dunked pieces of red rock-salt in the water as they drank. The rock-salt came from a secret place near by. There followed two hours' frantic work, during which the Arabs took turns to draw up the water and fill the trough. With the sun blazing overhead it seemed monstrously hard work, but I remembered that it happened only once every nine days. The rest of the time these Arabs needed their energy just to survive.

Later, after we had filled all our *girbas*, the Arabs made us tea. The woman emerged from the tent and collected a plateful of hard camel dung from around the well. Firewood was a luxury here, she explained. The fire required a surprising amount of dung and a great deal of puffing and blowing to keep it alight. But the tea that appeared half an hour later was excellent.

We left the well in the late afternoon and rode for two hours across the plain. As we made camp, Adam said, 'I told you we'd see people, didn't I? I read it in the sands. If we'd followed your angle, we'd have been on our way back to Rahib by now. I said we'd see people today.' This nettled me a little, though I had to admit that my compass bearing had not been as accurate as it might have been.

'There's only one person on this earth we have to thank for finding that well,' I told Adam, 'and that's my wife. And she's *not* a son of the Arabs.'

We awoke with the sun a thickening pearl over the hills. The morning was still, with no hint of cooling wind. The time of heat was upon us. Adam looked terrible and told me his eyes had pained him all night. For most of the day he rode with closed lids, obliging me to keep a steady watch on the compass. The hot sun seemed to bleach the colours out of the landscape till nothing remained but a chiaroscuro of grey and black. We moved through a science-fiction panorama of jagged, crumbling coxcombs of rock. Noon caught us on an endless plain where there was only a single, fungus-shaped pedestal a yard high. We couched the camels by the rock and ate our meal in the narrow rim of shade.

In the afternoon we continued across the plain. It was a moonscape, a timeless, eerie, twilight zone. Marinetta brooded silently in the simmering heat. I watched her anxiously knowing that the extremes of temperature could change your mood as easily as flicking a switch. In mid-afternoon she asked me for some dates. 'They're finished,' I told her. 'We finished them yesterday.'

'I never had any yesterday!' she said. 'Why didn't you save some for me?'

'There weren't many left,' I said vaguely, remembering that I had given some to Adam. 'Anyway, they're finished.'

'You miserly, greedy bastard!' she shouted. 'This is how you are!

I should never have married you!'

'Ah, we're back to *that* old white elephant.'

'I know you only married me because you thought I had money. You want me to keep you in luxury after the expedition.'

I knew by now that there was no point in talking to her during these obsessive moods. We hardly spoke for the rest of the day. The following day was our first wedding anniversary. It was exactly a year since those miserable days in Paris. 'Nothing's changed,' Marinetta grumbled to herself. 'Anyway, there won't be any more anniversaries. All I want now is to be free.'

That evening some flat splodges of cloud formed at sunset. Adam said that this meant heat.

His prediction proved true. The next day the heat was thick from sunrise onwards. We laboured up a steep escarpment, picking our way over a surface gashed with small stones. The rocks cut and scratched the camels' feet, and they were reluctant to go on. We scrambled over folds of hard ground and came into an area of low dunes, which closed in on us quickly, a glinting jigsaw of brilliant silicon. We tramped left and right to find a way through them, and the camels were further exhausted by the steep climb through the slipping sand. We struggled up a ridge and saw the desert stretching before us, a weft of dazzling colours. It seemed impossible that a giant river could exist in this emptiness.

We camped among dunes that night and in the morning reached firmer ground. We rode across a sandy plain decorated by blue volcanic lozenges and pieces of petrified wood. Millions of years ago there might have been a jungle here, a jungle of hunting reptiles and mammals and insects fighting tooth and claw, destroying life for life in the ferocious struggle to survive. Those creatures were our ancestors.

In the late afternoon we crossed a trench that might once have been a river. I remembered the strange formation from a previous journey. Or was it a previous life? I tried to remember, and my mind was filled with a cascade of images, the strange premonition in Tijikja, the stream of strange dreams that had followed me across the entire breadth of the Sahara. That place seemed to spark off a nebula of feelings and memories, to be a focus of all pasts and futures, a place where conscious and unconscious, dream and reality, came together. All seeking appeared to culminate here. I half expected to drop dead in the middle of the trench but, instead, as we climbed out of it, I heard the low wind-bag moan that announced the start of a sandstorm.

A blast of hot air pressed us sideways, and we dropped out of our saddles and tied the camels together. The rasp and whoosh of sand filled the air. There was a whine like the expiration of tortured lungs. Coils of dust flamed out of the desert, scourging us with cat-o'-nine-tails claws. A web of seething grey sand clamped down upon us, and we fought through its folds like drunken men. Marinetta clutched her compass tight, eyes riveted on the bouncing needle, while I led the camels. The net of dust drew tight around us, numbing our senses like abrasive cotton wool. I wrenched the headropes left and right, forcing the camels to walk in true. Adam followed on with his camel, a few yards behind.

We gritted our teeth to fight our last battle with the desert, trying its hungry best to cast us off its surface. We moved like warriors with every muscle tense, every sense alert, until night blackened the thick strands of flailing dust to darker shades. We thumped our baggage down. Adam took a blanket and went straight to ground like a burrowing creature. Marinetta and I plunged into the torrent of blown sand, tying the camels down and erecting our shelter. The cotton rattled, whipping out of our hands. 'Jesus!' Marinetta yelled. 'It's the wildest storm I've ever seen!' I held the leather ropes in my teeth, straining on the cotton to make it reach. The lash and roar of the sand was exhilarating. It was as if all the savage forces of the earth had been unleashed. The lashing wind made us gasp. We threw ourselves into our poor shelter, holding on to each other, feeling the same forces flowing through our veins. We scrabbled under each other's clothes, ripping them away, joining our bodies in the wild night. We rolled over, sobbing and grunting and crying in the maelstrom, two black demons wrestling in the darkness of the world. Fierce obsession drove us on, uncaring, as we released the pent-up frustration of 4,000 miles of hardship. A searing flash of crimson lighting ripped across the belly of the night, but no rain fell.

All was quiet at first light as we rolled from beneath drifts of sand.

We loaded and climbed a stony bank. From the top Adam pointed a bony finger to a line of green where none should have been. Then there was the miraculous quicksilver flash of water. Yellow cakes of hills stretched beyond the silver water to a far-off horizon. 'Those hills are in the Nubian desert,' Adam said. 'This is where the Sahara ends.'

I can hardly remember how we dragged the camels down the escarpment, through the noise and smell and bustle of Ed Debba. I recall that I took Marinetta's small hand and led her and our tiny caravan through streets where people stopped to stare at us. I remember someone shouting, 'Hey, those camels will bite you!' and a posse of children chanting, 'Christians with camels!' I remember vividly the great cool stream of the Nile, silent, grey and ancient, flowing in soothing flood through the harsh throat of the desert. The camels broke the rippled surface and the air was filled with the sounds of their drinking. Marinetta and I held hands and stared at the incredible sacrament of water. I took off my Moorish sandals. They were the ones I had bought in Chinguetti, 256 days, another lifetime, away. Those sandals had walked across the greatest desert on earth.

I looked at them once, then cast them into the swirling waters.

The Belly of Stones

We had reached the Nile, but our journey was not yet over. Our original plan had been to reach Cairo. That was impossible now, for the hot season was already well advanced, but we were determined not to give up until we had crossed the Egyptian border.

The police in Ed Debba did not share our enthusiasm. 'Your visas have expired,' said a fat, sour-faced security man who accosted us by the Nile. This was incorrect, I pointed out. The visas were valid from the date of entry, not the date of issue. This made him really mad. He marched us off to the tumble-down police station on the waterfront. He raged at us, and demanded, 'What are you doing with this girl?'

'This is my wife,' I said, 'so please speak with more respect.'

'Ahh! Don't tell me you're married!' the fat man jeered. 'She looks young enough to be your daughter!' I bit my lip. The Sudanese are the nicest people in Africa, but this was an example of what happened to perfectly nice people when they became 'security men'. 'You must report to the police in Dongola, the regional capital,' he told us. 'Explain your story to them.' He sent us off with our passports and without a guard.

'Like hell we will!' said Marinetta.

We sold Galil Al'Agl in the market and paid Adam the 800 Sudanese pounds we owed him. It must have been the most anyone had ever paid him for riding across the desert on a camel, but his face registered no pleasure.

He put the money away quickly. 'Don't tell anyone, Omar,' he begged me, 'or they'll all be asking for a loan.' Later he came back from the market with nothing but 2 pounds of tobacco in a plastic bag.

'Is that all you're going to get?' asked Marinetta. 'Why don't you buy a blanket or a new pair of shoes?'

'If I buy a new blanket, they'll say I'm rich and take money off me,' he moaned. 'And these shoes have still got plenty of life in them.' He looked down at his odd sandals, one blue, one red. 'I want to get out of this place as soon as I can,' he said. 'I don't like all this coming and going, all these people ready to take your money.' He had not been in a town for twenty years. I wondered if he would ever see one again.

We left for Egypt on 21 April, exactly one year after that near disastrous day when we had landed in Nouakchott, Mauritania. We spent a tranquil week riding through the adobe villages of Upper Nubia, where fat, green wheat waved in the fields and thick palm trees overshadowed the track. We filled our waterskins with river water and camped out in the desert at night. We made a wide circle around Dongola, concealing our camp fires in rocky crevices in the darkness. At the village of Mosho we sneaked into the market at the dead hour of late afternoon to buy a sack of sorghum for the camels. None of the villagers seemed surprised that we were going to Egypt.

North of Mosho the Nile enters the twisted series of ravines and canyons called the Belly of Stones. The character of the land and the people changes. The villages are remote, hemmed in by peaks and buttes of granite, separated from each other by narrow paths among the hills. Often it is difficult to get within 15 miles of the river by camel. Instead we followed the old stock route along which Sudanese camel men exported herds to Egypt. The track was well marked with camel grooves and with scores of bones of camels that had expired on the way.

The village I wanted most to avoid was Hamid. This, the last sizeable village on the west bank of the Nile, was where the Sudanese border police had their base. I had had trouble at Hamid before and wanted to take no chances this time. A few miles south of the village we headed our camels out into open desert. Only moments later two donkey riders emerged from the palm groves and began trotting north towards Hamid. I saw them turning their heads towards us as they rode. People riding out into the desert just south of the border

post must look suspicious to anyone, I supposed. I imagined word
being passed to the police sergeant in Hamid: 'Two strangers riding
out into the desert on camels!' I imagined the Land-Rover engine
churning, the constables jumping in excitedly with their old rifles. I
imagined the vehicle roaring across the desert to intercept us.

For an hour we travelled inside a deep groove in the rock, invisible
from the village. Then the groove suddenly fell away, and we saw
the tower of Hamid mosque hovering over the desert like a periscope.
It was easy to imagine hidden eyes watching us from within. Our
only advantage was the sun going down behind us, which would
blind any observer with its glare.

Darkness brought us invisibility. We found a depression carpeted
with sand and couched our camels there. A triangle of firestones was
waiting for us and a few pieces of unburned firewood, like a thoughtful
present from the previous occupants. As I lit a fire, I hoped no nosy
tribesmen would spot it and report us to the police.

Our sleep was undisturbed, and in the morning we headed back
to the river at Sagiet Al'Abd. We needed to fill our *girbas* before
pressing on into the rocky country ahead. On the riverbank was a
lump of shapeless mud brick that had once been an ancient fortress.
A sign saying 'Antiquity Area – Please Preserve' was lying flat on
its face in the dust. The wood-and-wire fence around it had also
collapsed. Marinetta wanted to use the posts as firewood.

We stalked through the soft sand looking for a gap in the hedge
of thorn and tamarix that obscured the steep riverbank. A little farther
on we found a clearing in the trees that would allow us to get down
to the water. I climbed down the loose, sandy bank. About half way
down I froze. Lying under a thorn tree was a very wizened old man
in a long shirt and layered headcloth. He was sound asleep. Or
perhaps he was dead. I didn't wait to find out but rushed back to the
camels, shushing Marinetta's questions until we had moved on. There
was something very eerie about finding a man asleep in such a lonely
place. It reminded me of stories from the *Arabian Nights*.

We pushed on for half an hour until we saw the village of Abri
standing on the opposite bank. Its yellow plaster buildings glittered
starkly through the trees. The bank was very steep here, but someone
had cleared a path down to the water's edge through the tangled

bush. We couched our camels in the shade of some acacias, and I carried our empty *girbas* and jerrycans down to the river. Crouching there, I could see the Sudanese flag dancing over the police station at Abri. I sincerely hoped that no inquisitive and keen-sighted policeman would look out across the river and notice the Arab with the incongruous red face. I filled all the vessels, dipping my travel-scarred feet into the cool stream. Then I manhandled the lightest *girba* up the steep slope. It was an excruciating task. My wet feet slipped in the sand, and I stumbled left and right, trying to balance the awkward shape of the goatskin. I was panting hard by the time I reached the top of the slope.

There was no possibility of hauling the heavier *girbas* up alone. I called Marinetta, and we shifted them, inch by grunting inch, hoping desperately that no one would see us. We slipped and floundered, cutting our feet on sharp slivers of bush, cursing and sweating. My arms ached and my legs burned like fire. Getting those water vessels up the incline seemed the most difficult task of the entire journey. At last we had them all at the top of the slope and we collapsed, snatching a moment's rest. In the same moment I saw a man in a clean white gandourah coming across a mud flat on the river. He looked lean and purposeful. 'Quick!' I hissed at Marinetta. Never had we loaded as fast as we loaded those water vessels. In less than five minutes we were mounted and moving out into the desert. When I looked behind, the man in the white shirt was examining our tracks.

The river was soon out of sight. We followed a trail of camel skeletons, which increased in number as we approached a natural gate in a rock wall. The pass was an ossuary of camels. Some lay in the sand with their heads bent back towards their shoulders. Others were still in the sitting position. Some of them had been deliberately arranged by the herdsmen into horrific configurations, guarding the pass with vacant occiputs and canine fangs polished sharp by the wind-blown sand. One of the camel skulls was clamped over the mummified remains of a great Nubian vulture.

We spent the night near the pass and woke to find ourselves in a wonderland of knolls and peaks. The rocks were sharks' jaws gaping at us across the void, pieces of grey Gruyère cheese, eaten away by time, the shapes of houses and tents and covered wagons laagered into circles. On the horizon we saw successive terraces of hills, each a subtly different shade of grey, black or silver, fitting into each other's shadow with serrated edges. At midday we heard a sound like the throbbing of an aircraft engine. It went on and on, though no aircraft passed over us. I stopped and listened carefully. It was like the boom of a great drum being pounded over and over again, stroke after stroke. There was no wind. It could not have been the river, which was too far away for us to hear. I suddenly realized what the sound was. It was the Drummer of Death.

In the afternoon we cut through another natural gate and saw the Nile beneath us, bluer than blue, like a vision from a dream. We came to a village standing on an alluvial beach which ran down to the water. The village was deserted. The people who had lived there had probably left when the opening of the High Dam in Aswan had swollen the Nile's banks in this area. Farther on, the river flexed and twisted through high cliffs of Nubian sandstone, the grain in the rock standing out like blood vessels.

We camped in some tamarix, and I led the camels down to drink. While they mooched about, nuzzling at the fuzz of grass, I sat on a rock and smoked my pipe. Two ibis skimmed across the surface and circled in a cloudless azure sky. Silver fish jumped out of the water, and when I dipped my feet into it I could feel them nibbling. The river seemed almost to whisper to me. It was the most beautiful, most tranquil, place I had ever seen.

Marinetta pulled her clothes off and bathed naked, standing up to her thighs in the stream. She looked cheerful, splashing water through her dark hair and over the smooth skin of her body. I stopped watching the water and looked at her instead. Just then I registered a flurry of movement far across the river. Through the binos I saw a man riding a donkey along the opposite bank. 'Get your clothes on!' I told Marinetta without thinking. 'There's someone coming!'

She splashed more water over herself and giggled. 'I can't see anyone!' she said. 'Anyway, what does it matter now?' I shrugged and went back to my pipe.

That night we camped in soft desert sand near Lamulay. Both of us felt sanctified after our wash in the Nile. After we had eaten Marinetta said, 'It's funny how being clean makes you feel hungry for sex, isn't it?' Then she took off her clothes for the second time that day. If there were any donkey riders that night, we didn't see them.

The following morning we found ourselves in the middle of a great expanse of grey earth, which had been cracked by the sunlight into a jigsaw of deep crevices. At first the cracks were narrow enough to step over, but soon they widened until they were a foot across and over a yard deep. The camels already had sore feet, and they refused to go on. I was just about to tell Marinetta to retreat when Wad An Nejma lost his footing. He squealed as his flat hooves pawed at the crumbling earth, but in a moment he was firmly wedged in. I hoped to God that his legs had not been broken. 'Go back!' I told Marinetta. Then her camel lost his balance too, and plunged into the cracks.

'God!' she moaned desperately. 'We'll never get them out.' I had to admit that this looked like the end.

No amount of pushing, pulling or beating would shift the camels. The brittle ground was as treacherous as a marsh, constantly crumbling and flaking. It was all we could do to maintain our own balance. Slowly we unloaded, piece by piece. We ferried the heavy baggage back to the roots of some tamarix bushes behind us. It was backbreaking work. The camels wheezed and whimpered and made periodic attempts to haul themselves out, managing only to wedge themselves more tightly in. We strained and strained on the headropes until their clumsy legs sprawled out and they stood trembling on the narrow ledges between the cracks.

There was still no way forward or back. I took the axe and began to smash my way through the cracked blocks, which shattered like porcelain. It was a slow, draining effort, but steadily the crests of the cracks got lower and the spaces higher as they filled up with clods of earth. It took an hour to make a very slim path to some firmer ground. Then we had to load the camels and lead them out. We stopped to examine the damage. Both camels had badly lacerated feet, and Wad An Nejma's forefoot was like a balloon. One *girba* had been punctured and two saddle bags broken.

The firmer ground gave us only brief respite. There were more of these curious expanses of cracked earth and each time we encountered one we had to stop and carve out a path with the axe. The work took hours, and all day we moved in fits and starts. Finally we came to a kind of island where a palm-frond hut stood on firm ground. There were four Nubians living there, drying fish and cultivating the hard soil. The men had come from Halfa Jadid in the eastern Sudan.

The ancestors of these men had lived along this reach of the Nile since Pharaonic times. When the High Dam was opened in Aswan, creating Lake Nasser, the rising water had drowned many of the old villages, together with their cultivation and palm groves. Thousands of Nubian families had been forcibly moved to the new town of Halfa Jadid, named after their old capital, Wadi Halfa. The men said that in recent years the level of water had fallen again, uncovering some of the original land. These regions of cracked earth were the places that had once been covered by water and were now exposed to the sun. The heat had dried out the wet mud until it had cracked like glass. The firm ground between them was where the spits and bays had been: the places not covered by water. These Nubians were determined to recultivate their ancestral land. I asked them why they preferred the harsher life here to their new homes. 'So many people!' one of them said. 'Here you can breathe.'

We drank tea with the men, and later they pointed out the direction of Semna, where we should be able to rejoin the old stock trail once more. 'Watch out near the border,' they told us. 'There are new Sudanese patrols there now, and they stop everyone going to Egypt.'

The following day we marched twelve hours and covered only 5 miles. There was no crossing the immense bays of cracked earth that we came to, and going around them cost us hours. We tried to take shortcuts by climbing over rocky slopes, but the sore-footed animals complained and pulled against the ropes. Soon my back was aching with the strain of hauling them. We made agonizing progress. Once we came to a chasm between the hills that was choked with tamarix. I actually had to cut a way through it with the machete. A splinter of wood gashed Marinetta's foot badly, and she sobbed with irritation. Near sunset we came to the top of a cliff where we could see the ribbon of the Nile and the bend at Semna far beneath us.

We descended through a watercourse, and at last pushed our way to a narrow shelf by the water's edge, where we made camp. We were hardly able to move. I felt sick and feverish with strain; my body was racked with spasms of hot and cold. I had a burning sensation in my legs and an ache in the back of my neck. My hands were blistered from the constant pulling of the headrope. Even my appetite had gone. The riverbank was covered in stinging plants and a species of bean that rattled all night. Just after dark I killed two tarantulas.

We felt better in the morning as we climbed the steep, sandy skirts of the valley. There was a pass in which we found camel grooves and the lump of a camel skeleton. It was the first skeleton we had found for two days, and it proved that we were back on the stock trail. I did a dance around it. For the rest of the day we followed carcasses and firestones, and in the evening we camped near a great wadi. The first thing we saw in the morning was the fresh tracks of camels, together with the distinct imprints of military boots. It could only be a Sudanese border patrol.

A little farther on, combing the horizon with the binoculars, I spotted a white tent with a camouflaged truck parked outside. The camp was a mile away, but the sun was in front of us now, giving the advantage to the observer. Through the binos I saw dark figures moving around the tent. 'Come on,' I told Marinetta. 'We don't want to get stopped now.' By then our visas really had expired.

We marched for fourteen hours that day. At last I realized that the distance was telling on me. My body was giving me signals to slow down and rest, signals that I had been ignoring for weeks. I no longer felt tired; I felt physically sick, racked with strange fever and constantly in pain. After sunset I managed to drag everything from the camels, then I collapsed and crawled into my sleeping-bag.

I felt strangely cold. Fits of shivering convulsed me. My teeth were chattering. I wondered blankly if I had malaria but rejected the idea. Marinetta made a fire and cooked a meal. She brought it to me and helped me to eat. I took a mouthful and was violently sick. I crawled back into my sleeping-bag. Marinetta knelt over me, cradling me and looking worried. 'Come on, Maik,' she crooned. 'You've got to eat. If you don't eat, you'll die. Remember what you used to say? When the going gets tough, the tough get going!'

'I've let you down,' I said, eaten up with misery.

Suddenly she began to cry. 'No, you haven't,' she sobbed. 'You've never let me down. We've lived a lifetime together already. I couldn't leave you now. Not ever. I love you, Maik.'

I had come 4,500 miles to hear the woman I loved say that.

In the morning we crossed the crust of a mountain and saw Lake Nasser beneath us, dotted with pelicans and herons. Above the inlet there was a military tent with a radio antenna, half hidden on top of a knoll. As we approached, two dark figures strolled down to meet us, followed by a barking dog. They were Egyptian border police.

The men were friendly and welcomed us to their tent, where they made us tea and fed us home-made bread. The patrol leader sent a message through to his HQ at Abu Simbel about our arrival. Marinetta and I relaxed, sitting on a camp bed and waiting for the next radio rendezvous. At noon the radio stuttered, and the patrol commander listened for a few moments. Then he laid the headphones down and said calmly, 'I'm afraid you'll have to go back.'

Go back! I felt my face flushing. Marinetta's mouth had fallen open in shock. 'We'll die if we go back,' I said. 'You see what a state the camels are in. They are finished and so are we.'

'It's orders,' the soldier said. 'It's illegal to cross the border from the Sudan without special permission.'

'We have visas.'

'Yes,' said he, examining our passports again. 'But these visas expired six days ago.'

For almost an hour we discussed the matter. I was adamant that we should not return to the Sudan. Our Sudanese visas had expired, and even if we survived, we would quickly be arrested by the Sudanese for illegal entry. The soldier, whose name was Hassan, said that he would query his HQ again during the next radio call. But when the time for the call came, conditions were too bad for contact. 'Look,' Hassan said, 'you may as well stay the night with us, and we'll establish contact in the morning.' Then he added, 'After all, we can't shoot you, can we?'

Just before sunset Marinetta and I walked down to the lake to wash. The water felt ice-cold. We sat in silence for long moments, watching the sun sinking across the lapping water. It was blissfully tranquil.

'Did you mean what you said last night?' I asked Marinetta.

'I'll always mean it,' she said. 'Thank you for taking me with you, Maik.'

I felt a sudden weight of sadness and nostalgia for the beauty we had seen, for the obstacles we had met and crossed, for the characters we had known. There might be good things to look forward to in the civilized world. But nothing would ever inspire either of us as the desert had.

When we arrived back in the camp the soldiers fed us on chicken and rice. Afterwards Hassan said, 'In the morning you should load your camels and go to Abu Simbel. Don't tell anyone there we let you go. Say that you went anyway. If you stay here, they will force us to send you back.' For a soldier, I thought, Hassan was a very reasonable man.

It took us twelve hours to reach Abu Simbel the next day, stumping on through endless chasms of rock and sand. We had almost despaired of reaching it when we spotted the white dome of the airport control tower standing out above the undulating rocks. Moments of our marathon journey across an entire continent on camels crowded again into our minds. This was journey's end, 271 days, nine months, after leaving Chinguetti. We had completed the longest trek ever made by Westerners in the Sahara.

We stopped outside the town and changed into Western clothes, knowing that it would improve our reception. Then we led our weary camels along the asphalt road to the police station. The young policemen there surrounded us, unloading our camels with great clamour and even taking snapshots. As we sat down with them some busloads of tourists passed by. I had a fleeting glimpse of white faces, grey hair and clean clothes. I realized that we hadn't seen another Westerner for two months. These were the ordinary people of our world, I thought, only a few days away from their offices and houses. At that moment they seemed as far away from us as the sky.

A young officer arrived and smiled at us truculently, commenting again that our visas had expired. He brought along a more senior officer from the Border Intelligence Section and some other men, who held a kind of court. In the end the officer said, 'You'll have to go back.'

Then I played my final card. 'I'm a writer,' I said, 'and your country is a very popular one among tourists. If you send us back and anything unpleasant happens to us, it would look very bad for your country.'

The officers listened politely, then walked away. Later the Border Intelligence officer called us. 'You want to get to Aswan, mister? Tomorrow you will go to Aswan. You will leave the camels here with us. You will be interrogated by the police and by the military intelligence people. If they agree, you will get your entry stamp.'

'Thank you very much,' I said.

We spent the night in the police station among piles of our equipment. The camels chomped on their grain outside, and in the morning a local herdsman came to take them away. I watched them limping off, feeling somehow guilty that I had forced them to bring us so far.

We picked up the few things that we could carry and left behind all those that were now useless yet had formed our home for ten months: the cooking pot, the milk bowl, the mugs, the good old *girbas*, the axe, the machete and all the other bits and pieces that had seemed so essential in our Adam-and-Eve world.

A policeman was waiting to take us to the bus. It was a tourist-company bus, crammed with French visitors. They looked well fed and sleepy, like contented pets. The air was full of their sickly perfume and the scent of suntan oil. How ironical, I thought, that we should end such a journey in a busload of tourists. I had spent years searching for the old ways and the hidden places, but in the end no one and nothing escaped change.

The bus slid across the desert on a smooth asphalt *piste*. The tourists turned drowsily to take in the view of the glittering, insubstantial, amber plain, the closing, rocky jaws of the hills. We turned too, for our last glimpse of the Sahara. For each of us on the bus the desert had its own special meaning. For me it was a void to which we ourselves had given life, an arena in which we had played out an incredible life-and-death game. Now it reverted to what it had always been: an illusion.

The bus gathered speed. My wife's hand sought mine, and the small, fragile fingers twined around my larger ones. The Sahara had wrought few changes in that hand. It was exactly as it had been on the day I had slipped a gold ring over one of the fingers and promised that I would protect her always. It was as small and soft and delicate as a child's. A nice hand, I thought.

Acknowledgements

The journey recorded in this book could not have succeeded without the help and goodwill of a great many people. I should like particularly to thank the following.

In London: Martin Soames, formerly of Penguin Books, for initial support; Anthony Goff, my agent, and his former assistant, Suzanne P. Breen, who performed the almost impossible task of sending us money in the Sahara; Lady Ewart-Biggs of the UK UNICEF Committee for allowing us to send films via the UNICEF pouch; Nick Cater and Caroline Penn for stimulating media interest; Professor Harry Norris of SOAS for advice on learning Tamasheq; Nigel and Shane Winser of the Expedition Advisory Centre for their advice; John Garvey, for being a friend for as long as I can remember; Omar Alim, of the Sudanese Embassy, for his enthusiastic assistance; all those who answered my letters, including Geoffrey Moorhouse, Squadron Leader Tom Sheppard, Ken and Julie Slavin, Jean Abdallahi and Ted Edwards.

In Paris: Philippe Davide and family for their hospitality and help; Professor Théodore Monod for advice and enthusiasm.

In Nouakchott: Charles and Mariana Habis, without whose help there might have been no expedition; Abbas of the USAID office; Peace Corps volunteers Nancy Lock, Cathy Chilson and Karen Targerson for their kindness; Lelio Bernardi, Mr Jacomini, David Fletcher, Malik Sene; Father Istifan Stirnemann and his colleagues at the Catholic Mission.

In Niamey: Mr Bashizi, UNICEF representative; Giovanni Di Cola of UNICEF for his hospitality; Auda for help in negotiating Nigérien bureaucracy; the British Honorary Vice-Consul, Mr A. Santoni.

In N'Jamena: Pamela Clifton for much kindness; Bob Reitmayer for the generous gift of binoculars; Ulf Kristoffersson, UNICEF representative, for his support; François and Susan Tissot of UNDP for the loan of a car for our return journey to Ati; Arthur Holdbrook of UNDP for carrying our films to Rome; all other members of UNICEF and UNDP Chad who gave us friendship and help.

In Ati: Maurie-Laure Glandor, Eva Hensel and Margrit Kapelli, nurses for UNICEF/INTERAID, for putting ourselves and our camels up in their house.

In Gineina: the District Commissioner for allowing us to stay in the rest-house there; Mohammid Zakkaria for customary help and generosity.

In El Fasher: Rob 'Rabi' Hydon for the loan of his house; Bob Siddell, UNDP, for interceding with the authorities on our behalf.

In Egypt: the four members of the military patrol at Jebel Ussa, but for whose kindness we might never have reached journey's end; Abdal Sayyid of Abu Simbel Border Intelligence for helping to persuade the authorities to let us stay; the manager of the Cleopatra Hotel, Aswan, for his generosity and hospitality.

In Stamford: Ms Susan Wheatley for typing the manuscript; Dr Mitchell for his advice and assistance with our medical kit.

In London: the staff of Cetaprint for their patient work on the photographs; Eleo Gordon for raising the book eighty-five notches!

Finally I should like to thank my parents for their invariable support and for their courage in meeting us in Cairo during an unusually hot summer. I am most grateful to General and Mrs Peru, not only for their support and for allowing me to write this book at their cottage in Sardinia but also for bringing into the world the bravest woman I have ever met, my wife. She was by my side constantly while I wrote this book, and for 4,500 miles across the greatest desert on earth. This work is dedicated to her.

M.J.A.

Frazione Agnata, Gallura, Sardinia   1 October 1987

Index